ISBN 978-1-330-11426-1
PIBN 10029194

1 MONTH OF
FREE
READING

at

www.ForgottenBooks.com

By purchasing this book you are eligible for one month membership to ForgottenBooks.com, giving you unlimited access to our entire collection of over 1,000,000 titles via our web site and mobile apps.

To claim your free month visit:

www.forgottenbooks.com/free29194

English
Français
Deutsche
Italiano
Español
Português

www.forgottenbooks.com

Mythology Photography **Fiction**
Fishing Christianity **Art** Cooking
Essays Buddhism Freemasonry
Medicine **Biology** Music **Ancient
Egypt** Evolution Carpentry Physics
Dance Geology **Mathematics** Fitness
Shakespeare **Folklore** Yoga Marketing
Confidence Immortality Biographies
Poetry **Psychology** Witchcraft
Electronics Chemistry History **Law**
Accounting **Philosophy** Anthropology
Alchemy Drama Quantum Mechanics
Atheism Sexual Health **Ancient History**
Entrepreneurship Languages Sport
Paleontology Needlework Islam
Metaphysics Investment Archaeology
Parenting Statistics Criminology
Motivational

GOLDSMITH'S History of GREECE.

Ones sc.

T. Stothard R.A. pinxt.   T. S. Engleheart sculpt.

CHISWICK.

Printed by C. & C. Whittingham,

for Thomas Tegg No 73 Cheapside

Sept 1826

THE

HISTORY OF GREECE.

BY

DR. GOLDSMITH.

Abridged.

CHISWICK:

PRINTED BY C. AND C. WHITTINGHAM.

SOLD BY THOMAS TEGG, 73, CHEAPSIDE;

N. HAILES, PICCADILLY;

BOWDERY AND KIRBY, OXFORD STREET, LONDON:

AND RICHARD GRIFFIN AND CO. GLASGOW.

1826.

CONTENTS.

CHAPTER I.

CHAPTER II.

CHAPTER III.

CHAPTER IV.

CHAPTER V.

CHAPTER IX.

CHAPTER X.

CHAPTER XIV.

CHAPTER XV.

THE

HISTORY OF GREECE.

CHAPTER I.

OF THE EARLIEST STATE OF GREECE.

THE History of ancient Greece, like that of modern Germany, is not so much the history of any particular kingdom, as of a number of petty independent states, sometimes at war, and sometimes in alliance with one another. Of these different states, therefore, we shall now give an account, with as much brevity as is consistent with perspicuity; and we shall begin our narrative at that period, where real and authentic history commences: for as to the more early, that is, the fabulous times of the Grecian republics, these belong to mythology rather than to history.

Sicyon, then, is said to have been the first kingdom that was established in Greece. The beginning of it is placed by historians in the year of the world one thousand nine hundred and fifteen, before Christ two thousand and eighty-nine, and before the first Olympiad one thousand three hundred and thirteen. Its first king was Ægialeus. It is said to have lasted a thousand years.

A. M. 2148.] The kingdom of Argos, in Peloponnesus, began a thousand and eighty years before the first Olympiad, in the time of Abraham. The first king was Inachus.

This was succeeded by the kingdom of Mycenæ, to which place the seat of government was transferred

B

from Argos by Perseus, the grandson of Acrisius, the king of Argos, whom Perseus unfortunately slew. Eurystheus, the third in succession from him, was expelled by the Heraclidæ, or descendants of Hercules, who made themselves masters of Peloponnesus.

A. M. 2448.] The kingdom of Athens was first formed into a regular government by Cecrops, an Egyptian. This prince having quitted Egypt, and spent some time in travelling through Phœnicia and other parts, came at last into Attica, where he married the daughter of Actæus, the king of that country, and, upon his death, succeeded to the throne. He taught the people, who had hitherto led a wandering life, the use of fixed habitations; restrained all licentious amours, by obliging every man to be content with one wife; and, for the better administration of justice, he instituted the celebrated court of Areopagus. Amphictyon, the third king of Athens, established the famous Amphictyon Council, which makes so capital a figure in the history of Greece. And Codrus, the last prince of this line, devoted himself for the good of his country. For in a war between the Athenians and the Heraclidæ, in which the latter had penetrated to the very gates of Athens, Codrus, hearing that the Oracle had declared, that that people should prove conquerors, whose king first fell in the contest, disguised himself in the habit of a peasant, and going over to the enemy's camp, provoked one of their common soldiers, who instantly slew him. The Heraclidæ, being informed of this circumstance, concluded that heaven had declared against them; and they therefore retreated to their own country without striking another blow. After the death of Codrus, the title of king was abolished at Athens, and that of Archon, or chief governor, substituted in its stead. The duration of this last office was at first for the possessor's life. It was afterwards limited to ten years, and finally to one.

A. M. 2549.] Cadmus was the founder of the kingdom of Thebes. To him are attributed sixteen letters of the Greek alphabet; though it is probable he borrowed them from the Phœnician characters, rather than invented them. The adventures of his unhappy posterity, Laius, Jocasta, Œdipus, Eteocles, and Polynices, are well known.

The kingdom of Sparta, or Lacedæmon, is supposed to have been first instituted by Lelexa. Helena, the tenth in succession from this monarch, is equally famous for her beauty and her infidelity to the marriage bed. She had not lived above three years with her husband Menelaus, when she was carried off by Paris, the son of Priam king of Troy. In revenge the Greeks invested that city, and took it after a siege of ten years, about the time that Jephtha was judge in Israel.

A. M. 2820.] Corinth began to be formed into a state at a later period than any of the kingdoms abovementioned. Its first sovereign was Sisyphus, the son of Æolus, and, upon the expulsion of his descendants, Bacchis assumed the reins of power. The government after this became aristocratical, a chief magistrate being annually chosen by the name of Prytanis. At last Cypselus usurped the supreme authority, which he transmitted to his son Periander, who was reckoned one of the seven wise men of Greece.

The kingdom of Macedon was first governed by Caranus, descended from Hercules, and subsisted from this time till the defeat of Perseus by the Romans, a space of six hundred and twenty-six years.

Such was the political situation of Greece in the early period of its history, during which we see that kingly government prevailed in all the states; but this was soon changed every where, except in Macedonia, for a republican mode of government, which however was diversified into as many various forms as there were different cities, according to the peculiar character of each respective people.

These different states, though totally independent, and sometimes at war with one another, were yet united by one common language and one religion; by the celebration of public games, at which they all assisted; and particularly by the famous Amphictyonic Council, which met twice a year at Thermopylæ, in order to deliberate about the general interest of those states of whose deputies it was composed. The states that sen deputies to this council were twelve, viz. the Thessalians, the Thebans, the Dorians, the Iönians, the Perhæbeans, the Magnetes, the Locrians, the Oëtans, the Phthiotes, the Maleans, the Phocians, and the Dolopians. Each of these states sent two deputies to the council, one of whom was named Hieromnemon, and took care of religion; the other was called Pylagoras, and attended to the civil interests of his community. After offering up sacrifices to Apollo, Diana, Latona, and Minerva, the deputies took an oath, importing, that they would never subvert any city of the Amphictyons, never stop the course of waters either in war or peace, and that they would oppose any attempts to lessen the reverence and authority of the gods, to whom they had paid their adoration.

These different motives to confederacy united the Greeks for a time into a body of great power, and greater renown. By this association a country, not half so large as England, was able to dispute the empire of the world with the greatest monarchs of the earth. By this association they were able not only to oppose, but even to rout and disperse the most numerous armies of Persia, reducing their power to so low an ebb, as to make them submit to the most mortifying conditions of peace. But of all the states of Greece, the two that made the most capital figure, were Athens and Lacedæmon; and of these, therefore, it will be necessary to give a more particular account than our limits will allow us to give of the rest.

CHAPTER II.

OF THE GOVERNMENT OF SPARTA, AND THE LAWS OF LYCURGUS.

LACEDÆMON, as we have already observed, was in the beginning governed by kings, of which thirteen in succession held the reins of power, of the race of the Pelopidæ. Under the Heraclidæ, who succeeded them, instead of one king, the people admitted two, who governed with equal authority. This change is said to have been owing to the following circumstance: Aristodemus dying, left two sons, Euristhenes and Procles, who were twins, and so very much alike, that it was hardly possible to distinguish the one from the other; and the mother, equally attached to both, and desirous of advancing both to the throne, pretended that she really could not tell which of them was first born, or which had the best claim. The people, therefore, invested both with the sovereign power; and this form of government, however strange, continued to subsist for several centuries.

It was during this latter period that the Helots, or peasants of Sparta, were enslaved; for these people having taken up arms, in order to vindicate their right to the same privileges as the citizens enjoyed, which the two first kings had bestowed upon them, and of which Agis had deprived them, they were, after a violent struggle, subdued; and, to punish them for their rebellion, they and their posterity were condemned to perpetual slavery; and, to render their condition as disgraceful as it was miserable, all other slaves were called by the general name of Helots.

To prevent the repetition of these and the like disorders, to which this little state was subject, Lycurgus instituted his celebrated body of laws, which makes so conspicuous a figure in the history of Greece; and which continued, for a long time, to render Lacedæmon at once the terror and the umpire of the neighbouring kingdoms. But before he gave this proof of his patriotism and his abilities as a legislator, he gave, if possible, a still more striking proof of his disinterestedness and love of justice. For having succeeded to the throne by the death of his elder brother, Polydectes, without issue, and the queen-dowager, his sister-in-law, afterwards proving with child, she offered to destroy the birth, provided he would marry her, and admit her into a share of power. Lycurgus dissembled his resentment at so unnatural a proposal, and fearing that she might use means to put her design in execution, assured her that, as soon as the child was born, he would take care to remove it out of the way. Accordingly, she was delivered of a boy, which Lycurgus commanded to be brought to him, and presenting him to the people, as their lawful sovereign, by the name of Charilaus, he continued thenceforward to act, not as king, but as regent.

The better to qualify himself for the office of a legislator, which he was now about to assume, he travelled into Crete, and afterwards into Asia, where he is said to have made the first discovery of the works of Homer. From thence, he went into Egypt; and having thus made himself acquainted with the customs and institutions of the various countries through which he passed, he at length returned home; and being assisted in his designs by some of the leading men of the state, he published his celebrated code of laws, by which it was enacted, that the kings should retain their right of succession as before: but their authority was considerably diminished by the institution of a senate, consisting of twenty-eight members, chosen from among the principal citizens, into which none were eligible till they were sixty years of age. The kings, however, still enjoyed all their outward marks of dignity and respect. They had the chief seats in every public assembly; they gave their votes first; they received ambassadors, and other strangers of distinction; and in time of war they had the command of the army; though upon these occasions they were subject to the control of the senate, who sometimes obliged them to march against the enemy, or return home, when they had least inclination to do either.

The senators, too, were the more respectable, as they held their places for life; and besides, being possessed of so considerable a share of the executive, were invested with the whole of the judicial power; and this last part of their duty they executed with such integrity and discretion, that though there lay an appeal from them to the people, yet their decrees were hardly ever reversed. Their authority, however, was about a century after tempered by the erection of a superior court, called the Court of the Ephori, consisting of but five members, chosen annually into office, and elected from among the people; and these had a power to arrest and imprison even the persons of their kings, if they acted in a manner unbecoming their station.

In order to reconcile the people to this mode of government, in which, though they had a nominal, they had no real share, Lycurgus fell upon two expedients, equally bold and decisive. These were to divide all the lands of the state equally among the citizens, and to abolish the use of money. The lands of Laconia he divided into thirty thousand parts, and those of Sparta into nine thousand; and these he portioned out to the respective inhabitants of each district. To abolish the use of money, he did not think it necessary to deprive those, who were possessed of gold and silver, of their property. He thought it sufficient to cry down the value of those metals, and to order that nothing but iron money should pass in exchange for any commodity. This coin also he made so heavy, and fixed at so low a rate, that a cart and two oxen were required to carry home a sum of ten minæ, or about twenty pounds sterling. As this coin had no currency among the other states of Greece, it soon fell into contempt even among the Spartans themselves; who despised it so much, that money was at last brought into disuse, and few troubled themselves with more than was necessary to answer their daily expenses.

To enforce the practice of temperance and sobriety, Lycurgus further ordained, that all the men should eat in one common hall in public. Every one was obliged to send thither his provisions monthly, consisting of one bushel of flour, eight measures of wine, five pounds of cheese, and two pounds and a half of figs; and this regulation was so rigidly observed, that a long time after, when Agis returned from a successful expedition, he was severely reprimanded for having eaten with his queen in private. Black broth was their favourite dish; of what ingredients it was composed is not known; but, as they used no flesh in their entertainments, it probably resembled those lenten soups which are still in use on the continent. Dionysius, the tyrant, found this fare very unpalatable; but, as the cook asserted, the broth was nothing without the seasoning of fatigue and hunger.

To accustom the youth to early habits of discipline
and obedience, Lycurgus took their education out of
the hands of their parents, and committed it to masters
appointed by the state. So desirous, indeed, was he
of having a hardy and robust race of citizens, that he
began the work of education, even from the time of the
mother's conception, making it her duty to use such
diet and exercise, as might fit her to produce a healthy
and vigorous offspring. Nay, such children as were
born with any capital defect, were not suffered to be
brought up, but were exposed to perish in a cavern
near mount Taygetus; and such as, upon a public view,
were deemed to be sound and healthy, were adopted as
children of the state, and delivered to their parents to be
nursed with rigour and severity. From their tenderest
years they were accustomed to make no choice in their
eating, not to be afraid in the dark, or when left alone;
not to be peevish or fretful; to walk barefoot; to lie
hard at nights; to wear the same clothes summer and
winter; and to fear nothing from their equals. At the
age of seven they were taken from their parents, and
delivered over to the classes for a public education.
Their discipline there was still more rigid and severe.
They were still obliged to go barefoot, their heads were
shaved, and they fought with one another naked.

To enable them the better to endure bodily pain without complaining, they were annually whipped at the
altar of Diana; and the boy that bore this punishment
with the greatest fortitude came off victorious. Plutarch tells us, that he has seen several children expire
under this cruel treatment; and he makes mention of
one, who having stolen a fox, and hid it under his coat,
chose rather to let the animal tear out his bowels than
discover the theft. In order to prepare them for the
stratagems of war, they were permitted to steal from
one another; but if they were caught in the fact, they
were punished for their want of dexterity. At twelve
years of age they were removed into a class of a more
advanced kind. There their labour and discipline
were increased with their years. They had now their
skirmishes between small parties, and their mock fights
between larger bodies; and in these they sometimes

fought with such obstinacy, that they were seen to lose their eyes, and even their lives, before they gave up the contest. Such was the constant discipline of their minority, which lasted till the age of thirty, before which they were not permitted to marry, to go into the troops, or to bear any office in the state.

The discipline of the virgins was as severe as that of the young men. They were inured to a life of labour and industry till they were twenty years of age, before which time they were not allowed to be marriageable. They had also their peculiar exercises. They ran, wrestled, and pitched the bar; and performed all these feats naked before the whole body of the citizens. Yet this was thought no way indecent, as it was supposed that the frequent view of the person would tend rather to check than excite every irregular desire. An education so manlike did not fail to bestow upon the Spartan woman equal vigour of body and mind. They were bold, hardy, and patriotic, filled with a sense of honour, and a love of military glory. Some foreign women, in conversation with the wife of Leonidas, saying, that the Spartan women alone knew how to govern the men, she boldly replied, "The Spartan women alone bring forth men." A mother was known to give her son, who was going to battle, his shield, with this gallant advice, "Return with it, or return upon it;" thereby in effect telling him, that, rather than throw it away in flight, he should be borne home upon it dead. Another hearing that her son was killed fighting for his country, she answered without any emotion, "It was for that I brought him into the world." After the battle of Leuctra, the parents of those who fell in the action went to the temples to thank the gods that their sons had done their duty, while those whose children survived that dreadful day were overwhelmed with grief.

Besides these general regulations, there were many other subordinate maxims, that, by long and constant practice, obtained the force of laws. The Spartans were expressly forbid to exercise any mechanic art. War was their chief occupation; and in time of peace they employed themselves in hunting, or bodily exercises. The Helots, or slaves, tilled their lands for them, and received for their labour a bare subsistence. Nor was this the only hardship to which these unhappy men were subject; they were in a manner bound to the soil, nor was it even lawful to sell them to strangers, or to make them free: nay, if at any time their numbers increased to such a degree as to excite the suspicion of their cruel masters, there was a *Cryptia*, or *secret act*, by which it was permitted to destroy them without mercy. Thucydides relates, that two thousand of these slaves disappeared at once, without ever after being heard of. Nor were they only thus wantonly put to death, they were even made a mockery of while living: they were frequently intoxicated on purpose, and in that condition exposed before the children, in order to deter them from this kind of debauchery.

As to the citizens themselves, being possessed, by means of their slaves, of competence and leisure, they were almost always in company in their large common halls, where they met and conversed with one another. The love of their country was their ruling passion, and all self-interest seemed lost in the general wish for the welfare of the public. Pedarctus, having missed the honour of being chosen one for the three hundred who had a certain rank in the city, converted his disappointment into joy, "that there were three hundred better men in Sparta than he."

The Spartans were forbid to make frequent war upon the same people, lest they should teach their discipline to others. When they had broken and routed their enemies, they never pursued them farther than was necessary to make themselves sure of the victory. This had an excellent effect; for the enemy, knowing that all who resisted were put to the sword, often fled, as they were convinced that this was the most effectual means of ensuring their safety. With the Spartans themselves the case was directly the reverse: for their first and most inviolable maxim was, never to turn their backs on the enemy, however unequal to them in numbers, nor ever to deliver up their arms till they resigned them with their life. Nay, they would not suffer the contrary notion to be propagated, or even mentioned among them. For when the poet Archilochus came to Sparta, he was obliged to quit the city, for having asserted in one of his poems, that it was better for a man to lose his arms than his life. Thus depending upon their valour alone, their legislator would not allow them to wall the city. It was his opinion, that a wall of men was preferable to a wall of brick, and that valour, which is obliged to take shelter within a fortification, is little better than cowardice.

Such was the general purport of the institutions of Lycurgus, which from their tendency gained the esteem and admiration of all the surrounding states. In order to render them as lasting as they were excellent, Lycurgus pretended that something was still wanting to the completion of his plan, and that it was necessary for him to go and consult the Oracle of Delphos. In the meantime, he persuaded his countrymen to take an oath for the strict observance of all his laws till his return, and then left Sparta with a firm resolution of never seeing it more. When he arrived at Delphos, he inquired of the Oracle, whether the laws he had made were sufficient to render the Lacedæmonians happy; and being told that they were, he sent this answer to Sparta, and then voluntarily starved himself to death. Others say, that he died in Crete, ordering his body to be burnt, and his ashes to be thrown into the sea. Whichever of these was the case, he equally obliged his countrymen, by the oath they had taken, to observe his laws for ever; which, indeed, they were sufficiently inclined to do, from a conviction of their real and intrinsic merit.

The first opportunity which the Spartans had to display the superiority of their power among the neighbouring states, was in the war between them and the Messenians. This war lasted twenty years, and is remarkable for two incidents that are well worthy of notice. The Spartans having drained their city of all its male inhabitants, in order to carry on the war, and having bound themselves by an oath not to return home till they had conquered the enemy; their women, in the meantime, remonstrated, that from their long absence all posterity would be at an end. To remedy this inconvenience, they detached fifty of their most promising young men from the army to go to Sparta, and to lie promiscuously with all the young women they pleased. The offspring of these virgins, were from them called Partheniæ, who finding themselves despised by the Spartans, on their return, as a spurious race, joined some years after in an insurrection with the Helots, but were soon suppressed. Being expelled the state, they went under the conduct of their captain, Phalantus, and settled at Tarentum in Italy.

The other incident is this. The Messenians having sent to consult the Oracle of Delphos, received for answer, that they must offer a virgin of the family of Æpytus as a sacrifice. The lot fell upon the daughter of Lyciscus; but she being thought to be supposititious, Aristodemus offered his daughter, whom all allowed to be his own. Her lover, however, attempted to avert the blow, by asserting that she was with child by him; but her father was so enraged at the imputation, that he ripped up her belly with his own hands publicly, in order to vindicate her innocence. The enthusiasm produced by this sacrifice, served for a while to give the Messenians the advantage; but being at last over-thrown and besieged in the city of Ithoë, they were obliged to submit to the Spartans, and Aristodemus slew himself on his daughter's grave.

After a rigorous subjection of thirty-nine years, the Messenians made one effort more for the recovery of their liberty under the conduct of Aristomenes, who thrice defeated the Spartan army, and as often merited the Hecatomphonia, a sacrifice due to those who had killed one hundred of the enemy hand to hand in battle. But the Spartans, being headed by the famous Athenian poet and school-master, Tyrtæus, who inflamed their courage by his songs and orations, the Messenians were at last obliged to abandon their country, which was added to the territory of Sparta [A. M. 3340]; and thus rendered that kingdom one of the most powerful states in all Greece.

CHAPTER III.

OF THE GOVERNMENT OF ATHENS, THE LAWS OF SOLON,
AND THE HISTORY OF THE REPUBLIC, FROM THE TIME
OF SOLON TO THE COMMENCEMENT OF THE PERSIAN
WAR.

THE happy effects produced at Sparta, by the institutions of Lycurgus, at last inspired the Athenians with
a desire of being governed by written laws; and the
first person they pitched upon for a legislator was
Draco [A. M. 3380], a man of equal integrity and wisdom, but rigid and severe in the highest degree. Draco
inflicted death on all crimes without exception, and
being asked why he did so, replied, "Small crimes
deserve death, and I have no higher punishment even
for the greatest." His laws, indeed, were so severe,
that they were said to be written not with ink, but
with blood. Their severity, however, defeated their
intention. It was impossible to carry them into execution. They therefore fell into disuse; and the people,
from the neglect and contempt of laws, soon grew more
licentious than ever they had been before any written
laws existed. It was in this distressful state of the
republic, that Solon was applied to for his advice and
assistance in regulating the government.

To mention all the proofs he had given of his wisdom, before he was advanced to the office of legislator,
would be foreign to our purpose. Suffice it to say,
that he was one of the seven wise men of Greece. The
others were, Thales the Milesian, Chilo of Lacedæmon,
Pittacus of Mitylene, Periander of Corinth, and Bias
and Cleobulus, whose birthplaces are uncertain. One
day at the court of Periander, a question was proposed,
Which was the most perfect popular government?
That, said Bias, where the laws have no superior.
That, said Thales, where the people are neither too
rich nor too poor. That, said Anacharsis the Scythian,
where virtue is honoured and vice detested. That,
said Pittacus, where dignities are always conferred
upon the virtuous, and never upon the base. That,

said Cleobulus, where the citizens fear blame more than punishment. That, said Chilo, where the laws are more regarded than the orators. But Solon's opinion seems to be best founded, who said, where an injury done to the meanest subject is an insult upon the whole community.

Nor must we omit his celebrated interview with Crœsus, king of Lydia. That monarch, who was reputed the richest prince of his time, having displayed before him his immense wealth and treasures, asked, whether he did not think him the happiest of mankind? No, replied Solon; I know one man more happy, a poor peasant of Greece, who, neither in affluence nor poverty, has but few wants, and has learned to supply them by his own labour. But at least, said the vain monarch, do you not think me happy? Alas, cried Solon, what man can be pronounced happy before he dies? The sagacity of Solon's replies appeared in the sequel. The kingdom of Lydia was invaded by Cyrus, the empire destroyed, and Crœsus himself taken prisoner. When he was led out to execution, according to the barbarous manners of the times, he then recollected the maxims of Solon, and could not help crying out, when on the scaffold, upon Solon's name. Cyrus, hearing him repeat the name with great earnestness, was desirous of knowing the reason; and, being informed by Crœsus of that philosopher's remarkable observation, he began to fear for himself, pardoned Crœsus, and took him for the future into confidence and friendship. Thus Solon had the merit of saving one king's life, and of reforming another.

Such was the man whom the Athenians now raised to the high dignity of archon, and invested with full power to new-model the government. Solon, however, was sensible that there were certain disorders in the state that were altogether incurable; and with these therefore he resolved not in the least to meddle. In a word, as he himself declared, he gave his countrymen not the best of all possible laws, but the best they were capable of receiving. His first step was in favour of the poor, whose debts he abolished at once, and who had been grievously oppressed by the rich, by the exorbitant interest they exacted from them. But to do this with the least injury he could to the creditor, he raised the value of money a little, and by that means nominally increased their riches. His next step was to repeal all the laws of Draco, except those against murder. He then proceeded to the regulation of offices, employments, and magistracies, all which he left in the hands of the rich. He divided the rich citizens into three classes, ranging them according to their incomes. Those that had five hundred measures yearly, as well in corn as liquids, were placed in the first rank; those that had three hundred were placed in the second; and those that had but two hundred made up the third. All the rest of the citizens, whose income fell short of two hundred measures, were comprised in a fourth and last class, and were considered as incapable of holding any employment whatever. But to compensate for this exclusion, he gave every private citizen a right to vote in the great assembly of the whole body of the people. And this, indeed, was a right of a most important nature. For by the laws of Athens it was permitted, after the decision of the magistrates, to appeal to the general assembly of the people; and thus, in time, all causes of weight and consequence came before them.

To counteract, however, the influence of a popular assembly, Solon gave greater weight to the court of Areopagus, and also instituted another council consisting of four hundred. Before his time the Areopagus was composed of such citizens as were most remarkable for their probity and wisdom. But Solon now ordained, that none should be admitted into it but such as had passed through the office of archon. By this means the dignity, and consequently the authority, of the court were greatly increased: and such was its reputation for integrity and discernment, that the Romans sometimes referred causes, which were too intricate for their own decision, to the determination of this tribunal. The business of the council of four hundred was to judge upon appeals from the Areopagus, and maturely to examine every question before it came before the general assembly of the people.

Such was the reformation in the general plan of government; his particular laws for the administration of justice were more numerous, and equally judicious. To promote a spirit of patriotism, and prevent all selfish indifference about the concerns of the republic, he ordained, that whoever in public dissensions espoused neither party, but remained neuter, should be declared infamous, condemned to perpetual exile, and to have all his estates confiscated. From a similar motive, he permitted every person to espouse the quarrel of any one that was injured or insulted. He abolished the custom of giving portions with young women, unless they were only children. He wished to render matrimony an honourable connexion, and not, as it formerly had too often been, and still continues to be, a mere matter of traffic. He allowed every one that was childless to dispose of his wealth as he pleased, without being obliged to leave it to the next of kin. By this means, the natural dependence of the young upon the old was strengthened and increased. He lessened the rewards of the victors at the Olympic and Isthmian games, whom he considered as a useless, and often a dangerous set of citizens, and bestowed the money thus saved upon the widows and children of those who had fallen in the service of their country.

To encourage industry, he empowered the Areopagus to inquire into every man's method of procuring a livelihood, and to punish such as had no visible way of doing so. With the like view he ordained, that a son should not be obliged to support his father in old age or necessity, if the latter had neglected to give him some trade or calling; and all illegitimate children were exempted from the same duty, as they owed nothing to their parents but the stigma of their birth. No one was allowed to revile another in public; the magistrates were obliged to be particularly circumspect in their behaviour; and it was even death for an archon to be taken drunk. Against the crime of parricide he made no law, as supposing it could never exist in any society. To preserve the sanctity of the marriage bed, he permitted any one to kill an adulterer, if he was taken in the fact; and though he allowed of public brothels, he branded both the women and men who frequented them with an indelible mark of disgrace.

Such were the chief institutions of this celebrated lawgiver, which he bound the Athenians, by a public oath, to observe religiously, at least for the space of a hundred years; and having thus completed the task assigned him, he set out on his travels, leaving his countrymen to become habituated to the new form of government. But it was not easy for a people long torn by civil dissensions to yield implicit obedience to any laws, however wisely framed; their former animosities began to revive, when that authority was removed which alone could hold them in subjection. The factions of the state were headed by three different leaders, Pisistratus, Megacles, and Lycurgus. Of these Pisistratus was at once the most powerful, the most artful, and in the end the most successful. He had many virtues, and hardly a single vice, except that of an inordinate ambition. He was learned himself, and an encourager of learning in others. Cicero says, he was the first that made the Athenians acquainted with the works of Homer; that he disposed of them in the order in which we now have them, and first caused them to be read at the feasts called Panathenæa.

By his promises, his professions, his liberality, and address, he so far gained upon the affections of his countrymen, that he was just upon the point of making himself master of the government, when he had the mortification to see Solon return, after an absence of ten years, fully apprized of his treacherous designs, and determined, if possible, to prevent their completion. This, however, he could not do for any length of time; for Pisistratus, now finding his schemes ripe for execution, gave himself several wounds, which he pretended to have received in the cause of the people; and in that condition, with his body all bloody, he ordered himself to be carried in his chariot to the marketplace, where, by his complaints and eloquence, he so inflamed the minds of the populace, that he obtained a guard of fifty persons for the security of his person. This was all he aimed at; for, having now got the rudiments of a standing army, he soon increased it to such a degree, as to enable him to set all opposition at defiance. In a little time, therefore, he seized upon the citadel, and in effect usurped the supreme power. Solon did not long survive the liberties of his country. He died about two years after at the age of eighty, admired and lamented by all the states of Greece, as the greatest legislator, and, excepting Homer, the greatest poet that had hitherto appeared.

By adhering to the same arts by which he had acquired his power, Pisistratus contrived to maintain himself in the possession of it to his dying day, and transmitted it to his two sons, Hippias and Hipparchus. These young men seemed to tread in the footsteps of their father; they encouraged learning and learned men; they invited to their court Anacreon, Simonides, and other poets, and honoured them with their friendship, and loaded them with presents. They established schools for the improvement of youth, and caused Mercuries to be erected in all the highways, with moral sentences written upon them, for the instruction of the lowest vulgar. Their reign, however, lasted but eighteen years, and terminated upon the following occasion.

Harmodius and Aristogiton, two citizens of Athens, had contracted a most sincere and inviolable friendship, and resolved to consider any insult that should be offered to either as an injury done to both. Hipparchus, being naturally of an amorous disposition, debauched the sister of Harmodius, and afterwards published her shame as she was about to walk in one of the sacred processions, alleging that she was not in a condition to assist at the ceremony. Such an indignity was not to be borne; and they therefore resolved to destroy the tyrant, which, after various efforts, they at last effected, though they themselves fell in the attempt. Hippias naturally wreaked his resentment upon all whom he supposed privy to the conspiracy, and, among others, upon a courtesan of the name of Leona, whose courage and constancy deserve to be mentioned. When put to the torture, she bore all the cruelty of her executioners with invincible fortitude; and lest she should, in the agony of pain, be induced to a confession, she bit off her tongue, and spit it in the tyrant's face. To perpetuate her memory, the Athenians erected a statue, representing a lioness without a tongue.

Hippias, dreading the fate of his brother, endeavoured to fortify himself by foreign alliances, and particularly by one with the Lacedæmonians; but in this he was prevented by the family of the Alcmæonidæ, who had been banished from Athens at the beginning of the usurpation, and who, having rebuilt the temple of Delphos in a most magnificent manner, had secured the priestess in their interest. Whenever, therefore, the Spartans came to consult the Oracle, they never received any promise of the God's assistance, but upon condition of setting Athens free. This task, therefore, they resolved to undertake; and, though unsuccessful in their first attempt, they at last dethroned the tyrant the very same year in which the kings were expelled from Rome [A. M. 3496]. The family of Alcmæon were chiefly instrumental in this great work; but the people seemed fonder of acknowledging their obligations to the two friends who struck the first blow. The names of Harmonius and Aristogiton were ever after held in the highest veneration; and their statues were erected in the marketplace, an honour which had never been paid to any one before.

CHAPTER IV.

FROM THE EXPULSION OF HIPPIAS TO THE DEATH OF MILTIADES.

Though Hippias, upon being driven from the throne, was obliged to abandon his native country, he did not, however, abandon all hopes of being able, some time or other, to recover his lost power. He first applied to the Lacedæmonians, and that people seemed suffi-

ciently willing to espouse his cause; and they thought
that they might the more easily effect his restoration,
as Athens was at this time thrown into confusion, by
the introduction of the new mode of voting by ostra-
cism, that is, of procuring the banishment of any citizen
for ten years, whose wealth or popularity rendered
him dangerous to the state, by allowing every one
above sixty years of age to give in the name of the
obnoxious person written upon a tile or oyster-shell.
Before they undertook, however, to assist Hippias in
reascending the throne, they thought it prudent to
consult the other states of Greece with regard to the
propriety of the measure, and finding them all to be
totally averse to it, they abandoned the tyrant and his
cause for ever.

Hippias, disappointed in his hopes of aid from the
Lacedæmonians, had recourse to one whom he considered as a much more powerful patron. This was
Artaphernes, governor of Sardis, for the king of Persia.
To him he represented the facility with which an entire
conquest might be made of Athens; and the Persian
court, influenced by the prospect of gaining such an
addition of territory, and particularly such an extent
of seacoast, readily adopted the proposal. When the
Athenians, therefore, sent a messenger into Persia to
vindicate their proceedings with regard to Hippias,
they received for answer, "That if they wished to be
safe, they must admit Hippias for their king." But
these gallant republicans had too ardent a passion for
liberty, and too rooted an aversion to slavery, patiently
to submit to so imperious a mandate. They, therefore,
returned to it a flat and peremptory refusal. And from
that time forward the Athenians and Persians began to
prepare for commencing hostilities against each other.

The gallantry, indeed, of the Athenians upon this
occasion is the more to be admired, as their numbers
and resources bore no proportion to those of the prince
whom they thus set at defiance. The Persian monarch
was, at that time, the most powerful sovereign in the
universe; whereas the small state of Athens did not
contain above twenty thousand citizens, ten thousand

strangers, and about fifty or sixty thousand servants. The state of Sparta, which afterwards took such a considerable share, and made so capital a figure in the war against Persia, was still more inconsiderable with respect to numbers. These did not amount to above nine thousand citizens, and about thirty thousand peasants. And yet these two states, with very little assistance from the inferior republics, were able not only to resist, but even to baffle and defeat all the attempts of the Persian monarch; a memorable instance what acts of heroism may be performed by men animated by a love of freedom, and inspired with a passion for military glory.

The restoration of Hippias was not the only cause of quarrel between the Persians and the Athenians. The Greek colonies of Ionia, Æolia, and Caria, that had been settled for above five hundred years in Asia Minor, were at length subdued by Crœsus, king of Lydia; and he, in turn, sinking under the power of Cyrus, his conquests, of course, fell in with the rest of his dominions. These colonies, however, had not yet lost all memory of the liberty they had formerly enjoyed; and they therefore seized every opportunity of delivering themselves from the Persian yoke, and recovering their ancient independence. In this they were now encouraged by Histiæus, the governor, or tyrant, as he was called, of Miletus; for all the Persian governors of these provinces were by the Greeks called tyrants. This man, having rendered his fidelity suspected at the Persian court, had no other way of providing for his own safety, than by exciting the Ionians to a revolt. By his direction, therefore, Aristagoras, his deputy, first applied to the Lacedæmonians for assistance; and failing of success in that quarter, he next had recourse to the Athenians, where he met with a more favourable reception. The Athenians were at this time inflamed with the highest resentment against the Persian monarch, on account of his haughty mandate with regard to the restoration of Hippias; and they therefore supplied the Ionians with twenty ships, to which the Eretrians and Euboeans added five more.

Thus supported, Aristagoras entered the Persian territories, and penetráting into the heart of Lydia, he burned Sardis, the capital city; but being soon after deserted by the Athenians, on account of some checks he received, he found himself altogether unable to make head against the power of Persia; and though he contrived to maintain the struggle for the space of six years, yet he was at last obliged to fly into Thrace, where he was cut off with all his followers. As to Histiæus himself, being taken prisoner with a few of the insurgents, he was conducted to Artaphernes, and that inhuman tyrant immediately ordered him to be crucified, and his head to be sent to Darius.

The commencement of this war naturally tended to widen the breach between the Athenians and Persians, and the conclusion of it was no less calculated to inflame the pride and presumption of the latter, than to inspire them with the ambitious thoughts of making an entire conquest of Greece. To pave the way for this grand project, Darius, in the twenty-eighth year of his reign, having recalled all his other generals, sent his son-in-law, Mardonius, to command throughout the maritime parts of Asia, and particularly to revenge the burning of Sardis, which he could neither forgive nor forget. But his fleet being shattered in a storm in doubling the cape of Mount Athos, and his army repulsed, and himself wounded, by the Thracians, who attacked him suddenly by night, Mardonius returned to the Persian court, covered with shame and confusion for having miscarried in his enterprise both by sea and land. Darius, therefore, displaced him, and appointed two older and abler generals, namely, Datis, a Mede, and Artaphernes, son of the late governor of Sardis, in his stead. At the same time he exerted himself with unwearied diligence, in furnishing them with such an army and navy as might render them morally certain of success.

Previous, however, to his invasion of Greece, he thought it became his dignity and humanity to send heralds into that country to require submission from the different states, or to threaten them with his vengeance in case of refusal. The lesser states, intimidated by his power, readily submitted; but the Athenians and Spartans nobly disdained to acknowledge subjection to any earthly sovereign. When, therefore, the heralds demanded earth and water, the usual method of requiring submission from inferior states, these spirited republicans threw the one into a well, and the other into a ditch, and tauntingly bid them take earth and water from thence. Nay, they went still farther; they resolved to punish the Æginetans for having basely submitted to the power of Persia, and by that means betrayed the common cause of Greece. These people, indeed, made some resistance; they even carried on a naval war against the Athenians; but these last, having at length overcome them, increased their own navy to such a degree, as to render it almost an equal match for that of Persia.

In the mean time Darius, having completed his levies, sent away his generals, Datis and Artaphernes, to what he considered as a certain conquest. They were furnished with a fleet of six hundred ships, and an army of a hundred and twenty thousand men; and their instructions were to give up Athens and Eretria to be plundered, to burn all the houses and temples of both, and to lead away the inhabitants into captivity. The country was to be laid desolate, and the army was provided with a sufficient number of chains for binding the prisoners.

To oppose this formidable invasion, the Athenians had only about ten thousand men, but all of them animated with that invincible spirit which the love of liberty ever inspires. They were at this time headed by three of the greatest generals and statesmen their country ever produced, though no country ever produced more. These were Miltiades, Themistocles, and Aristides. The first was looked upon as the ablest commander; the second was so fond of a popular government, and so eager to ingratiate himself with his fellow-citizens, that he was frequently accused of acts of partiality. Indeed, he seemed to glory in the charge; for one day, when somebody was talking to him on the subject, and saying that he would make an excellent magistrate if he had more impartiality: "God forbid," replied he, "that I should ever sit upon a tribunal, where my friends should find no more favour than strangers." As to Aristides, he was so rigidly and inflexibly just, that his name has descended to posterity as almost another term for justice itself.

The first brunt of the war fell upon the Eretrians, who, being utterly unable to oppose so mighty a force in the field, shut themselves up in the town; but, although they defended the place with great gallantry, yet, after a siege of seven days, it was taken by storm, and reduced to ashes. The inhabitants were put in chains, and sent as the first fruits of victory to the Persian monarch; but he, contrary to their expectation, treated them with great lenity, and gave them a village in the country of Cissa for their residence; where Apollonius Tyanæus found their descendants six hundred years after.

Elated with this success, the Persians advanced into the heart of the country, and, being directed in their march by Hippias, the expelled tyrant of Athens, they soon arrived in the plains of Marathon, about ten miles distant from that city. There, however, it was that the Athenians resolved to oppose them; but not thinking themselves singly equal to such an undertaking, they first sent to the Spartans for assistance, and would certainly have obtained it, had it not been for a foolish superstition which prevailed among that people, and which would not allow them to begin a march before the full moon. They then applied to the other states of Greece; but these were too much intimidated by the power of Persia to venture to move in their defence.

Obliged, therefore, to depend upon their own courage alone, they collected all their forces, to the number of ten thousand men, and intrusted the command of them to ten generals, of whom Miltiades was the chief; and each of these was to have the direction of the troops for one day at a time in regular succession. But this arrangement was soon found to be so very inconvenient that, by the advice of Aristides, the chief command was vested in Miltiades alone, as the ablest and most experienced of all the generals. At the same time it was resolved in a council of war, though only by a majority of one vote, to meet the enemy in the open field, instead of waiting for them within the walls of the city.

Miltiades, sensible of the inferiority of his numbers when compared to those of the enemy, endeavoured to make up for this defect by taking possession of an advantageous ground. He, therefore, drew up his army at the foot of a mountain, so that the enemy should not be able to surround him or charge him in the rear. At the same time he fortified his flanks with a number of large trees that were cut down for the purpose. Datis saw the advantage which the Athenians must derive from this masterly disposition; but, relying on the superiority of his numbers, and unwilling to wait till the Spartan succours should arrive, he resolved to begin the engagement. The signal for battle, however, was no sooner given, than the Athenians, instead of waiting for the onset of the enemy, according to their usual custom, rushed in upon them with irresistible fury. The Persians regarded this first step as the result of madness and despair, rather than of deliberate courage; but they were soon convinced of their mistake, when they found that the Athenians maintained the charge with the same spirit with which they had begun it. Miltiades had purposely and judiciously made his wings much stronger than his centre, which was commanded by Themistocles and Aristides. The Persians, availing themselves of this circumstance, attacked the centre with great bravery, and were just upon the point of making it give way, when the two wings, having now become victorious, suddenly wheeled about, and, falling upon the enemy in both flanks at once, threw them into disorder. The rout in a moment became universal, and they fled to their ships with great precipitation. The Athenians pursued them as far as the beach, and even set several of their ships on fire. It was on this occasion that Cynægyrus, the brother of the poet Æschylus, seized one of the enemy's ships with his right hand, as they were pushing it off from the shore. When his right hand was cut off, he laid hold of the vessel with his left; and that likewise being lopped off, he at last seized it with his teeth, and in that manner expired.

Seven of the enemy's ships were taken, and above six thousand of them left dead on the field of battle, not to mention those who were drowned as they were endeavouring to escape, or were consumed in the ships that were set on fire. Of the Greeks there fell not above two hundred, and among these was Callimachus, who gave the casting vote for fighting the enemy in the field [A. M. 3514]. Hippias, who was the chief cause of the war, is thought to have perished in this battle, though some say he escaped, and afterwards died miserably at Lemnos.

Such was the famous battle of Marathon, one of the most important that is to be found in history, as it first taught the Greeks to despise the power of the Persian monarch, and bravely to maintain their own independence; and thus to go on cultivating those arts and sciences, which had so evident a tendency to polish and refine their own manners, and have since diffused their benign influence over all the rest of Europe.

Of the marble which the Persians had brought with them to erect a monument in memory of their expected victory, the Athenians now caused a statue to be made by the celebrated sculptor Phidias, to transmit to posterity the remembrance of their defeat. This statue was dedicated to the goddess Nemesis, who had a temple near the place. Monuments were at the same time erected to the memory of all those who had fallen in the battle; and upon these were inscribed their own names, and the name of the tribe to which they belonged. Of these monuments there were three kinds; one for the Athenians, one for the Platæans their allies, and one for the slaves, who had been enrolled into the troops upon this pressing emergency. To express their gratitude to Miltiades, the Athenians caused a picture to be painted by one of their most eminent artists, named Polygnotus, in which that great commander was represeated at the head of the other generals, animating the troops, and setting them an example of bravery.

But their gratitude to this celebrated warrior, however sincere, was by no means lasting. The Athenians, with all their good qualities, were naturally fickle, and apt to be jealous of such as, either by their merit, their power, or popularity, had, in their opinion, rendered themselves dangerous to the state. Of this Miltiades had very soon after a mortifying proof: for having received a wound in an expedition against the Parians, and being thereby prevented from appearing in public to defend himself from a charge of bribery, which was brought against him by one Xanthippus, sentence was of course passed upon him in his absence, and he was condemned to lose his life. This severe sentence, however, the Athenians had not the effrontery to execute upon one who had done them such essential services, and they therefore changed it into a fine of fifty talents; and as this was a sum which Miltiades could not pay, he was thrown into prison, where he soon after died. But the Athenians would not suffer his body to be buried till the fine was paid. His son Cimon, therefore, by exerting all his interest among his friends and relations, was at last able to raise the requisite sum to pay the fine, and to procure his father an honourable interment.

CHAPTER V.

FROM THE DEATH OF MILTIADES TO THE RETREAT OF XERXES OUT OF GREECE.

DARIUS, rather enraged than intimidated by the loss he had sustained in the battle of Marathon, was preparing to invade Greece in person, when, happily for the peace of that country, death put an end to his ambitious project. His son Xerxes, however, who succeeded him on the throne, was determined to execute the plan which his father had formed. Having just returned from a successful expedition he had made into Egypt, he expected to meet with the like good fortune in Europe.

Confident of victory, he did not choose, he said, for
the future to buy the figs of Attica; he would possess
himself of the country, and thus have figs of his own.
But before he would engage in so important an enterprise, he thought proper to consult the principal officers
of his court. Mardonius, his brother-in-law, well knowing his secret sentiments, and willing to flatter him in
his favourite pursuits, highly applauded the resolution
he had taken. But Artabanus, his uncle, whom years
and experience had rendered wise, used every argument he could think of, in order to divert him from his
rash design, and he addressed himself to the king in
the following terms:

"Permit me, Sir," said he, "to deliver my sentiments
upon this occasion with that liberty which becomes my
age, and my regard for your interest. When Darius,
your father, and my brother, first thought of making
war upon the Scythians, I used all my endeavours to
divert him from it. The people you are going to attack
are infinitely more formidable than they. If the Athenians
alone could defeat the numerous army commanded by
Datis and Artaphernes, what ought we to expect from
an opposition of all the states of Greece united? You
design to pass from Asia into Europe, by laying a bridge
over the sea. But what if the Athenians should advance
and destroy this bridge, and so prevent our return? Let
us not expose ourselves to such dangers, especially as
we have no sufficient motives to induce us to run such
risks; at least let us take time to reflect upon the matter.
When we have maturely considered an affair, whatever
happens to be the success of it, we have nothing to
regret. Precipitation is imprudent, and is usually
unsuccessful. Above all, do not suffer yourself, great
prince, to be dazzled with the splendour of imaginary
glory. The highest trees have the most reason to dread
being struck with the thunder. As for you, Mardonius,
who so earnestly urge this expedition, if it must be so,
lead it forward. But let the king, whose life is dear
to us all, return into Persia. In the meantime, let
your children and mine be given up as a pledge to
answer for the success of the war. If the issue be

favourable, I consent that mine be put to death; but if it be otherwise, as I foresee it will, then I desire that you and your children may receive the reward of rashness."—The pride of the Persian monarch could not easily bear such a plain but honest speech, even from an uncle; and he therefore sternly replied, "Thank the gods that thou art my father's brother; were it not for that, thou shouldest this moment receive the just reward of thy audacious behaviour. But you shall have your punishment; remain here behind among the women; these you but too much resemble in your cowardice and fear. Stay here, while I march at the head of my troops, where my duty and glory call me."

Xerxes, having thus resolved upon his expedition into Greece, began to make preparations for carrying it forward; and the greatness of these showed the high sense he entertained of the power and bravery of the enemy. Sardis was the place of general rendezvous for his land forces: and the fleet was ordered to advance along the coasts of Asia Minor, towards the Hellespont. In its way thither, in order to shorten its passage, he cut a canal through the neck of land that joined Mount Athos to the continent; and while this was doing, he addressed the mountain, with all that pomp and ostentation for which the Eastern princes have ever been so remarkable. "Athos," said he, "thou proud aspiring mountain, that liftest up thy head unto the heavens, be not so audacious to put obstacles in my way: if thou dost, I will cut thee level with the plain, and throw thee headlong into the sea."

In his march to Sardis, he gave a shocking proof of the extreme acts of cruelty he was capable of committing whenever his authority was called in question. Having required the eldest son of Pythias, a Lydian prince to attend him in the war, the father offered him all his treasure, amounting to about four millions sterling, to purchase his exemption; and as the young man seemed desirous of staying at home, Xerxes commanded him immediately to be put to death before his father's eyes. Then causing the body to be cut in two, and one part of it to be placed on the right, and the other on the left, he made his whole army pass between them; a terrible example of what every one had to expect that dared to dispute his orders.

His army was composed not merely of Persians, but of Medes, Lydians, Bactrians, Assyrians, Hyrcanians, in a word, of every people that either acknowledged his authority, dreaded his power, or courted his alliance. It is said to have amounted to above two millions of men. His fleet consisted of fourteen hundred and twenty-seven ships, besides a thousand lesser vessels, that were employed in carrying provisions. On board of these were six hundred thousand men; so that the whole army might be said to amount to above two millions and a half; which, with the women, slaves, and sutlers, always attending a Persian camp, might make the whole about five millions of souls—a force which, if rightly conducted, might have given law to the universe: but being commanded by ignorance and presumption, was soon after repulsed, and finally defeated by the small but gallant states of Greece.

A. M. 3523.] With this mighty armament Xerxes set out on his expedition into Greece, ten years after the battle of Marathon. Upon reviewing his forces his heart was naturally elated with joy, from a consciousness of his superior power: but this soon gave place to the feelings of humanity, and he burst into tears, when he reflected that, a hundred years hence, not one of so many thousands would be alive. He had previously given orders for building a bridge of boats across the Hellespont, or, as it is now called, the Dardanelles, which separates Asia from Europe, and is about an English mile over. But this bridge, when completed, being carried away by the current, Xerxes, like a tyrant, wreaked his vengeance upon the workmen, and, like a lunatic, upon the sea. He caused the heads of the former to be struck off, and a certain number of lashes to be inflicted upon the latter, to punish it for its insolence; and fetters to be thrown into it, to teach it for the future, obedience to his will: a striking proof how much the possession of despotic power tends not only to corrupt the heart, but even to weaken and blind the understanding. Another and a stronger bridge was soon after built, and over this the army passed; though, such was its immense number, the whole could not cross in less than seven days.

Xerxes having thus reached Europe, began his march directly for Greece, receiving every where the submission of the countries through which he passed. Even the smaller states of Greece, overawed by his power, submitted at the first summons. Athens and Sparta alone, those glorious republics, nobly disdained such pusillanimous conduct. They gallantly resolved to oppose the invader of their country, and either to preserve their liberties entire, or to perish in the attempt. From the moment that Xerxes began his preparations, they had received intelligence of his designs; and they, in their turn, began to take measures for rendering them abortive. They had also sent spies to Sardis, in order to bring them an exact account of the number and quality of the enemy's forces. The spies, indeed, were seized, but Xerxes, instead of punishing, or even detaining them, ordered them to be conducted through his camp, and then dismissed, desiring them at the same time, on their return home, to give a faithful relation of what they had seen. The Athenians and Spartans, however, neither intimidated by the mighty force that now came against them, nor by the base submission of the inferior states, nobly resolved to face the common danger with joint forces. These forces did not amount to above eleven thousand two hundred men; and yet with this handful of troops, they determined to oppose the almost innumerable army of Xerxes.

Their first care was to appoint a general; and they wisely made choice of Themistocles, the ablest commander that had appeared in Greece since the death of Miltiades. They likewise recalled Aristides, who had been driven into banishment by the faction of his enemies; at the head of which, indeed, was Themistocles: such is the jealousy that sometimes prevails between great men, though equally attached to the interests of their country! It was upon the occasion of his banishment that a peasant, who could not write, and did not know Aristides personally, applied to him, and desired him to write the name of that citizen upon the shell, by which his vote was given against him. "Has he done you any wrong," said Aristides, "that you are for condemning him in this manner?" "No," replied the peasant, "but I hate to hear him always praised for his justice." Aristides, without saying a word more, calmly took the shell, wrote down his name upon it, and contentedly retired into exile. Themistocles, however, convinced of his uncommon merit, and willing to have the benefit of his counsels, was now as desirous of having him recalled, as ever he had been to see him banished; and these two great men, generously forgetting all their private feuds and animosities, resolved to exert their joint efforts in promoting the good of the public.

Themistocles saw that the enemy must be opposed by sea as well as by land; and to enable him to do this with the greater effect, he had lately caused a hundred galleys to be built, and turned all his thoughts towards the improvement of the navy. The Oracle had declared some time before, that Athens should only defend herself with wooden walls; and he took the advantage of this ambiguity to persuade his countrymen, that by such walls was only meant her shipping. The Lacedæmonians used no less industry in improving their navy; so that, upon the approach of Xerxes, the confederates found themselves possessed of a squadron of two hundred and eighty sail, the command of which was conferred upon Eurybiades, a Spartan.

The next point to be determined was, which was the most proper place for making the first stand against the enemy; and after some deliberation, the straits of Thermopylæ were pitched upon for the purpose. This was a narrow pass of twenty-five feet broad, between Thessaly and Phocis, defended by the remains of an old wall, with gates to it, and remarkable for some hot baths, from whence the place had its name. The command of this important pass was given to Leonidas, one of the kings of Sparta, who led thither a body of six thousand men. Of these three hundred only were Spartans: the rest consisted of Bœotians, Corinthians, Phocians, and other allies. This chosen band were taught from the beginning to look upon themselves as a forlorn hope, only placed there to check the progress of the enemy, and give them a foretaste of the desperate valour of Greece; nor were even oracles wanting to inspire them with enthusiastic ardour. It had been declared, that to procure the safety of Greece, it was necessary that a king, one of the descendants of Hercules, should die; and this task was now cheerfully undertaken by Leonidas, who, when he marched out of Lacedæmon, considered himself as a willing sacrifice offered up for the good of his country.

In the meantime, Xerxes advanced with his immense army, the very sight of which he thought would terrify the Greeks into submission, without his being obliged to strike a single blow. Great, therefore, was his surprise, when he found that a few desperate men were determined to dispute his passage through the Straits of Thermopylæ. At first he could not believe they would persevere in their resolution; and he therefore gave them four days to reflect on their danger, hoping they would at last think it most prudent to retire. But when he found them remain immoveable at their post, he sent them a summons to deliver up their arms. Leonidas, with a true Spartan contempt, desired him "to come and take them." And when some people said that the Persian forces were so numerous that their very darts would darken the sun, "Then," replied Dieneces, a Spartan, "we shall fight in the shade."

Xerxes, provoked at these sarcasms, resolved to begin the attack immediately. The first assault was made by a body of Medes, but these were instantly repulsed with great slaughter. A body of ten thousand Persians, commonly known by the name of the Immortal Band, made another attempt to dislodge the Grecians, but with no better success than the former. In a word, the Greeks maintained their ground against the whole power of the Persian army for two days together; and would probably have maintained it much longer, had it not been for the treachery of Epialtes, a Trachinian, who, having deserted to the enemy, conducted a body

D

of twenty thousand Persians through a by-path to the top of a mountain that overhung the straits.

Leonidas seeing the enemy in this situation, plainly perceived that his post was no longer tenable. He therefore advised his allies to retire, and reserve themselves for better times, and the future safety of Greece. As for himself and his fellow Spartans, they were obliged by their laws not to fly; that he owed a life to his country, and that it was now his duty to fall in its defence. Thus, having dismissed all but his three hundred Spartans, with some Thespians and Thebans, in all not a thousand men, he exhorted his followers in the most cheerful manner to prepare for death. "Come, my fellow soldiers," says he, "let us dine cheerfully here, for to-night we shall sup with Pluto." His men, upon hearing his determined purpose, set up a loud shout as if they had been invited to a banquet, and resolved every man to sell his life as dearly as he could. The night now began to advance, and this was thought the most glorious opportunity of meeting death in the enemy's camp, where darkness, by hiding the smallness of their numbers, would fill the Persians with greater consternation. Thus resolved, they made directly to the Persian tents, and, in the silence of the night, had almost penetrated to the royal pavilion, with hopes of surprising the king. The obscurity added much to the horror of the scene; and the Persians, incapable of distinguishing friend from foe, fell furiously upon each other, and rather assisted than opposed the Greeks. Thus success seemed to crown the rashness of their enterprise, until the morning beginning to dawn, the light soon discovered the smallness of their numbers. They were soon, therefore, surrounded by the Persian forces, who fearing to fall in upon them, flung their javelins from every quarter, till the Greeks, not so much conquered, as tired with conquering, fell amidst heaps of the slaughtered enemy, leaving behind them an example of courage, to which there is no parallel to be found in history. Leonidas was one of the first that fell; and the endeavours of the Lacedæmonians to defend his dead body were incredible. It was found,

after the battle, buried under a mountain of the dead ;
and was nailed to a cross, by way of infamy, by the
brutal victor. Of all the train two only escaped, whose
names were Aristodemus and Panites. The latter was
treated with such contempt on his return to Sparta, that
he killed himself in despair. Aristodemus recovered
his lost honour by his gallant behaviour at the battle
of Platæa. The loss of the Persians on this occasion
is supposed to have amounted to twenty thousand men,
among which were two of the king's brothers.

The very day on which the battle of Thermopylæ
was fought there was a naval engagement between the
fleets of Greece and Persia, in which the former took or
sunk thirty of the enemy's ships, and forced a hundred
and seventy of them to sea, where, by stress of weather,
they were all soon after either sunk or stranded.

Xerxes, however, having now passed the straits,
found nothing capable of opposing his progress in the
open country, and he therefore directed his march
towards Athens, on which he was determined to take
a signal vengeance. Themistocles, seeing the impos-
sibility of defending this place, used all his eloquence
and address in persuading his countrymen to abandon
it for the present ; and this he was at last able, though
with no little difficulty, to effect. A decree was therefore passed, by which it was ordained, that Athens for
a while should be given up in trust to the Gods ; and
that all the inhabitants, whether in freedom or slavery,
should go on board the fleet. The young and adven-
turous set sail for Salamis ; the old, the women and
children, took shelter at Trezene, the inhabitants of
which generousl offered them an asylum. But in this
general desertion of the city, that which raised the
compassion of all was, the great number of old men
they were obliged to leave in the place, on account of
their age and infirmities. Many also voluntarily remained behind, believing that the citadel, which they
had fortified with wooden walls, was what the Oracle
pointed out for general safety. To heighten this scene
of distress, the matrons were seen clinging with fond
affection to the places where they had so long resided ;

the women filled the streets with lamentations; and even the poor domestic animals seemed to take a part in the general concern. It was impossible to see those poor creatures run howling and crying after their masters, who were going on shipboard, without being strongly affected. Amongst these the faithfulness of a particular dog is recorded, who jumped into the sea after his master, and continued swimming as near as he could to the vessel, till he landed at Salamis, and died the moment after upon the shore.

Those few inhabitants that remained behind retired into the citadel, where literally interpreting the Oracle, they fortified it as well as they could, and patiently awaited the approach of the invader. Nor was it long before they saw him arrive at their gates, and summon them to surrender. This, however, they refused to do, or even to listen to any terms he proposed to them. The place was therefore taken by assault; all who were found in it were put to the sword, and the citadel was reduced to ashes.

But though the confederates had been thus obliged to abandon Athens to the fury of the enemy, they were by no means disposed to let them overrun the whole country. They took possession of Peloponnesus, built a wall across the isthmus that joined it to the continent, and committed the defence of that important post to Cleombrotus, the brother of Leonidas. In adopting this measure they were all of them unanimous, as being the most prudent that could be embraced. The case was not the same with regard to the operations of the fleet. Eurybiades was for bringing it into the neighbourhood of the isthmus, that so the sea and land forces might act in conjunction. Themistocles was of quite a different opinion, and maintained, that it would be the height of folly to abandon so advantageous a post as that of Salamis, where they were now stationed. They were now, he said, in possession of the narrow seas, where the number of the enemy's ships could never avail them; that the only hope now left the Athenians was their fleet, and that this must not capriciously be given up by ignorance to the enemy. Eurybiades, who considered himself as glanced at, could not contain his resentment, but was going to strike Themistocles for his insolence —"Strike me," cried the Athenian, "strike me, but hear me." His moderation and his reasoning prevailed; and it was therefore resolved to await the enemy's fleet at Salamis. Fearful, however, that the confederates might change their mind, Themistocles had recourse to one of those stratagems which mark superior genius. He contrived to have it privately intimated to Xerxes that the confederates were now assembled at Salamis, preparing for flight, and that it would be an easy matter to attack and destroy them. The artifice succeeded. Xerxes gave orders to his fleet to block up Salamis by night, in order to prevent an escape, that would have baffled his views of vengeance.

Even Themistocles himself was not sensible, for some time, of the success of his scheme, and of his seemingly dangerous situation. Aristides, who then commanded a small body of troops at Ægina, no sooner heard it, than, ignorant of the real cause of all these manœuvres, and actually thinking Themistocles in danger, he ventured in a small boat by night through the whole fleet of the enemy. Upon landing he made up to the tent of Themistocles, and addressed him in the following manner: "If we are wise, Themistocles, we shall henceforth lay aside all those frivolous and puerile dissensions which have hitherto divided us. One strife, and a noble one it is, now remains for us, which of us shall be most serviceable to our country. It is yours to command as a general; it is mine to obey as a subject; and happy shall I be, if my advice can any way contribute to your and my country's glory." He then informed him of the fleet's real situation, and warmly exhorted him to give battle without delay. Themistocles felt all that gratitude, which so generous and disinterested a conduct deserved; and eager to make a proper return, he immediately let him into all his schemes and projects, particularly this last, of suffering himself to be blocked up. After this they exerted their joint influence with the other commanders to persuade them to engage; and accordingly both fleets prepared themselves for battle.

The Grecian fleet consisted of three hundred and eighty ships, the Persian fleet was much more numerous. But whatever advantage they had in numbers, and the size of their ships, they fell infinitely short of the Greeks in their naval skill, and their acquaintance with the seas where they fought; but it was chiefly on the superior abilities of their commanders that the Greeks placed their hopes of success. Eurybiades had nominally the command of the fleet, but Themistocles directed all its operations. He knowing that a periodical wind, which would be favourable, would soon set in, delayed the attack till that time; and this had no sooner arisen, than the signal was given for battle, and the Grecian fleet sailed forward in exact order.

As the Persians now fought under the eye of their sovereign, who beheld the action from a neighbouring promontory, they exerted themselves for some time with great spirit; but their courage abated when they came to a closer engagement. The numerous disadvantages of their circumstances and situation then began to appear. The wind blew directly in their faces; the height and heaviness of their vessels rendered them unwieldy and useless; and even the number of their ships in the narrow sea only served to embarrass and perplex them. The Ionians were the first that fled; the Phœnicians and Cyprians were soon after driven on shore; and in a little time their whole fleet was thrown into confusion. In the general consternation which this occasioned, Artemisia, queen of Halicarnassus, who had come to the assistance of Xerxes with five ships, exerted herself with so much spirit, that that monarch was heard to say, that his soldiers behaved like women in the conflict, and the women like soldiers. Nothing, however, could repair the disorder that had now taken place in the Persian fleet. They instantly fled on all sides; some of them were sunk, and more taken; above two hundred were burnt, and all the rest were entirely dispersed.

Such was the issue of the battle of Salamis, in which the Persians received a more severe blow than any they had hitherto experienced from Greece. Themistocles is said to have been so elated with this victory, that he proposed breaking down the bridge on the Hellespont, and thus cutting off the retreat of the enemy; but from this he was dissuaded by Aristides, who represented the great danger of reducing so powerful an army to despair. Xerxes, however, seems to have been so apprehensive of some such step being taken, that, after leaving about three hundred thousand of his best troops behind him under Mardonius, not so much with a view of conquering Greece, as in order to prevent a pursuit, he hastened back with the rest to the Hellespont, where finding the bridge broken down by the violence of the waves, he was obliged to pass over in a small boat; and this manner of leaving Europe, when compared to his ostentatious method of entering it, rendered his disgrace the more poignant and afflicting.

CHAPTER VI.

FROM THE RETREAT OF XERXES OUT OF GREECE TO THE BATTLE OF MYCALE.

NOTHING could exceed the joy of the Greeks upon the victory they had obtained at Salamis [A. M. 3524]. It was a custom among them, after a battle, for the commanding officers to declare who had distinguished themselves most, by writing the names of such as merited the first and second rewards. On this occasion, each officer concerned adjudged the first rank to himself, but all allowed the second to Themistocles, which was in fact allowing him a tacit superiority. This was farther confirmed by the Lacedæmonians, who carried him in triumph to Sparta; and who having adjudged the reward of valour to their own countryman, Eurybiades, adjudged that of wisdom to Themistocles. They crowned him with olive, presented him with a rich chariot, and conducted him with three hundred horse to the confines of their state. But there was an homage paid him that flattered his pride yet more; when he appeared at the Olympic games, that is before all the states of Greece assembled, the spectators received him with uncommon acclamations. As soon as he appeared the whole assembly rose up to do him honour; nobody regarded either the games or the combatants; Themistocles was the only object worth their attention. Struck with such flattering honours, he could not help crying out, that he had that day reaped the fruits of all his labours.

Mardonius, having passed the winter in Thessaly, led his forces in the spring into the province of Bœotia, and from thence sent Alexander, king of Macedonia, with very tempting proposals to the Athenians, hoping by that means to detach them from the general interests of Greece. He offered to rebuild their city, to present them with a considerable sum of money, to allow them to enjoy their laws and liberties, and to bestow upon them the government of all Greece. The Spartans were afraid that the Athenians might be apt to accept of these proposals, and they therefore sent ambassadors to Athens, in order to dissuade them from so base a conduct. But Aristides, who was then chief archon of Athens, needed no other monitor than the dictate of his own heart. Receiving Alexander and the ambassadors at the same time, he addressed them in the following terms: "For men," said he, "bred up in pleasure and ignorance, it is natural to proffer great rewards, and to hope by bribes to undermine virtue. Barbarians, who make silver and gold the chief object of their esteem, may be excused for thinking to corrupt the fidelity of a free people; but that the Lacedæmonians, who came to remonstrate against these offers, should suppose they could prevail, is indeed surprising. The Athenians have the common liberty of Greece entrusted to their care, and mountains of gold are not able to shake their fidelity: No; so long as that sun, which the Persians adore, continues to shine with wonted splendour, so long shall the Athenians be mortal enemies to the Persians; so long shall they continue to pursue them for ravaging their lands, for burning their houses, and polluting their temples. Such is the answer we return to the Persian proposal. And you," continued he, addressing himself to Alexander, "if you are really their friend, refrain for the future from being the bearer of such proposals; your honour, and perhaps even your safety demands it."

Mardonius, provoked at the rejection of his offers, invaded Attica, which the Athenians, unable to resist the torrent, were once more obliged to abandon to his fury. Nothing, however, could reconcile that people to any terms of accommodation. They even stoned Lycidas, a senator, to death, for proposing a submission; and his wife and children met with the same fate from the women. In the meantime the Spartans were in danger of falling into the same error from which they had been so anxious to preserve the Athenians; I mean that of consulting their own private safety, without regarding the general interests of Greece. They proposed to fortify the isthmus of Peloponnesus: but the Athenians remonstrating against so partial and ungenerous a proceeding, the Spartans readily gave up the point.

The Grecian army was now assembled to the number of seventy thousand men. Of these five thousand were Spartans, attended by thirty-five thousand Helots. The Athenians amounted to eight thousand, and the troops of the allies made up the rest. With this army the Greeks resolved to oppose Mardonius, though at the head of no less than three hundred thousand men. That general, fearing to be attacked in the hilly country of Attica, where he could not avail himself of his great superiority of numbers, had lately returned into Bœotia, and encamped his troops on the banks of the river Asopus. Thither he was pursued by the Grecians; but as neither side could begin the attack without encountering great disadvantage, the two armies continued in sight of each other for the space of ten days, both of them equally eager for a battle, and yet both afraid to strike the first blow.

It was during this interval that a mutiny had like to have arisen in the Grecian army about the post of honour. All parties allowed the Spartans the command of the right wing; but the Tegæans alleged that they were better entitled, by their past services, to the command of the left, than the Athenians, who now occupied it. This dissension might have produced very-fatal effects, had it not been for the moderation and magnanimity of Aristides, who commanded the Athenians, and who addressed himself to the Spartans and the rest of the confederates in the following manner: "It is not now a time, my friends, to dispute about the merit of past services; for all boasting is vain in the day of danger. Let it be the brave man's pride to own, that it is not the post or station which gives courage, or which can take it away. I head the Athenians; whatever post you shall assign us, we will maintain it, and will endeavour to make our station, wherever we are placed, the post of true honour and military glory. We are come hither not to contend with our friends, but to fight with our enemies; not to boast of our ancestors, but to imitate them. This battle will distinguish the merit of each city: each commander, and the lowest sentinel will share the honour of the day." This speech determined the council of war in favour of the Athenians, who thereupon were allowed to maintain their former station.

Meanwhile the Grecians, beginning to be straitened for want of water, resolved to retreat to a place where they might be more plentifully supplied with that necessary article. As their removal was made in the night, much disorder ensued; and in the morning, Mardonius, construing their retreat into a flight, immediately pursued them, and coming up with them near the little city of Platæa, he attacked them with great impetuosity. His ardour, however, was soon checked by the Spartans, who brought up the rear of the Grecian army, and who, throwing themselves into a phalanx, stood impenetrable and immoveable to all the assaults of the enemy. At the same time, the Athenians being informed of the attack, quickly turned back, and after defeating a body of Greeks in Persian pay, they came to the assistance of the Spartans, just as these last had completed the overthrow of the enemy. For Mardonius, enraged at seeing his men give way, rushed into the thickest of the ranks, in order to restore the battle; and while he was doing so, he was killed by Aimnestus, a Spartan. Upon this the whole army betook. themselves to flight. Artabazis, with a body of forty thousand men, fled towards the Hellespont; the rest retreated to their camp, and there endeavoured to defend themselves with wooden ramparts. But these being quickly broken down, the confederates rushed in upon them with irresistible fury; and eager to rid their country of such terrible invaders, they sternly refused them all quarter, and put upwards of a hundred thousand of them to the sword. Thus ended the invasion of the Persians into Greece; nor ever after was an army from Persia seen to cross the Hellespont. We have already observed, that Aristides commanded the Athenians in this important action. The Spartans were headed by Cleombrotus, and Pausanias, a Lacedæmonian, was the chief commander.

The battle was no sooner over, than the Greeks, to testify their gratitude to heaven, caused a statue of Jupiter to be made at the public expense, and placed in his temple at Olympia. On the right side of the pedestal were engraved the names of the several nations of Greece that were present in the engagement. The Spartans had the first place, the Athenians the second, and all the rest succeeded in order.

The successes of the Greeks were as rapid as they were important. On the very evening of the day on which the victory at Platæa was won, another, equally glorious, was obtained at Mycale on the coast of Ionia. After the defeat at Salamis, the remains of the Persian fleet retired to Samos; but the Greeks were not long in pursuing them. The confederates, on this occasion, were headed by Leotychides, the Spartan, and Xanthippus, the Athenian. The Persians were no sooner informed of their approach, than, conscious of their own inferiority by sea, they drew up their ships upon dry land at Mycale, and fortified them with a wall and a deep trench, while they were at the same time protected by an army of sixty thousand men, under the command of Tigranes. But nothing could secure them from the fury of the Grecians, who immediately coming on shore, and dividing themselves into two bodies, the

Athenians and Corinthians advanced directly on the
plain, while the Lacedemonians fetched a compass over
hills and precipices, in order to take possession of a
rising ground. But before these last arrived, the former
had entirely put the enemy to flight, and now being
joined by the Spartans, they soon forced their way
through the Persian ramparts, and set all their ships on
fire; so that nothing could be more complete than the
victory now obtained. Tigranes, the Persian general,
with forty thousand of his men, lay dead upon the field
of battle; the fleet was destroyed; and of the great
army which Xerxes brought into Europe, scarce a
single man remained to carry back to him the news of
its defeat.

CHAPTER VII.

FROM THE VICTORY AT MYCALE TO THE PEACE CONCLUDED BETWEEN THE GREEKS AND PERSIANS.

No sooner were the Greeks freed from the apprehensions
of a foreign foe [A. M. 3526], than they began to entertain jealousies of each other; and the first symptoms
of this dangerous spirit appeared in a misunderstanding
that took place between the Athenians and Spartans.
The former, with their families, being returned to their
own country, begun to think of rebuilding the city;
and as its late state of weakness had rendered it so easy
a prey to the Persians, they now formed a plan for
strengthening and extending the walls, and giving it,
for the future, a greater degree of security. This
excited the jealousy of the Lacedæmonians, who could
not bear to see any of the other states of Greece upon
an equal footing with themselves. They therefore sent
ambassadors to dissuade the Athenians from this undertaking; but being ashamed to avow their real motive,
they alleged the great detriment which these fortifications would be of to the general interests of Greece,
if ever they should fall into the hands of the enemy.
Themistocles, who then guided all the councils of
Athens, at once saw through their design, and resolved

to meet their duplicity with equal dissimulation. He therefore told them that the Athenians would soon send an embassy to Sparta, and fully satisfy all their scruples; and having procured himself to be chosen for this purpose, he accordingly went thither, and by studied delays kept the Spartans in suspense until the works were completely finished. He then boldly threw off the mask, and declared that Athens was now in a condition to keep out any enemy, either foreign or domestic; and that what she had done was perfectly consistent with the laws of nations, and the common interests of Greece. He further added, that if any violence were offered to his person, the Athenians would retaliate upon the Spartan ambassadors, who were now in their hands; in consequence of which the ambassadors on both sides were suffered quietly to depart, and Themistocles, upon his arrival in Athens, was received as if he had been returning from a triumph.

Encouraged by his success in this undertaking, Themistocles projected another scheme, far less justifiable indeed, for increasing the power and importance of his country. This scheme, however, he declared, in a full assembly of the people, would not admit of being publicly mentioned, as its execution required secrecy and despatch. He therefore begged that some person might be appointed, to whom he might communicate his design, one who was qualified to judge at once of the utility and the practicability of the project. Aristides was pitched upon for this purpose. To him Themistocles privately signified his intention of burning the fleet belonging to the rest of the Grecian states, which then lay in a neighbouring port, and thus rendering Athens the undisputed sovereign of the sea. Aristides, shocked at so base a proposal, made no answer, but returning to the assembly, informed them, that nothing could be more advantageous to Athens than what Themistocles proposed, but that nothing, at the same time, could be more unjust. The people, adopting the magnanimous sentiments of their magistrate, unanimously rejected the proposal, without knowing its contents, and bestowed upon Aristides the surname of *Just*, which he so well deserved.

The confederates being thus left at liberty to turn their arms against their foreign foes, instead of drawing their swords against one another, fitted out a powerful fleet. Pausanias commanded the Spartans; the Athenians were conducted by Aristides and Cimon the son of Miltiades. They first directed their course to the isle of Cyprus, where they set all the cities free. Then steering towards the Hellespont, they attacked the city of Byzantium, of which they made themselves masters; and, besides the vast quantity of plunder which they found in it, they took a great number of prisoners, many of whom were of the richest and most considerable families of Persia.

But whatever the Greeks gained upon this occasion in fame and authority, they lost in the purity and simplicity of their manners. The deluge of wealth poured in upon them from this quarter, naturally tended to corrupt their minds; and from this time forward, neither the magistrates nor the people valued themselves, as formerly, on their personal merit, but merely on account of their riches and possessions. The Athenians, being a polite people, bore this change for some time with tolerable moderation; but the contagion immediately broke out among the Spartans with all its native virulence. It seems to have inspired Pausanias, who was naturally of a haughty and imperious temper, and who had forfeited the good opinion not only of the neighbouring states, but also of his own subjects, with the ambitious hopes of raising himself to a still higher rank than he had yet attained. He offered to deliver up Sparta, and even all Greece, to Xerxes, provided that prince would give him his daughter in marriage. How long this conspiracy was carried on is uncertain. Pausanias was twice tried, and twice acquitted for want of sufficient evidence against him. His guilt, however, became at length too apparent to be any longer concealed; but just as the Ephori were upon the point of seizing him, he took refuge in the temple of Minerva, where the sanctity of the place preventing his being dragged forth, the people blocked up the entry with large stones, and tearing off the roof, left him in that manner to die of cold and hunger. This he in a little time did; and thus perished the man who had led on the victorious troops of Greece in the battle of Platæa.

The fate of Pausanias soon after involved that of Themistocles, who had some time before been banished, and lived in great esteem at Argos. The occasion of his banishment was this: he had built near his house a temple in honour of Diana, with this inscription, " To Diana, the goddess of good counsel;" thereby insinuating the benefit his own counsels had been of to his country, and the little gratitude his fellow-citizens had shown in rewarding them. He was now accused, not only of having been privy to the designs of Pausanias, without revealing them to the state, which part of the charge, indeed, seems to have been well founded, but likewise of having approved and favoured those designs, a crime, it would appear, of which he was altogether guiltless. The Spartans, however, who had always been his enemies, now declared themselves his accusers before the assembly of the people of Athens; and all those of his countrymen, who had formerly either dreaded his power, or envied his popularity, joined in the general charge against him. In a word, the people were wrought up to such a degree of rage, that they clamoured for his death with great vehemence; and persons were actually sent to seize and bring him before the general council of Greece. Fortunately, however, he had notice of their design, and saved himself by a precipitate flight. He first took refuge in the island of Corcyra; from thence he repaired to the court of Admetus, king of the Molossians; but that prince not being able to afford him any long or certain protection, he at last went over to Sardis, where, throwing himself prostrate before the Persian monarch, he boldly declared his name, his country, and his misfortunes. " I have done," cried he, " my ungrateful country services more than once, and I am now come to offer those services to you. My life is in your hands: you may now exert your clemency, or display your vengeance. By the former you will preserve a faithful suppliant; by the latter you will destroy the greatest enemy of Greece." The king made him no answer at this audience, though he was struck with admiration at his eloquence and intrepidity ; but he soon gave a loose to his joy for the event. He told his courtiers, that he considered the arrival of Themistocles as a very happy incident, and wished that his enemies would always pursue the same destructive policy of banishing from among them the good and wise. His joys were continued in a dream, In the night he was seen to start from his sleep, and three times to cry out, " I have got Themistocles the Athenian." He even gave him three cities for his support, and had him maintained in the utmost affluence and splendour. It is said, that such was his interest at the Persian court, and so great was the estimation in which he was held by all ranks of people, that one day at table he was heard to cry out to his wife and children, who sat near him, " Children, we should certainly have been ruined, if we had not formerly been undone."

But nothing could erase from the breast of Themistocles the love he entertained for his country. Indeed the spirit of patriotism appears to have prevailed among the Greeks in a higher degree than ever it did among any other people. This was no doubt owing to the many violent struggles they had been obliged to make in defence of their country. And perhaps it will be found, that the value we set upon any thing, is always in proportion to the pains we have taken in acquiring or preserving it. When Xerxes, therefore, proposed fitting out an expedition against Athens, and entrusting the command of it to Themistocles, that patriot, rather than carry arms against the place of his nativity, put an end to his own life by poison.

In the meantime, Aristides, instead of incurring the jealousy of his countrymen by his ambitious and interested views, continued every day to acquire a larger share of their esteem and veneration by his integrity and love of justice. So great, indeed, was his character in this respect, that when it was deliberated among the states of Greece who was the most proper person to be entrusted with the care of the public treasure for carrying on the war, all eyes were fixed upon him as the most upright man to be found in the country; and his discharge of this most important office, to which he was immediately appointed, only served to confirm the high opinion the world already entertained of him. His merit, besides, in this particular was so much the greater, as he himself was extremely poor; but it appeared from the following incident that he was voluntarily poor, and might have been richer, if he had chosen it. Callias, an intimate friend and relation of his, being summoned before the judges for some offence, one of the chief objections urged against him was, that while he rolled in affluence and luxury, he suffered his friend and relation, Aristides, to remain in poverty and want. But Callias appealing to Aristides himself, it appeared that he had generously offered to share his fortune with him, which the other had absolutely refused to accept, asserting that he only might be said to want, who permitted his appetites to transgress the bounds of his income; and that he who could dispense with a few things, thus rendered himself more like the gods, that want for nothing.

In this manner he lived, just in his public, and independent in his private capacity, and universally esteemed and beloved by all that knew him. History does not acquaint us with the time or place of his death; but it bears the most glorious testimony to his character, in telling us that he who had the absolute disposal of the public treasures, died poor. It is even asserted, that he did not leave money enough behind him to defray the expense of his funeral, but that the government was obliged to bear the charge of it, and to maintain his family. His daughters were portioned, and his son subsisted at the expense of the public; and some of his grand-children were supported by a pension equal to that bestowed upon those who had been victorious at the Olympic games.

The first man that began to make a figure at Athens after the death of Themistocles and Aristides, was Cimon, the son of Miltiades. In his earlier years he had led a very dissolute life; but Aristides perceiving in him, amidst all his dissipation, the seeds of many

E

great and good qualities, advised him to change his conduct, and to raise his mind, from the pursuit of low and ignoble pleasures, to the ambition of directing the affairs of the state. He did so, and in a little time, became equal to his father in courage, to Themistocles in sagacity, and even not much inferior to his instructor himself in integrity. The first specimen he gave of his military talents was in scouring the Asiatic seas, and delivering all the Greek cities on the coast of Asia Minor from their dependance upon the Persian crown, and making them join in the general confederacy of Greece against that very power to which they had formerly acknowledged allegiance. Some of these, however, that were strongly garrisoned by Persian troops, made a desperate defence. The city of Eion deserves to be particularly mentioned. Boges, the governor, resolved either to preserve it, or to perish in the attempt. He accordingly defended the place with incredible fury, till finding his station no longer tenable, he killed his wife and children, and laying them on a funeral pile, which he had erected for the purpose, he immediately set it on fire, and rushing into the midst of the flames, in that manner expired.

While Cimon was employed in these operations, he received intelligence that the whole Persian fleet was anchored at the mouth of the river Eurymidon. He accordingly sailed thither, and pursuing the enemy up the stream, where they endeavoured to take shelter, he destroyed all their ships; and his men jumping on shore in pursuit of the Persian mariners, who had abandoned their vessels, they soon put them to flight; thus obtaining a complete victory both by sea and land on the same occasion. This severe blow at last compelled the Persians to agree to a peace, the terms of which were as mortifying to them, as they were honourable to the Grecians. It was stipulated that the Greek cities in Asia should be left in quiet possession of their liberty, and that neither the sea nor the land forces of Persia should approach so near the Grecian coasts, as to give the least occasion for any kind of jealousy.

The treasures taken in this expedition Cimon laid

out in beautifying his native city; and the Athenians gave examples in the art of architecture, that continue to be admired to this very day. About the same time lived the poet Simonides, some of whose works still remain; and these only leave us room to regret that the rest are long since irretrievably lost.

CHAPTER VIII.

FROM THE PEACE WITH PERSIA TO THE PEACE OF NICIAS.

THOUGH Cimon was for some time, after the death of Aristides, the most considerable man at Athens, he did not remain long without a rival. He was soon opposed by Pericles, who was much younger than he, and was a man of a very different character. Pericles was descended from the greatest and most illustrious families of Athens; his father Xanthippus defeated the Persians at Mycale : and his mother Agarista was niece to Calisthenes, who expelled the tyrants, and established a popular government in Athens. In the earlier part of his life he applied himself with success to all the different branches of philosophy; but the chief bent of his mind was directed to the study of eloquence, in which he is said to have outshone all his contemporaries. Even his great opponent, Thucydides, was often heard to say, that though he had frequently overthrown him, the power of his eloquence was such, that the audience could never perceive him fallen. He resembled the tyrant Pisistratus, not only in the sweetness of his voice, but the features of his face, and his whole air and manner. To these natural and acquired endowments he added those of fortune; he was very rich and intimately connected with all the most powerful families of the state.

The established reputation of Cimon, however, was for some time a bar to the rise of Pericles; but as the former was generally abroad, commanding the fleets or armies of the country; and the latter was always at home, haranguing and making interest with the people, he soon found means to overcome this obstacle. The first use he made of his popularity was to lessen the power, and consequently the character of the court of Areopagus. This he did chiefly by the assistance of one Ephialtes, another popular leader, who contrived to take away the decision of almost all causes from that celebrated tribunal, and to bring them before the assembly of the people. Cimon's interest, however, was still able to counteract, and even to overpower, that of Pericles, in a very important question. This was, Whether the Athenians should assist the Lacedæmonians in suppressing an insurrection of their Helots, or slaves, who had taken up arms to rescue themselves from bondage? Cimon gave his opinion in the affirmative; Pericles in the negative. But Cimon's opinion, as being the most generous, was for this time adopted, and he was allowed to conduct a large body of troops to Sparta, with which he effectually quelled the insurrection. But the Helots taking up arms a second time, and possessing themselves of the strong fortress of Ithome, the Spartans were once more obliged to apply to Athens for assistance. The influence, however, of Pericles now prevailed in its turn, and all kind of aid was denied them. Thus left to finish the war by themselves, they besieged Ithome, which held out for ten years; at the end of which, however, they made themselves masters of it, though they spared the lives of those who defended it, upon condition of their leaving Peloponnesus for ever.

The conduct of the Athenians upon this occasion, and some insults they pretended to have received from the Lacedæmonians, revived a jealousy that had long subsisted between these rival states, and which continued thenceforward to operate with greater or less influence, till both of them were reduced to such a low ebb of power, that neither of them was able to withstand the slightest invasion from abroad. The first instance the Athenians gave of their resentment, was to banish Cimon, who had been a favourer of the Spartan cause, for ten years, from the city; they next dissolved their alliance with Sparta, and entered into a treaty with the Argives, the professed enemies of the former. The slaves banished from Peloponnesus were taken under the protection of Athens, and settled with their families at Naupactus : and all the privileges of Spartan subjects were demanded in behalf of those Athenians that resided in Lacedæmon. But what contributed to widen the breach still more, the city of Megara, breaking off its alliance with Sparta, was protected and garrisoned by the Athenians; and thus was laid the foundation of an inveterate hatred, that terminated in the destruction of both these states.

The chief motive to this insolent and treacherous conduct of the Athenians, was the high opinion they entertained of themselves ever since the battle of Platæa. That victory had raised them to the same national eminence with the Lacedæmonians. But they were not satisfied with being their equals; they wanted to be their superiors. They, therefore, called themselves the *Protectors of Greece;* they desired that the convention of the states should be held at Athens, and they resolved to declare open war against any power that should dare to insult them.

Exasperated, however, as these two states were against each other, they did not immediately come to a rupture. They first endeavoured to strengthen themselves by leagues and alliances with the neighbouring states. At last the armies of the two republics came to an engagement near Tangara; and though Cimon, forgetting the injury he had received from his country, came to its assistance, yet the Athenians suffered a defeat. A month or two after another action happened, and the Athenians were, in their turn, victorious. The conduct of Cimon upon this occasion reestablished him in the public favour; he was restored to his country, after a banishment of five years; and his rival Pericles, was the first that proposed the decree for his recall.

Cimon's first care, after his return, was to compromise all differences between the rival states; and this was so far outwardly effected, that a truce was concluded for the space of five years. This furnished an opportunity for exerting the power of the state upon a

more distant enemy. A fleet of two hundred sail was
fitted out, and the command of it given to Cimon, for
conquering the island of Cyprus. He accordingly
sailed thither, overran the island, and laid siege to the
capital, Citium. But being either wounded by some
of the defendants, or wasted by sickness, he began to
perceive the approaches of death. Still mindful, however, of his duty, he ordered his attendants to conceal
his decease till their schemes were crowned with success. They did so; and thirty days after he was dead,
the army, which still supposed itself under his command,
obliged the place to surrender. Thus he not only died
in the arms of victory, but he even gained battles by
the terror of his name. In so great awe, indeed, did
the Persians stand of him, that they universally deserted
the seacoasts, and would not come within four hundred
leagues of any place where he could possibly be expected.

Pericles, being now freed from the opposition of so
powerful a rival, resolved to complete the work of
ambition he had begun; and by dividing the conquered
lands among the people, amusing them with shows,
and adorning the city with public buildings, he at last
acquired such an ascendancy over the minds of the
populace, that he may actually be said to have been
possessed of sovereign power in a free state. The
buildings, indeed, which he raised, have endeared his
memory to all the lovers of the fine arts. Some small
remains of them are still to be seen; and these are
allowed by the best judges to be so perfect in their
kind, that they have never since been excelled, and
hardly ever equalled. True it is, that, to complete
these works, he was guilty, in some measure, of injustice; for he applied to this purpose part of the money
that had been raised by the different states of Greece
for carrying on the war against Persia: but when any
of these states complained of this embezzlement of the
public treasure, Pericles boldly replied, that the Athenians were not accountable to any for their conduct;
and that they had the best right to the treasures of the
confederate states, who took the greatest care to defend

them. He added, that it was fit that ingenious artisans should have their share of the public money, since there was still enough left for carrying on the war.

These arguments, however, were by no means sufficient to satisfy the other states of Greece, and least of all the Spartans, who beheld the present prosperity of Athens with envy, and the insolence of Pericles with indignation. And these passions were still further inflamed by an expedition which the Athenians undertook against Samos, in favour of the Milesians, who had craved their assistance. It is said, that Pericles fomented this war, to please a famous courtesan named Aspasia, of whom he was particularly enamoured. After several skirmishes not worth mentioning, Pericles besieged the capital of Samos with tortoises and battering rams, which was the first time these military engines had been employed in sieges. The Samians, after sustaining a nine month's siege, surrendered. Pericles razed their walls, dispossessed them of their ships, and exacted immense sums for defraying the expenses of the war. Elated with this success, he returned to Athens, buried all those who had fallen in the most splendid manner, and pronounced their funeral oration.

Though the jealousy and rivalship that subsisted between Athens and Sparta, was the true cause of the Peloponnesian war, yet neither of them was willing to avow their real motive; a petty quarrel among the inferior states of Greece, their allies, furnished them with an ostensible reason. The Corcyreans, resenting the conduct of the Corinthians with regard to one of their dependent colonies named Epidamnus, took up arms to revenge the affront; but being worsted in some naval engagements, they had recourse to the Athenians for support, who sent them some naval succours, which, however, were of no great service. From this war arose another; for Potidæa, a city belonging to Athens, declaring for Corinth, these two states immediately came to a rupture, and drawing their forces into the field near Potidæa, a battle ensued, in which the Athenians gained the victory. It was in this battle that Socrates saved the life of Alcibiades, his pupil; and after the battle was over, procured him the prize of valour, which he himself more justly deserved. The city of Potidæa was soon after besieged in consequence of this victory, and the Corinthians complained to the states of Greece against the Athenians, as having infringed the articles of peace. The Lacedæmonians gave them an audience, and after hearing what the Athenians had to urge in reply, they came to a resolution, that the Athenians were the aggressors, and ought to be reduced to a sense of their duty.

To give a colour of justice, however, to their proceedings, they began by sending ambassadors to Athens; and while they made preparations for acting with vigour, they still kept up a show of seeking redress by treaty. They required the Athenians to expel from their city some persons that had been guilty of profaning the temple of Minerva at Ceylon; they demanded that the siege of Potidæa should be raised; and that the Athenians should cease for the future to encroach upon the liberties of Greece.

Pericles now saw, that as he had drawn his countrymen into a war, he ought to inspire them with courage to support it. He accordingly showed them, that even trifles extorted from them with an air of command, were in themselves a sufficient ground for war; that they might hope to derive considerable advantage from the divided councils of their opponents; that they had shipping to invade the enemy's coasts; and that their city, being well fortified, could not easily be taken. The people, influenced by the force of his eloquence, naturally fond of change, and unterrified by distant dangers, readily came into his opinion; but in order to meet the duplicity of the Spartans with equal address, they returned an evasive answer, declaring that they wished for nothing more than to settle all differences in an amicable manner; but that, if they were attacked, they would defend themselves with their wonted valour.

Pericles is thought to have had a personal interest in hurrying his countrymen into this unhappy quarrel. He was deeply indebted to the state, and knew that a time of peace was the only opportunity in which he could be called upon to account for his management of the public treasure. It is said that Alcibiades, his nephew, seeing him one day very pensive, and asking the reason, was answered, that he was considering how to make up his accounts. "You had better," said he, "consider how to avoid being accountable." Besides this, Pericles finding no happiness in domestic society, gave himself up to the allurements of his mistress, Aspasia, whose wit and vivacity had captivated all the poets and philosophers of the age, Socrates himself not excepted. She was inclined to oppose the Spartan state; and he, in some measure is thought to have been guided by her counsels.

A. M. 3572.] A war between the two principal states of Greece naturally drew all the inferior ones into the quarrel; and these chose their party, as interest, inclination, or ideas of justice led them. The majority declared in favour of the Lacedæmonians, who were considered as the deliverers of Greece. On their side were ranged the Achaians, the inhabitants of Pellene excepted, the people of Megara, Locris, Bœotia, Phocis, Ambracia, Leucadia, and Anactorium. On the side of Athens were the people of Chios, Lesbos, Platæa, many of the islands, and several maritime tributary states, including those of Thrace, Potidæa excepted.

The Lacedæmonians were not long in taking the field. Their army, including their allies, amounted to sixty thousand men, and was commanded by Archidamus, one of their kings. The forces of the Athenians were not near so numerous. These did not exceed thirteen thousand heavy armed soldiers, sixteen thousand inhabitants, twelve hundred horse, and about double that number of archers. Unable, therefore, to meet the enemy in the field, Pericles advised them to shut themselves up in the city, which could not easily be stormed. This advice at first was but very ill relished; but at last necessity compelled them to adopt it. Removing, therefore, all their valuable effects out of the open country, which they abandoned to the mercy of the enemy, they took refuge within their walls, where they

seemed determined to defend themselves to the last
extremity. To compensate, however, for the weakness
of the land army, they had a great superiority over the
Spartans in their naval force. This consisted of three
hundred ships, and with these they continually infested
and plundered the enemy's coasts, and raised contribu-
tions sufficient for defraying the expenses of the war.

In the meantime the Lacedæmonians entered the
country of Attica at Œnoue, and meeting with no
opposition, marched forward to Acharne, within seven
miles of Athens. The Athenians, enraged at the mortification to which they were now exposed, turned the
edge of their resentment from the enemy, and directed
it against Pericles, whom they regarded as the author
of their disgrace. They, therefore, insisted upon being
led out into the open field, where, notwithstanding the
inferiority of their numbers, they said they would boldly
face the enemy. But Pericles chose the wiser part;
he shut up the city gates, placed sufficient guards at
all the posts around, sent out parties of horse to keep
the enemy employed, and at the same time dispatched
a fleet of a hundred sail to infest the coasts of Peloponnesus. These expedients had the desired effect. The
Lacedæmonians, finding the place to be altogether
impregnable, gave up the siege, after laying waste the
country around, and insulting the defenders by their
numbers and reproaches. To revenge this injury, the
Athenians, in their turn, invaded the enemy's country
with their whole force, and reduced Nisæa, a strong
seaport, with walls reaching as far as Megara. Elated,
with this success, they expressed their joy by celebrating funeral games, in honour of those who had fallen
in battle. It was upon this occasion that Pericles
delivered his famous funeral oration, which has come
down to our times, and is generally considered as a
proof at once of his eloquence and his gratitude.

In the beginning of the next year the Lacedæmonians
invaded Attica with the same number of forces as
before, and the Athenians were once more obliged to
take refuge within their walls. But a more dreadful
calamity, than even that of war, now began to visit the

unhappy Athenians. A plague, and one of the most terrible that is recorded in history, now broke out among them. It is said to have begun in Ethiopia, whence it descended into Egypt, from thence travelled into Libya and Persia, and at last broke like a flood upon Athens. This pestilence baffled the utmost efforts of art; the most robust constitutions were unable to withstand its attacks; no skill could obviate, nor no remedy dispel the infection. The instant a person was seized he was struck with despair, which quite disabled him from attempting a cure. The humanity of friends was as fatal to themselves, as it was useless to the unhappy sufferers. The prodigious quantity of baggage, which had been removed out of the country into the city, increased the calamity. Most of the inhabitants, for want of better lodging, lived in little cottages, in which they could scarce breathe, while the burning heat of the summer inflamed the malignity of the distemper. They were seen confusedly huddled together, the dead as well as the living; some crawling through the streets, some lying along by the sides of fountains, whither they had endeavoured to repair to quench the raging thirst which consumed them. Their very temples were filled with dead bodies, and every part of the city exhibited a dreadful scene of mortality, without the least remedy for the present, or the least hopes with regard to futurity. It seized the people with such violence, that they fell one upon another as they passed along the streets. It was also attended with such uncommon pestilential vapours, that the very beasts and birds of prey, though perishing with hunger round the walls of the city, would not touch the bodies of those who died of it. Even those who recovered, received such a terrible shock from it, as affected not only their senses, but the very faculties of their mind. It effaced the memory of all the occurrences of their past lives, and they knew neither themselves nor their nearest relations. The effects of this disease are described at large by Thucydides, who was sick of it himself; and he observes, among other things, that it introduced into the city a more licentious way of living. For the people at first had recourse to their gods to avert this judgment; but finding they were all equally infected, whether they worshiped them or not, and that the disease was generally mortal, they abandoned themselves at once to despair and riot; for since they held their lives but as it were by the day, they were resolved to make the most of their time and money. The cause of it was generally imputed to Pericles, who, by drawing such numbers into the city, was thought to have corrupted the very air. Yet, though this was raging within, and the enemy wasting the country without, he still continued of the same mind as before, that they ought not to risk all their fortunes on the event of a battle. In the meantime, the Lacedæmonians, advancing towards the coast, laid waste the whole country, and returned after having insulted the wretched Athenians, already thinned by pestilence and famine.

It is not to be supposed that Pericles, the reputed author of all these calamities, could long escape the popular resentment. In fact, he began to be as much hated by the people as ever he had been beloved by them, and they had actually deposed him from the command of the army; though, actuated by that fickleness for which they were remarkable, they soon reinstated him with more than former authority. But he did not live long to enjoy his honours. He was seized with the plague, and in a little time died of it; a man certainly possessed of many great and amiable qualities, and hardly addicted to a single vice, except that of an inordinate ambition.

The most memorable transaction of the following years, was the siege of Platæa, one of the most famous that is to be found in antiquity, on account of the vigorous efforts of both parties, but chiefly for the glorious resistance made by the besieged, and the stratagems they employed to elude the fury of the assailants. The Lacedæmonians besieged this place in the beginning of the third campaign, and surrounded it with a strong wall, on which to erect their battering engines. The besieged seeing the works begin to rise round them, threw up a wooden wall upon the walls of the city, in order that they might always outtop the besiegers. Thus both walls seemed to vie with each other for superiority, till at last the besieged, without amusing themselves at this work any longer, built another within, in the form of a half moon, behind which they might retire in case their other works were forced. In the meantime, the besiegers, having mounted their engines of war, shook the city wall in a very terrible manner; which, though it alarmed the citizens, did not however discourage them; they employed every art that fortification could suggest against the enemy's batteries. They caught with ropes the heads of the battering-rams that were played against them, and deadened their force with levers. The besiegers finding their attack did not go on successfully, and that a new wall was raised against their platform, despaired of being able to take the place by storm; and therefore changed the siege into a blockade, after having in vain attempted to set fire to the city, which was suddenly quenched by a shower. The city was now surrounded by a brick wall, suddenly erected, strengthened on each side by a deep ditch. The whole army was successively engaged upon this wall, and when it was finished, they left a guard over half of it; the Bœotians offering to guard the other half while the rest of the army returned to Sparta.

In this manner the wretched Platæans were cooped up by a strong wall, without any hopes of relief, and only awaited the mercy of the conquerors. There were now in Platæa but four hundred natives, and fourscore Athenians, with a hundred and ten women to dress their victuals, and no other person, whether freeman or slave; all the rest having been sent to Athens before the siege. At last, the inhabitants of Platæa, having lost all hopes of succour, and being in the utmost want of provisions, formed a resolution to cut their way through the enemy. Half of them, however, struck with the greatness of the danger, and the boldness of the enterprise, entirely lost courage when they came to the execution; but the rest, who were about two hundred and twenty soldiers, persisted in their resolution, and effected their escape in the following manner. Having taken the height of the wall, by counting the rows of bricks that composed it, and having made a sufficient number of ladders of a proper length, they set out in the middle of a dark night, and during a violent storm of wind and rain, so that it was hardly possible either to see or hear them. Having crossed the first ditch, which they did with one of their legs bare, in order to prevent their sliding in the mud, they advanced to the bottom of the wall, and fixing their ladders to it, in a place where they knew it to be unguarded, a party of them ascended, and instantly made themselves masters of the two next towers, by killing those that defended them. This gave an opportunity to their comrades to follow them undisturbed; and as soon as they came up on one side, they went down on the other, and actually crossed the outer ditch without being attacked, though not entirely without being discovered. For while they were coming over the wall, one of them happened to throw down a tile from the parapet, which alarmed the enemy, and their whole army advanced towards the place; but the night was so very dark, that it was absolutely impossible to distinguish one object from another. Nay, before they crossed the outer ditch, a corps de reserve of three hundred men, that were kept for any unforeseen accident, came up to them with lighted torches; but these, instead of discovering them, served only to render the enemy visible. After passing the ditch, they directed their course for some time towards Thebes, well knowing the enemy would never pursue them that way, as not thinking it possible they should march towards a hostile city; but after proceeding about six or seven stadia, they turned short towards the mountains, and struck into the road to Athens, where two hundred and twelve of them actually arrived, the rest having returned to the city through fear, one archer excepted, who was taken on the side of the outer ditch.

In the meantime, the Platæans, who remained in the city, supposing that all their companions had been killed, because those who returned, to justify themselves, affirmed they were, sent a herald to demand their dead bodies; but being told the true state of the affair, he withdrew. At the end of the following campaign, the Platæans, being in absolute want of provisions, and unable to make any farther resistance, surrendered upon condition that they should not be punished till they had the benefit of a regular trial. Five commissioners came for this purpose from Sparta; and these, without charging them with any crime, barely asked them, Whether they had done any service to the Lacedæmonians and the allies in this war? The Platæans were much surprised, as well as puzzled at this question, and knew it must have been suggested by the Thebans, their professed enemies, who had vowed their destruction. They therefore, put the Lacedæmonians in mind of the services they had done to Greece in general, both at the battle of Artemisium and that of Platæa; and particularly in Lacedæmonia, at the time of the earthquake, which was followed by the revolt of their slaves. The only reason they assigned for their having joined the Athenians afterwards, was to defend themselves from the hostilities of the Thebans, against whom they had implored the assistance of the Lacedæmonians to no purpose: that if that was imputed to them as a crime, which was only their misfortune, it ought not, however, entirely to obliterate the memory of their former services. "Cast your eyes," said they, "on the monuments of your ancestors which you see here, to whom we annually pay all the honours which can be rendered to the manes of the dead. You thought fit to intrust their bodies with us, as we were eyewitnesses of their bravery. And yet you will now give up their ashes to their murderers, in abandoning us to the Thebans, who fought against them at the battle of Platæa. Will you enslave a province where Greece recovered its liberty? Will you destroy the temples of those gods to whom you owed the victory? On this occasion, we may venture to say, our interest is inseparable from your glory, and you cannot deliver up your ancient friends and benefactors to the unjust hatred of the Thebans, without eternal infamy to yourselves." One would imagine, that these arguments would have

had a proper effect upon the Lacedæmonians; but they
were biased by the answer which the Thebans made,
and which was expressed in the most haughty and
bitter terms; and besides they had brought their instructions from Lacedæmon. They stood therefore to
their first question, Whether the Platæans had done
them any service in this war? and making them pass
one after another, as they severally answered No, each
was immediately butchered, and not one escaped.
About two hundred were killed in this manner; and
twenty-five Athenians, who were among them, met with
the same unhappy fate. Their wives, who had been
taken prisoners, were made slaves. The Thebans afterwards peopled their city with exiles from Megara and
Thebes, but the next year they demolished it entirely.
It was in this manner the Lacedæmonians, in hopes of
reaping great advantages from the Thebans, sacrificed
the Platæans to their fury, ninety-three years after their
first alliance with the Athenians.

The Lacedæmonians, however, were not so elated
with this success, as to make them unwilling to agree
to a peace, provided it could be obtained upon honourable terms; and several overtures for this purpose were
made by their ambassadors, but without effect; for
Cleon, who now guided the councils of the Athenians,
boasted, that he would take all the Spartans in the
island of Spacteria within twenty days. He accordingly sailed thither in company with Demosthenes,
the Athenian admiral (whose courage and conduct his
eloquent descendant, of the same name, afterwards
celebrated); and, having landed their troops, they
attacked the enemy with great vigour, drove them from
post to post, and gaining ground perpetually, at last
forced them to the extremity of the island. The Lacedæmonians had stormed a fort that was thought inacces-
sible. There they drew up in order of battle, and facing
about to that side where alone they imagined they could
be attacked, they defended themselves like so many
lions. But a body of troops having clambered over
some steep rocks, and come upon their rear, they were
soon obliged to surrender at discretion. They were

carried to Athens, where they were told they should be allowed to remain in safety till a peace was concluded, provided the Lacedæmonians did not invade the Athenian territories; for in that case, they were informed, they should all be put to death. This tended greatly to pave the way for a general pacification; as the Lacedæmonians were extremely desirous of procuring the release of these men, who were some of the chief of the city. The war, however, continued for two or three years longer, though without being productive of any remarkable event. The Athenians, indeed, took the island of Cythera; but, in their turn, were defeated by the Lacedæmonians at Dellion. At last both nations began to be weary of a contest, that put them to so great an expense, without procuring them any solid advantage. A truce for a year was therefore concluded between them, which afterwards terminated in a more lasting reconciliation. This happy event was considerably facilitated by the death of the two generals that commanded their armies, and who had hitherto opposed a peace, though from very different motives. Brasidas, the Lacedæmonian, was killed in a sally, which he was conducting when besieged in Amphipolis; and Cleon, the Athenian, despising an enemy, to whom he knew himself superior, was set upon unawares, and flying for safety, was killed by a soldier who happened to meet him. Brasidas was possessed of courage and conduct, of moderation and integrity; and his opposition to a peace seems to have proceeded merely from a true Spartan zeal for the honour of his country. Courage, indeed, seems to have been hereditary in his family, as it no doubt was in the whole Spartan nation : for when his mother received the news of his death, she asked the persons who brought her the intelligence, whether he died honourably; and when they began to launch out into encomiums on his gallantry and heroism, and to prefer him to all the generals of his time; " Yes," said she, " my son was a brave man, but Sparta has still many citizens braver than he."

Cleon was a man of a very different character. He was rash, arrogant, obstinate, and contentious : and though he succeeded in his expedition to Sphacteria, he was by no means fitted for war. He only made use of it as a cloak for his ill practices, and because he could not carry on his other views without it. He had, indeed, a readiness of wit, with a kind of low drollery, that took with the populace, though with better judges it only passed for impudence and buffoonery. But what he chiefly depended upon was his eloquence; yet even this was of the noisy and boisterous kind, and consisted more of the vehemence of his utterance, and the violence of his action and gesture, than in the elegance of his style, or the strength of his reasoning.

Matters being now brought into this happy train, a peace was concluded in the tenth year of the war, between the two states and their confederates, for fifty years. The chief articles of it were, that the forts should be evacuated, and the towns and prisoners restored on both sides. This was called the Nician peace, because Nicias, who was just the reverse of his rival, Cleon, was the chief instrument in effecting it. Besides the tender concern he always entertained for his country, he had more particular ends in view in bringing it about. He wished by this means to secure his reputation. For though he had succeeded in most of the expeditions in which he had been engaged, he well knew how much he owed to his good fortune and his cautious management, and he did not choose to risk the fame he had already acquired by any attempts to procure more.

CHAPTER IX.

FROM THE PEACE OF NICIAS TO THE END OF THE PELOPON-
NESIAN WAR.

TREATIES of peace, however solemn or sincere, are but feeble barriers against the interests, the inclinations, or the prejudices of rival states, or even against the ambitious views of those that have the chief direction of their councils. This was fatally experienced in the war, that, notwithstanding their late agreement, soon after broke out between the Athenians and Spartans, not to promote the welfare, or advance the power of either people, but merely to gratify the pride and vanity of Alcibiades, who was now become the most popular man in Athens. Many things contributed to make him so. He was as remarkable for the beauty of his person, as the endowments of his mind. He was descended from one of the greatest families in Athens; he was the richest man in the place; and his style and manner of living was equal to his income. Add to this, that though he was frequently drawn into irregularities by the pernicious advice of flatterers, with whom he was naturally surrounded, and the violence of his own passions, which were ever in the extreme, yet he was as often recalled from these vicious courses, and brought back into the paths of virtue, by the salutary counsels of Socrates, for whose character he had conceived the highest regard, and to whose lessons he always gave the greatest attention.

Nor was the philosopher less fond of him, than he was of the philosopher. For perceiving in him, amidst all his irregularities, the seeds of many great and amiable qualities, he was extremely desirous of cultivating these, and bringing them to maturity, that so, when he grew up, instead of being a curse and disgrace, he might prove an honour and a blessing to his country. And so fully was he convinced of the ascendency he had acquired over the mind of this young man, that whenever he heard he was indulging himself in any low or vicious pleasures, he would pursue him as a master does a fugitive slave, and severely reprimand him for his folly; and the other would listen to him with all the submission of a dutiful son to the best of fathers. Hence proceeded the inequality of his conduct, which was sometimes agreeable to the most rigid rules of morality, and at others was marked with all the extravagance of the wildest passions.

His ruling passion, indeed, seems to have been the love of power, and a desire of superiority; and of this he is said to have given several striking instances, even while a boy. One day being rather overmatched in

wrestling, and fearing to be thrown down, he got the
hand of his antagonist in his mouth, and bit it with all
his force; upon which the other let go his hold, and
said, "Alcibiades, you bite like a woman."—"No,"
replied he, "I bite like a lion." At another time,
when he was playing in the street at some game of
chance, a loaded cart happened to come that way when
it was his turn to throw. At first he called out to the
driver to stop, because he was going to throw in the
road over which the cart was to pass. But the fellow
did not seem to mind him, but still drove on, upon
which all the rest of the boys divided and made way;
but Alcibiades throwing himself on his face before the
cart, and stretching out his limbs, bid the carter drive
on if he would; at which the man was so startled, that
he put back his horse, and Alcibiades was allowed to
have his throw before the cart passed. His ambition
naturally increased with his years, and when he came
to be a man, like Pompey in later times, instead of
being able to bear a superior, he could not even endure
an equal. For this reason it was, that he set himself in
opposition to Nicias, who was as much respected by his
own countrymen, and much more by the Lacedæmonians, who esteemed him for his moderation and love
of justice. And on the same account, he conceived an
incurable prejudice against the Lacedæmonians themselves for this preference given to his rival, and did
every thing in his power to excite a quarrel between
them and the Athenians.

The first step he took for this purpose was, to insti-
gate the people of Argos to break with the Lacedæmonians; assuring them, that, if they did so, they should
soon be supported by the whole power of Athens; and
the fact is, every thing was in a fair way for a treaty
between the Athenians and Argives, when the Lacedæmonians, informed of these negotiations, sent ambassadors to Athens, in order to remonstrate, and invested
them with full power to settle all matters in dispute
in an amicable manner. This commission seemed to
satisfy the council, to whom it was first communicated;
and the people were to assemble the next day, to give

the ambassadors an audience. Alcibiades, fearing that this would mar his schemes, had recourse to the following artifice. He contrived to have a private conference with the ambassadors, and persuaded them, under colour of friendship, not to let the people know at first what full powers they possessed, but merely to intimate that they came to treat and make proposals; for that otherwise the people would grow exorbitant in their demands, and endeavour to extort from them such unreasonable terms as they could not with honour consent to. The stratagem succeeded. The ambassadors, believing him sincere, withdrew their confidence from Nicias, and reposed it in him; and the next day, when the people were assembled, and the ambassadors introduced, Alcibiades, with a very obliging air, demanded of them with what powers they were come. They made answer, that they were not come as plenipotentiaries. Upon which he instantly changed his voice and countenance, and exclaiming against them as notorious liars, bid the people take care how they transacted any thing with men, on whose veracity they could have so little dependance. The people dismissed the ambassadors in a rage; and Nicias, knowing nothing of the deceit, was confounded and in disgrace. To redeem his credit, he proposed being sent once more to Sparta; but not being able to obtain such terms as the Athenians demanded, they immediately, upon his return, struck up a league with the Argives for a hundred years, including the Eleans and Mantenæans; which yet did not in terms cancel that with the Lacedæmonians, though it is plain, that the whole scope of it was levelled against them. Upon this new alliance Alcibiades was declared general; and though even his best friends could not commend the method by which he had accomplished his designs, yet it was looked upon as a great stroke in politics thus to divide and shake almost all Peloponnesus, and to remove the war so far from the Athenian frontier, that even success would profit the enemy but little, should they be conquerors; whereas, if they were defeated, Sparta itself would hardly be safe.

The Spartans, however, were determined to crush the evil in the bud; and accordingly drawing out their whole force both of citizens and slaves, and being joined by their allies, they encamped almost under the walls of Argos. The Argives were not slow in meeting them; they immediately marched out, and offered them battle. But just as the two armies were going to engage, a truce was concluded for four months, as a previous step towards an amicable settlement of all differences.

The Athenians, thinking they had now found the Spartans sufficient employment by the troubles they had excited in Peloponnesus, began to extend their views to more distant objects, and they actually formed a design of adding the island of Sicily to their empire. The people of Egesta supplied them with a plausible pretext for executing this project. They applied to the Athenians, in quality of their allies, craving their aid against the inhabitants of Selinuta, who were assisted by the Syracusans. This opportunity was greedily laid hold of; but not to engage in a war without being sure of the means of carrying it on with spirit, the Athenians sent deputies to Egesta, to inquire into the state of affairs, and see whether there was money enough in the treasury to defray the expense of so great an undertaking. The people of that city had lately borrowed from the neighbouring states a great number of gold and silver vases, of an immense value; and of these they now made a splendid display to the Athenian deputies. Upon the return, therefore, of these last, a resolution was immediately taken to comply with the request of the Egestans; and Alcibiades, Nicias, and Lamachus were appointed to command the fleet, with full power not only to succour Egesta, and restore the inhabitants of Leontium to their city, of which they had been deprived by the Syracusans, but also to regulate the affairs of Sicily in such a manner, as might best suit the interests of the republic.

Nicias was extremely uneasy at his being appointed to this command, partly because he disapproved of the war itself, but chiefly because he was joined in com-

mission with Alcibiades. But the Athenians thought
it necessary to temper the ardour and impetuosity of
the one, with the coolness and deliberation of the other.
Nicias, therefore, not daring to oppose the war openly,
endeavoured to do it indirectly, by representing the
great number of difficulties with which it would be attended. He said, that a fleet would not be sufficient;
that a land army must likewise be raised, and subsisted
at an immense expense; for as to the pompous promises
made them by the Egestans, these might probably fail
them at a time when they stood most in need of pecu-
niary aid: that they ought to weigh well the great
disparity between them and the enemy, with regard to
the conveniences they would respectively enjoy: that
the Syracusans would be in their own country, in the
midst of powerful allies, disposed by inclination, as well
as engaged by interest, to assist them with men, money,
horses, and provisions; whereas the Athenians would
carry on the war in a remote country, possessed by
their enemies, where, in winter, news could not be
brought them from home in less than four months; a
country where all things would oppose the Athenians,
and nothing be procured but by force of arms: that, even
if the expedition succeeded, it would not be productive
of the mighty advantage expected from it; and, if it
failed, it would reflect eternal disgrace upon the Athenian name: and that, for his own part, he was determined not to go, unless he was supplied with every
thing necessary for carrying on the war, as he would
not depend upon the caprice or precarious promises of
allies. This speech, however, instead of cooling the
ardour of the Athenians, as Nicias expected, served
only to inflame it more: and orders were immediately
given for raising as many troops, and fitting out as
many galleys as the generals thought necessary; and
the levies accordingly were carried on in Athens, and
other places, with incredible spirit.

Before we enter upon the narration of the important
events that took place in the expedition to Sicily, it
will be proper to say a few words respecting Syracuse,
the capital of that island. About the year of the world

2920, Corinth had acquired considerable reputation as a maritime power. As the improvement of navigation generally leads to discovery, so it leads to commerce also, and to colonization. It had this effect on the Corinthians. They had not been long acquainted with Sicily, before they projected the scheme of peopling part of it with the natives of Peloponnesus. Archias, therefore, a descendant of Hercules, was sent thither with a fleet, furnished with every thing necessary for such an enterprise. He built and peopled Syracuse, which, from the peculiar advantages it derived from its rich soil and capacious harbour, soon became the most flourishing city in Sicily: in size, indeed, and beauty, it yielded not to any city in Greece. It was long subject to Corinth, and governed by nearly the same laws. But as it increased in power, it aimed at independence, and by degrees renounced its allegiance to Corinth. To its emancipation are owing the occurrences which we are now to recite.

The levies being by this time completed, the generals resolved to set sail immediately, after having appointed Corcyra as the place of rendezvous for most of the allies, and such ships as were to carry the provisions and warlike stores. All the citizens, as well as foreigners, in Athens, flocked by daybreak to the port of Pyræus, in order to behold this magnificent sight. It was, indeed, a spectacle well worth their curiosity; for neither Athens, nor any other city had ever fitted out such a grand and gallant fleet as the present. True it is, that those which had been sent against Epidaurus and Potidæa were as considerable with respect to the number of soldiers and ships; but then they were not equipped with so much magnificence, neither was their voyage so long, nor the enterprise so important. The city had furnished a hundred empty galleys, that is, threescore light ones, and forty to transport the heavy-armed soldiers. Every mariner received daily a drachma, or ten-pence English, for his pay, exclusive of what the captains of ships gave the rowers of the first bench. When the ships were loaded, and the troops got on board, the trumpet sounded, and solemn prayers

were offered up for the success of the expedition.
Gold and silver cups were filling every where with
wine, and their accustomed libations were poured out;
the people, who lined the shore, shouting at the same
time, and lifting up their hands to heaven, to wish their
fellow citizens a good voyage and success. And now
the hymn being sung and the ceremonies ended, the
ships sailed one after another out of the harbour; after
which they strove to outsail one another, till they all
arrived at Ægina. From thence they made to Corcyra,
where the army of the allies was assembled with the
rest of the fleet.

Upon their arrival at Sicily, the generals were divided
in their opinions with regard to the place where they
should make a descent. Lamachus was for sailing
directly to Syracuse, and attacking the town, before
the inhabitants had time to recover from their first consternation; but his proposal was rejected, and it was
thought more expedient to reduce the smaller cities
first. Detaching, therefore, ten galleys to take a view
of the harbour and situation of Syracuse, they landed
with the rest of their forces, and surprised Catana.

In the meantime, the enemies of Alcibiades took
advantage of his absence to traduce his character,
which, indeed, was sufficiently open to attack. They
accused him of having neglected the proper method of
invading Sicily, and they further charged him with
impiety in profaning the mysteries of Ceres. This was
sufficient to induce the giddy multitude to recall their
general; but for fear of exciting a tumult in the army,
they only sent him orders to return to Athens, that so he
might pacify the people by his presence. Alcibiades
pretended to obey the order with great submission; but
reflecting on the inconstancy and caprice of his judges,
he no sooner reached Thurium than he disappeared;
and the galley, therefore, returned without him. For
this act of contumacy he was condemned to death, his
whole estate was confiscated, and all the orders of religion were commanded to curse him. Some time after
upon news being brought him that the Athenians had
condemned him to death, "I hope one day," said he,
" to make them sensible that I am still alive."

The Syracusans had by this time put themselves in a posture of defence, and finding that Nicias did not advance towards them, they talked of attacking him in his camp; and some of them asked, in a scoffing way, Whether he was come into Sicily to settle at Catana? He was roused by this insult, and determined to show them that he was deficient neither in courage nor conduct. He was afraid, however, of attacking the place by land for want of cavalry; and it was almost equally hazardous to make a descent by sea: nevertheless, he chose the latter method, and succeeded in it by a stratagem. He had gained a citizen of Catana to go as a deserter to the Syracusans, and to inform them, that the Athenians lay every night in the town without their arms; and that early in the morning, on a certain day appointed, they might surprise them, seize on their camp, with all their arms and baggage, burn their fleet in the harbour, and destroy their whole army. The Syracusans gave credit to this intelligence, and marched with all their forces towards Catana, which Nicias was no sooner informed of than he embarked his troops, and steering away for Syracuse, landed them there the next morning, and fortified himself in the outskirts of the town. The Syracusans were so provoked at this trick being put upon them, that they immediately returned to Syracuse, and presented themselves without the walls in order of battle. Nicias marched out of his trenches to meet them, and a very sharp action ensued, in which the Athenians at length got the better, and forced the enemy back to the city, after having killed two hundred and sixty of them and their allies, with the loss of fifty of their own men. They were not, however, yet in a condition to attack the city, and they, therefore, took up their winter quarters at Naxus and Catana.

Next spring, having received a supply of horse from Athens, together with provisions and other warlike stores, Nicias resolved to block up the place both by sea and land. The first thing he did for this purpose was to take possession of Epipolæ, a high hill which commanded the city, and could only be ascended by one very steep and craggy passage. The Syracusans

were so sensible of the importance of this post, that
they did every thing in their power to prevent his
seizing it; but Nicias landed his troops so secretly and
so suddenly, that he made himself master of it before
they were aware. He even repulsed a body of seven
hundred men who were coming to dislodge him, having
killed three hundred of them together with their leader.
Here he built a fort, and began to invest the town in
such a manner, as to cut off all communication between
it and the country. In the course of this work several
skirmishes happened, in one of which Lamachus was
slain, so that the sole command now devolved upon
Nicias. The Syracusans made another attempt to regain
this post. Nicias was then sick in the fort, and in bed,
with only his servants about him. But when he found
the enemy were forcing his intrenchments, he got up,
and set fire to the engines, and other wood that lay
scattered about the fort; which had so good an effect,
that it served as a signal to his own troops to come up
to his relief; and so terrified and confounded those of
the enemy, that they retreated into the city.

From this time Nicias began to conceive great hopes
of taking the place, the rather as several of the other
cities of Sicily came over to his interest, and supplied
his troops with all kinds of provisions. The Syracusans, on their side, seeing themselves blocked up both
by sea and land, and despairing of being able to hold
out much longer, were already beginning to think of a
surrender. Nay, they had actually summoned a council
to settle the terms of a capitulation, when, to their
great joy and surprise, because contrary to their expectation, they saw Gylippus, the Lacedæmonian general,
arrive with a force, that soon relieved them from all
their fears, and in a little time reduced the Athenians
to a more deplorable situation than that in which they
themselves were now placed. Gylippus, conscious of his
own strength, and perhaps a little actuated by Spartan
pride, sent a herald to the Athenians, to acquaint them
that he would allow them five days to leave Sicily.
Nicias did not deign to give any answer to this proposal,
and both sides therefore prepared themselves for battle.

In the first engagement the Spartans were defeated, chiefly on account of the narrowness of ground where they fought, which was between the two walls which the Athenians had raised to invest the city; and as this prevented Gylippus from extending his lines, or making use of his horse, the Athenians got the better. Gylippus, however, had the magnanimity, or rather indeed good policy, to take the whole blame of the miscarriage upon himself. He declared, that he, and not his men, were in fault; and that he would soon give them an opportunity of recovering his honour and their own; and, accordingly, the very next day attacking the enemy in a more advantageous spot he obtained over them a more complete victory than they had done over him: so much does the event of a battle depend upon the nature of the ground where it is fought.

Nicias being by this means obliged to act upon the defensive, took possession of Plemmyrium near the great harbour, where he built three forts, and almost shut himself up in garrison. Besides, the Lacedaemonians were now considerably strengthened by a reinforcement they received from Corinth. In this state of affairs, Nicias wrote home a most melancholy account of his present situation. He told his countrymen, that, instead of besieging the Syracusans, he himself was now besieged by them and their allies: that the towns revolted from him, the slaves and mercenaries deserted, and his troops were employed in guarding the forts and bringing in provisions, in which last service many of them were cut off by the enemy's horse. He added, that unless a reinforcement was sent him equal to that with which he had originally set out, it was in vain to think of attempting any thing farther: and, in any event, he begged, that he himself might be recalled, as his health was so much impaired as to render him incapable of going on with the service. This last part of his request, however, the Athenians would by no means consent to: but they resolved to send out Eurymedon and Demosthenes with fresh supplies; the former immediately with ten galleys, and the other early in the spring with a stronger force. At the same time they appointed Menander and Euthydemus as assistants to Nicias; and these immediately joined him.

But Gylippus was determined to be beforehand with the Athenians, and to crush, if possible, the force they now had in Sicily, before the succours should arrive. For this purpose he persuaded the Syracusans to hazard a battle by sea, while he should endeavour to storm the forts of Plemmyrium. The former part of this scheme failed; the latter succeeded. The Athenians had only sixty ships to oppose to eighty of the Syracusans; but as they were greatly superior to them in naval skill, they at last got the better, though victory seemed at first to incline to the side of the enemy. The Athenians lost three ships in this engagement; but the Syracusans had nine sunk, and three taken. In the meantime, Gylippus attacking the forts at Plemmyrium, while many of those who defended them were gone to the shore, in order to view the sea fight, he carried the greatest of them by storm; and this so intimidated the garrisons of the other two, that they abandoned them in a moment.

Encouraged by this success; he resolved to repeat his blow before the arrival of the Athenian succours. He therefore persuaded the Syracusans to venture another battle by sea. They did so, and with a greater degree of good fortune than had attended them on the former occasion. Nicias would willingly have declined this engagement; but he was overruled, or rather overpersuaded, by his two colleagues, Menander and Euthydemus. The Athenians had seventy-five galleys, the Syracusans eighty. The first day the two fleets continued in sight of each other, without coming to a general engagement, and only a few skirmishes passed between them. The Syracusans did not make the least motion the second day. But on the third they came up much sooner than usual, when a great part of the day was spent in skirmishing, after which they retired. The Athenians not imagining they would return again that day, did not keep themselves in readiness to receive them. But the Syracusans having refreshed themselves in great haste, and gone on board their galleys, attacked the Athenians unawares, and in a little time threw them into irretrievable confusion. These last, indeed, would have received a much more severe blow, had they not taken shelter behind their transports, which had been previously drawn up in a line to protect them. They lost, however, on this occasion seven galleys; and a great number of their soldiers were either killed or taken prisoners.

While Nicias was reflecting with grief upon his present unhappy situation, and looking forward with terror to the still more melancholy prospect that lay before him, he was relieved from all his uneasiness, by the arrival of Demosthenes' fleet, which now came forward in great pomp and splendour. It consisted of seventy-three galleys, on board of which were five thousand fighting men, and above three thousand archers, slingers, and bowmen. This was a force, which, if properly managed, might have turned the scale of victory yet once more in favour of the Athenians; but by the precipitancy of Demosthenes and the other generals, in opposition to the more cautious measures recommended by Nicias, it only served to heighten their disgrace and the enemy's triumph.

It was resolved, in a council of war, to attack the town immediately; and as a previous step to it, to make themselves masters of Epipolæ. In their first assault upon this latter place, which was made by night, they stormed the outer intrenchment; but as they were advancing towards the second, they were suddenly attacked by the forces of the city, which had marched under arms out of their lines, and were supported by Gylippus. These, however, being seized with astonishment, which the darkness increased, were soon put to flight; but a body of Bœotians, who followed them, made a more vigorous stand, and marching against the Athenians with their pikes presented, repulsed them with great shouts, and committed a most dreadful slaughter. This spread a universal terror through the rest of the army. Those who fled either forced along such as were advancing to their assistance, or else, mistaking them for enemies, turned their arms against them. They were now all mixed indiscriminately, it being impossible, amidst the horrors of so dark a night, to distinguish friend from foe; and death was frequently inflicted by that hand, from which, in the daytime, protection would have been received. The Athenians sought for one another to no purpose; and from their often asking the word, by which only they were able to know one another, a strange confusion of sounds was heard, which occasioned no little disorder; not to mention that they by this means divulged their watch-word to the enemy, and could not learn theirs; because, by their being together, and in a body, they had no occasion to repeat it. In the meantime, those who were pursued, threw themselves from the top of the rocks, and many were dashed to pieces by the fall: and as most of those who escaped straggled from one another up and down the fields and woods, they were cut to pieces the next day by the enemy's horse who pursued them. Two thousand Athenians were slain in this engagement, and a great quantity of arms was taken; those who fled having thrown them away, that they might be the better able to escape over the pre-cipices.

Thus were at once blasted all the flattering hopes which the Athenians had conceived on the arrival of Demosthenes; and Gylippus having soon after made the tour of Sicily, and brought in with him a great number of fresh troops, acquired by that means such an undisputed superiority over the Athenians, that these last, convinced of their utter inability to make any further head against him, resolved immediately to abandon the island, and return to their own country. But just as they were upon the point of embarking, (wholly unsuspected by the enemy, who never supposed they would quit the island so soon) the moon was sud-denly eclipsed: and as this was a phenomenon, with the real cause of which they were utterly unacquainted, they concluded it to be a prodigy or portent, and there-fore dreaded the consequences of it. It had been cus-tomary, upon former occasions, to suspend the execution of any enterprise for three days after such an accident happened. But the soothsayers, being now consulted, said, that the Athenians must not sail till nine times three days were past (these are Thucydides' words); which doubtless was a mysterious number in the opinion of the people. Nicias, scrupulous to a fault, and full of a mistaken veneration for those blind interpreters of the will of the gods, declared that he would wait a whole revolution of the moon, and not set sail till the same day of the next month, as if he had not seen the planet shine with her usual brightness the moment she emerged from the shadow of the earth by which she had been darkened.

The Syracusans, however, being informed of the intended departure of the Athenians, were determined not to let them retire in peace, and, if possible, not even retire at all; but either to cut them off entirely, or oblige them to surrender as prisoners of war. For this purpose, they attacked the intrenchments immediately, and gained a slight advantage over them. The next day they made a second attack, and at the same time sailed with seventy-six galleys against eighty-six of the Athenians. After an obstinate dispute, the Athenians were defeated with the loss of eighteen of their ships, which were taken by the enemy, and their crews cut to pieces. Eurymedon too, their commander, lost his life in the engagement.

In order to prevent their escaping by sea, the enemy shut up the mouth of the great harbour, which was about five hundred paces wide, with galleys placed cross-wise, and other vessels, fixed with anchors and iron chains, and at the same time made the requisite preparations for a battle, in case they should have courage to engage again. The Athenians seeing themselves cooped up in this manner, and having no other means of procuring provisions but by being masters of the sea, were obliged to hazard another engagement upon that element. Both commanders exerted all their eloquence to animate their men, and none could be actuated by stronger motives than now influenced them; for upon the issue of the battle, which was going to be fought, depended not only their own lives and liberties, but even the fate of their native country. This battle was more obstinate and bloody than any of the preceding ones. The Athenians, being arrived at the mouth of the port, easily took the first ships they came to; but when they attempted to break the chain of the rest, the enemy poured in upon them from all quarters. As near two hundred galleys came rushing on each side into a narrow place,· there must necessarily be very great confusion; and the vessels could not easily advance, or retire, or turn about to renew the attack. The beaks of the galleys, for this reason, did little execution; but there were very furious and frequent discharges. The Athenians were overwhelmed with a shower of stones, which always did execution from whatever place they were thrown; whereas they defended themselves only by shooting darts and arrows, which, by the motion of the ships, were diverted from their aim, and seldom hit the mark at which they were levelled. Ariston, the Corinthian, had given the Syracusans this counsel. These discharges being over, the heavy-armed soldiers attempted to board the enemy's ships, in order to fight hand to hand: and it frequently happened, that while they were climbing up one side of these, their own ships were entered on the other, so that two or three ships were sometimes grappled together, which occasioned great confusion. Add to this, that the noise of the ships which dashed against one another, and the different cries of the victors and vanquished, prevented the orders of the officers from being distinctly heard. The Athenians wanted to force a passage, whatever might be the consequence, in order to secure their return to their own country; and this the enemy endeavoured to prevent, that they might thereby gain a more complete victory. The two land armies, which were drawn up on the highest part of the shore, were spectators of the action, while the inhabitants of the city ran to the walls in order to behold it. All these saw clearly, because of their little distance from the fleets, every thing that passed, and contemplated the battle as from an amphitheatre, but not without great anxiety and terror. Attentive to, and shuddering at every movement, and the several changes of fortune that happened, they discovered the concern they had in the battle, their fears, their hopes, their grief, their joy, by different cries and different gestures; stretching out their hands sometimes towards the combatants to animate them, at other times towards heaven, to implore the succour and protection of the gods. At last, the Athenian fleet, after making a long and vigorous resistance, was put to flight, and driven against the shore. The Syracusans on the walls, seeing their countrymen victorious, conveyed the news to the whole city by a universal shout. The victors immediately sailed towards Syracuse, where they erected a trophy, while the Athenians were so much dejected, that they did not even request the dead bodies of their fellow soldiers to be delivered to them, in order to honour them with the rites of burial.

There now remained but two methods for them to choose; either to attempt the passage a second time, for which they had still ships and soldiers sufficient; or to abandon their fleet to the enemy, and retire by land. Demosthenes recommended the former plan; but the soldiers were so much intimidated by their late defeat, that they had not courage to undertake it. The second method was therefore adopted; and they accordingly prepared to set out in the night, the better to conceal their march from the enemy. Hermocrates, however, the Syracusan general, was extremely unwilling that so large a body of men (amounting to near forty thousand) should be suffered to depart, lest they should fortify themselves in some corner of the island, and renew the war. At the same time he knew it would be impossible to persuade the Syracusans to oppose their marching that evening, as they were then engaged in celebrating their late victory, and solemnizing the festival of Hercules. He therefore fell upon another expedient. He sent out a few horsemen, who were to pass for friends of the Athenians, and ordered them to tell Nicias not to retire till daylight, as the Syracusans lay in ambush for him, and had seized on all the passes.

Nicias was so weak as to believe this intelligence,

and accordingly delayed his departure not only that
evening but the whole of the next day, in order that
the soldiers might have more time to prepare for their
march, and carry off whatever might be necessary for
their subsistence. But this delay afterwards proved
fatal to them: for early next morning the enemy took
possession of all the difficult avenues, fortified the
banks of the rivers in those parts where they were
fordable, broke down the bridges, and spread detach-
ments of horse up and down the plain, so that there
was not one place which the Athenians could pass without fighting.

They set out upon their march the third day after
the battle, with a design to retire to Catana. Their
army was divided into two bodies, both drawn up in
the form of a phalanx, the first being commanded by
Nicias, and the second by Demosthenes, with the baggage in the centre. In this manner they proceeded for
several days, during which they were terribly harassed
by the enemy, who hung upon their rear, and overwhelmed them with showers of darts and arrows, but
never would stand a general engagement, when the
Athenians wheeled about.

Finding, therefore, their numbers daily decrease, and
being at the same time in extreme want of provisions,
they altered their plan, and, instead of continuing their
march to Catana, they directed their route towards
Camerina and Gela. As this scheme was executed in
the night, it was attended with so much confusion, that
the rear guard, under Demosthenes, soon parted from
the main body, and lost their way. Next day the Syracusans came up with them, and surrounded them in a
narrow place; and though they defended themselves
for some time with incredible bravery, yet finding it
impossible to effect their escape, they were at last
obliged to surrender prisoners of war, which they did
upon condition that they should not be put to death,
nor condemned to perpetual imprisonment. About six
thousand men surrendered on these terms.

In the meantime, Nicias proceeded on his march, and
crossing the river Erineus, encamped on a mountain,

where the enemy overtook him the next day, and summoned him to surrender, as Demosthenes had done. Nicias at first could not believe what they told him concerning Demosthenes, and therefore begged leave to send some horse to inquire into the truth; and when he found that matters really were so, he offered to defray all the expenses of the war, provided they would suffer him to quit the island with his forces. But this proposal was rejected by the enemy, who immediately renewed the attack; and though Nicias defended himself during the whole night, and even continued his march next day to the river Asinarus, yet he was quickly pursued thither by the Syracusans, who threw most of the Athenians into the stream; the rest having already thrown themselves into it in order to quench their burning thirst. Here the most terrible havock was committed; so that Nicias, finding all things desperate, was obliged to surrender upon this single condition, that Gylippus should discontinue the fight, and spare the lives of his men. The lives of the men, indeed, were spared; but Nicias and Demosthenes, after being scourged with rods, were cruelly put to death; a striking proof of the barbarity of the age. By this savage act, the Syracusans tarnished the glory they had acquired by the gallant defence of their city, and the signal victory they had won.

It must be owned, indeed, that Gylippus, and even many of the Syracusans themselves, did all they could to save the lives of the Athenian generals; but the great body of the people, egged on by their orators, and particularly by Diocles, one of their most popular leaders, could be satisfied with nothing less than the blood of these two illustrious men. The fate of Nicias is the more to be lamented, as no man was ever more remarkable for humanity and goodnature; and though he headed this expedition in obedience to the commands of his countrymen, yet he did every thing in his power to prevent them from undertaking it. Demosthenes too was a man of so respectable a character, that the famous orator of the same name, many years after valued himself on account of his being of the same family.

As to the prisoners, they were shut up in the dun-
geons of Syracuse, where many of them perished through
want and bad treatment: and those that survived, being
afterwards sold for slaves, recommended themselves so
strongly to their masters by their modest, prudent, and
ingenuous behaviour, that many of them soon obtained
their liberty; and some of them even owed that favour
to their being able to repeat the finest scenes of Euripides' tragedies, of which the Sicilians were passion-
ately fond: so that when they returned to their own
country they went and saluted the poet as their deliverer,
and informed him of the great advantage they had derived from their being acquainted with his verses.

The Athenians were so little prepared to receive the
news of this defeat, or rather, indeed, they were so
confident of receiving news of a contrary nature, that
they condemned to death the man that first brought the
intelligence; but when they found that matters were
really worse than fame had reported, they were at once
overwhelmed with grief and despair. They had never
indeed been reduced to so deplorable a condition as
they were now, having neither horse, foot, money, ships,
nor mariners: in a word, they sunk into the deepest
despondency, and expected every moment, that the
enemy, elate with so great a victory, and strengthened
by the junction of the allies, would come and invade
Athens both by sea and land with all the forces of
Peloponnesus. Cicero therefore had reason to say,
when speaking of the battles in the harbour of Syracuse, that it was there the troops of Athens, as well as
their galleys, were ruined and sunk; and that in this
harbour the power and glory of the Athenians were
miserably shipwrecked.

The Athenians, however, did not suffer themselves
to be wholly dejected, but assumed courage from
despair. They raised money on every side for building new ships; they retrenched all superfluous expenses; and they established a council of old men, to
examine every matter before it was brought into the
assembly of the people. In a word, they took every
step that could possibly tend to retrieve their ruined
affairs, or at least prevent them from growing worse

than they were. But nothing could restore them to their former splendid condition; for from this time forward, the Athenians present us with a very different picture from what they have hitherto done. We are no longer to behold them making a figure in arts and arms; giving lessons on politeness, humanity, philosophy, and war, to all the nations around; and aiming at the erection of an empire, which, if once thoroughly established, would have bid defiance to all the neighbouring states. Instead of aspiring to the conquest of their neighbours, they are now content with defending their own territories at home : instead of directing the councils, and conducting the confederate armies of Greece, they now confine all their attention to their own private affairs; they in a manner become annihilated; they fade from the eye of the historian; and other nations, whose names have hitherto been scarcely mentioned, emerge from obscurity.

It was in this deplorable state of the Athenian affairs, that Alcibiades made proposals of returning home, provided the administration of the republic was put into the hands of the great and powerful, and not left to the populace, who had expelled him. In order to induce his countrymen to agree to these terms, he offered to procure them not only the favour of Tissaphernes, the king of Persia's lieutenant, with whom he had taken refuge, but even that of the king himself, upon condition they would abolish the democracy, or popular government; because the king, he said, would place more confidence in the engagements of the nobility, than in those of the giddy and capricious multitude. The chief man who opposed his return, was Phrynicus, one of the generals, who, in order to accomplish his purpose, sent word to Astyochus, the Lacedæmonian general, that Alcibiades was using his utmost endeavours to engage Tissaphernes in the Athenian interest. He offered, further, to betray to him the whole army and navy of the Athenians. But his treasonable practices being all detected by the good understanding between Alcibiades and Astyochus, he was stripped of his office, and afterwards stabbed in the marketplace.

In the meantime the Athenians proceeded to complete

that change of government which had been proposed to them by Alcibiades; the democracy began to be abolished in several of the smaller cities, and soon after the scheme was carried boldly into execution in Athens itself by Pysander, who had the chief hand in this transaction. To give a new form to the government, he caused ten commissaries, with absolute power, to be appointed, who were, however, at a certain fixed time, to give the people an account of what they had done. At the expiration of that term, the general assembly was summoned, in which the first resolution was, that every one should be admitted to make such proposals as he thought fit, without being liable to any accusation, or consequent penalty, for infringing the law. It was afterwards decreed, that a new council should be formed, with full power to administer the public affairs, and to elect new magistrates. For this purpose five presidents were established, who nominated one hundred persons, including themselves. Each of these chose and associated three more at his own pleasure, which made in all four hundred, in whom an absolute power was lodged. But to amuse the people, and gratify them with the shadow of a popular government, whilst they instituted a real oligarchy, it was said, that the four hundred would call a council of five thousand citizens to assist them, whenever they should find it necessary. The assemblies of the people, indeed, were still held as usual; but nothing was done in them but by order of the four hundred. In this manner were the Athenians deprived of their liberty, after having enjoyed it almost a hundred years, from the time of destroying the tyranny of the Pisistratidæ.—This decree having passed without opposition, after the breaking up of the assembly, the four hundred, armed with daggers, and attended by a hundred and twenty young men, whom they made use of when any emergency required it, entered the senate, and compelled the senators to retire, after having paid them the arrears of their salaries that were still due. They elected new magistrates out of their own body, observing the usual ceremonies upon such occasions. They did not think proper to recall those who had been banished, lest they should authorize the return of Alcibiades, whose uncontrollable spirit they dreaded, and who would soon have made himself master of the government. Abusing their power in a tyrannical manner, they put some to death; others they banished, and confiscated their estates with impunity. All who ventured to oppose this change, or even to complain of it, were butchered upon false pretexts, and those were intimidated who demanded justice of the murderers. The four hundred, soon after their establishment, sent ten deputies to Samos for the army's approbation of their conduct.

The army, in the meantime, which was at Samos, protested against these proceedings in the city; and, by the persuasion of Thrasybulus, recalled Alcibiades, and created him general, with full power to sail directly to the Pyræus, and crush this new tyranny. Alcibiades, however, would not give way to this rash opinion, but went first to show himself to Tissaphernes, and let him know, that it was now in his power to treat with him, either as a friend or an enemy. By which means he awed the Athenians with Tissaphernes, and Tissaphernes with the Athenians. When, afterwards, the four hundred sent to Samos to vindicate their proceedings, the army was for putting the messengers to death, and persisted in the design upon the Pyræus; but Alcibiades, by opposing it, manifestly saved the commonwealth.

Meanwhile the innovation in Athens had occasioned such factions and tumults, that the four hundred were more intent upon providing for their own safety, than carrying on the war; and, the better to accomplish this purpose, they fortified that part of the Pyræus which commands the mouth of the haven, and resolved, in case of extremity, rather to let in the Lacedæmonians, than expose their persons to the fury of their fellow citizens. The Spartans took occasion, from these disturbances, to hover about with forty-two galleys, under the conduct of Hegesandrides; and the Athenians, with thirty-six, under Timochares, were forced to engage them, but lost part of their fleet, and the rest were dispersed. To add to which, all Eubœa, except Oreus, revolted to the Peloponnesians.

This failure of success gave the finishing blow to the

power of the four hundred. The Athenians, without delay, deposed them, as the authors of all the calamities under which they groaned. Alcibiades was recalled by unanimous consent, and earnestly solicited to make all possible haste to the assistance of the city. But judging that if he returned immediately to Athens, he should owe his recall to the compassion and favour of the people, he resolved to render his return glorious and triumphant, and to deserve it by some considerable exploit.

For this purpose, leaving Samos with a small number of ships, he cruised about the islands of Cos and Cnidos; and having learned that Mindarus, the Spartan admiral, had sailed to the Hellespont with his whole fleet, and that the Athenians were in pursuit of him, he steered that way with the utmost expedition to support them, and arrived happily with his eighteen vessels at the time the fleets were engaged near Abydos, in a battle which lasted till night, without any advantage on either side. His arrival gave new courage to the Spartans at first, who believed he was still their friend; but Alcibiades, hanging out the Athenian flag in the admiral's galley, immediately fell upon them, and put them to flight; and, pursuing his blow, sunk many of their vessels, and made a great slaughter of their soldiers, who had leaped into the sea, to save themselves by swimming. The Athenians, after having captured thirty of their galleys, and retaken those they had lost, erected a trophy.

Alcibiades, after this victory, went to visit Tissaphernes, who was so far from receiving him as he expected, that he immediately caused him to be seized, and sent away to Sardis, telling him that he had orders from the king to make war upon the Athenians; but the truth is, he was afraid of being accused to his master by the Peloponnesians, and thought, by this act of injustice, to purge himself from all former imputations. Alcibiades, after thirty days, made his escape to Clazomenæ, and soon after bore down upon the Peloponnesian fleet, which rode at anchor before the port of Cyzicus. With twenty of his best ships he

broke through the enemy, pursued those who abandoned their vessels, and fled to land, and made a great
slaughter. The Athenians took the enemy's whole fleet,
and made themselves masters of Cyzicus, while Mingi-
mis, the Lacedæmonian general, was found among the
number of the slain.

Alcibiades well knew how to make use of the advantage he had gained; and, at the head of his victorious
troops, took several cities which had revolted from the
Athenians. Calcedon, Salymbria, and Byzantium were
among the number. Thus flushed with success, he
seemed to desire nothing more than to be once more
seen by his countrymen, as his presence would be a
triumph to his friends, and an insult to his enemies.
He accordingly set sail for Athens. Besides the ships
covered with bucklers and spoils of all sorts, in the
manner of trophies, a great number of vessels were also
towed after him by way of triumph; he displayed likewise the ensigns and ornaments of those he had burnt,
which were more than the others, the whole amounting to about two hundred ships.

It is said, that reflecting on what had been done
against him, upon approaching the port, he was struck
with some apprehensions, and was afraid to quit his
vessel, till he saw from the deck a great number of his
friends and relations, who were come to the shore to
receive him, and earnestly entreated him to land. As
soon as he was landed, the multitude who came out to
meet him fixed their eyes upon him, thronged about
him, saluted him with loud acclamations, and crowned
him with garlands. He received their congratulations
with great satisfaction; he desired to be discharged from
his former condemnation, and obtained from the priests
an absolution from all their former denunciations.

Yet, notwithstanding these triumphs, the real power
of Athens was now no more: the strength of the state
was gone; and even the passion for liberty was lost in
the common degeneracy of the times. Many of the
meaner sort of people earnestly desired Alcibiades to
take upon him the sovereign power, and to set himself
above the reach of envy, by securing all authority in

his own person. But the great were neither so warm nor so injudicious in their expressions of gratitude. They contented themselves with appointing him generalissimo of all their forces; they granted him whatever he demanded, and gave him for colleagues the generals most agreeable to him. He set sail accordingly, with a hundred ships, and steered for the island of Andros, that had revolted, where having defeated the inhabitants, he went from thence to Samos, intending to make that the seat of war. · In the mean time, the Lacedæmonians, alarmed at his success, made choice of a general every way qualified to make head against him. This was Lysander, who, though born of the highest family, had been inured to hardships from his earliest youth, and was strongly attached to the manners and discipline of his country. He was brave, ambitious, circumspect, but, at the same time, cunning, crafty, and deceitful; and these latter qualities ran so much through his whole life that it was usually said of him, that he cheated children with foul play, and men with oaths: and it is reported to have been a maxim of his, that when the lion's strength fails, we must make use of the subtilty of the fox.

Lysander, having brought his army to Ephesus, gave orders for assembling ships of burden from all parts, and erected a dock for the building of galleys; he made the ports free for merchants, and, by encouraging trade of every kind, he laid the foundation of that splendour and magnificence to which Ephesus afterwards attained. Meanwhile, receiving advice that Cyrus, the king of Persia's son, was arrived at Sardis, he went thither to pay him a visit, and at the same time to complain to him of the conduct of Tissaphernes, whose duplicity, he said, had proved fatal to their common cause. Cyrus was sufficiently disposed to listen to any complaints against Tissaphernes, to whom he himself had a personal enmity; and he therefore came readily into the views of Lysander, and at his request increased the pay of the seamen. This last circumstance had a surprising effect. It almost instantly unmanned the galleys of the Athenians, and supplied the Lacedæmonian fleet with plenty of sailors, who, without inquiring into the justice of the cause on either side, went over to that party which gave the best pay.

Nor was this the only misfortune which the Athenians now met with. For Alcibiades, being obliged to leave the fleet, in order to raise the supplies, gave the command of it to Antiochus, with strict orders not to attack or engage the enemy in his absence. But Antiochus, desirous of distinguishing himself by some great action before the return of Alcibiades, sailed away directly for Ephesus, and used every art to provoke the enemy to an engagement. Lysander at first contented himself with sending out a few ships to repel his insults; but the Athenian galleys advancing to support their commander, other Lacedæmonian vessels likewise came on, till at last both fleets arrived, and the engagement became general. After a sharp struggle Lysander obtained the victory, having killed Antiochus, and taken fifteen of the Athenian galleys. It was in vain that Alcibiades soon after came up to the relief of his friends; it was in vain that he offered to renew the combat; Lysander was too wise to hazard the advantage he had gained by venturing on a second engagement.

This misfortune proved fatal to the reputation of Alcibiades, though indeed it was his own glory that ruined him; for the people, from his uninterrupted success, had conceived such a high opinion of his abilities, that they thought it impossible for him to fail in any thing he seriously undertook: and they therefore now began to question his integrity, and deprived him of the command of the army.

About the same time Callicratidas was appointed to succeed Lysander, whose year was expired. This man was equal to his predecessor in courage, and greatly superior in probity and justice, being as open and ingenuous, as the other was cunning and crafty. His first attempt was against Methymna in Lesbos, which he took by storm. He then threatened Conon, who had succeeded Alcibiades, that he would make him leave off *debauching* the sea: and accordingly soon after pursued

him into the port of Mitylene with a hundred and
seventy sail, took thirty of his ships, and besieged him
in the town, from which he cut off all provisions. He
soon after took ten ships more out of the twelve that
were coming to the relief of Conon. Then hearing that
the Athenians had fitted out their whole strength, consisting of a hundred and fifty sail, he left fifty of his
ships under Etonicus, to carry on the siege of Mitylene,
and with a hundred and twenty more met the Athenians
at Arginusæ, over against Lesbos. His pilot advising
him to retreat because the enemy were superior in
number, "Sparta," replied he, "will be never the worse
inhabited though I should be slain." The fight accordingly was immediately begun, and was maintained for
a long time with equal bravery on both sides, till at
last the ship of Callicratidas, charging through the
midst of the enemy, was sunk, and the rest fled. The
Peloponnesians lost about seventy sail, and the Athenians twenty-five, with most of the men in them.

The Athenian admirals, instead of being rewarded
for the victory they had gained, were severely punished
for a supposed neglect of duty: they were accused of
not having done their utmost to save their men who
had been shipwrecked; and they were accordingly
sent home in irons, to answer for their conduct. They
alleged in their defence, that they were pursuing the
enemy; and, at the same time, gave orders about taking
up the men to those whose business it more peculiarly
was; particularly to Theramenes, who now appeared
against them; but yet that their orders could not be
executed, on account of a violent storm which happened
at that time. This plea seemed so satisfactory that
several stood up and offered to bail them: but, in
another assembly, the popular incendiaries demanded
justice, and so awed the judges that Socrates was the
only man who had courage enough to declare, that he
would do nothing contrary to law, and accordingly
refused to act. After a long debate, eight of the ten
were condemned, and six of them were put to death;
among whom was Pericles, the son of the great statesman of the same name. He maintained, that they had

failed in nothing of their duty, as they had given orders
for the dead bodies being taken up; that if any one
were guilty, it was Theramenes himself, who, being
charged with these orders, had neglected to put them
in execution: but that he accused nobody, and that
the tempest, which came on unexpectedly at the very
instant, was a sufficient apology, and entirely freed the
accused from all kind of guilt. He demanded that a
whole day should be allowed them to make their defence, a favour not denied to the most criminal, and
that they should be tried separately. He represented,
that they were not in the least obliged to precipitate a
sentence, in which the lives of the most illustrious
citizens were concerned; that it was in some measure
attacking the gods, to make them responsible for the
winds and weather; that they could not, without the
most flagrant ingratitude and injustice, inflict death
upon the conquerors, to whom they ought rather to
decree crowns and honours, or give up the defenders
of their country to the rage of those who envied them;
that if they did so, their unjust judgment would be
followed by a sudden, but vain repentance, which
would leave behind it the sharpest remorse, and cover
them with eternal infamy.

Among the number also was Diomedon, a person
equally eminent for his valour and his probity: as he
was carrying to execution, he demanded to be heard.
"Athenians," said he, "I wish the sentence you have
passed upon us may not prove the misfortune of the
republic; but I have one favour to ask of you in
behalf of my colleagues and myself, which is, to acquit
us before the gods of the vows we made to them for
you and ourselves, as we are not in a condition to discharge them; for it is to their aid, invoked before the
battle, we acknowledge, that we are indebted for the
victory gained by us over the enemy." There was not
a good citizen that did not melt into tears at this discourse, so full of piety and religion, and behold with
surprise the moderation of a person, who, seeing himself unjustly condemned, did not, however, express the
least resentment, nor even utter a complaint against

his judges, but was solely intent, in favour of an ungrateful country, which had doomed them to perish, upon what it owed to the gods in common with them for the victory they had lately obtained.

This complication of injustice and ingratitude gave the finishing blow to the affairs of the Athenians: they struggled for a while after the defeat at Syracuse, but from this time forward they rapidly declined, though seemingly in the arms of victory. The enemy, after their defeat, had once more recourse to Lysander, who had so often led them to conquest; in him they placed their chief confidence, and earnestly solicited his return. The Lacedæmonians, therefore, to gratify their allies, and yet to observe their laws, which forbade that honour being twice conferred on the same person, sent him with an inferior title, but with the power of admiral. Thus appointed, Lysander sailed towards the Hellespont, and laid siege to Lampsacus, which he took by storm, and abandoned it to the mercy of the soldiers. The Athenians who followed him close, upon the news of his success, steered forward towards Olestus, and from thence sailing along the coast, halted over against the enemy at Ægos Potamos, a place fatal to the Athenians.

The Hellespont is not above two thousand paces broad in that place. The two fleets seeing themselves so near each other, expected only to rest that day, and hoped to come to an engagement on the next. But Lysander had another design in view. He commanded the seamen and pilots to go on board their galleys, and hold themselves in readiness, as if they were really to fight next morning. He likewise commanded the land army to be drawn up in battle array upon the coast, and to wait his orders in profound silence. On the morning, as soon as the sun was risen, the Athenians rowed towards them with their whole fleet, and offered them battle. This, however, Lysander did not think proper to accept, even though his ships were ranged in perfect order, with their heads towards the enemy. The Athenians, ascribing this conduct to fear or cowardice, retiring in the evening, and, thinking they were in no danger, went ashore to amuse and regale themselves, as if no enemy had been nigh. Of this last circumstance Lysander was fully informed, by some galleys he sent out to observe their motions. To throw them, therefore, into still greater security, and put them more off their guard, he allowed the three following days to pass in the same manner, during each of which the Athenians came regularly up, and offered him battle, which he as regularly persisted to decline.

In the mean time Alcibiades, who since his disgrace had lived in Thrace, and was much better acquainted with the character of the Lacedæmonians, and particularly with that of Lysander, than the present Athenian generals, came and warned them of their danger : he even offered, with a body of Thracian troops, to attack the enemy by land, and thus force them to a battle. But the Athenian generals, jealous of their honour, and thinking that, if the event proved successful, Alcibiades would enjoy all the glory, and, if otherwise, the whole blame would fall upon them, not only refused his assistance, but even rejected his salutary advice. The consequence was, that on the evening of the fifth day, when they had retired as usual, and their men were all gone on shore, and dispersed up and down the country, Lysander came suddenly upon them with his whole force, and, attacking them in this unprepared and defenceless condition, he easily made a capture of their whole fleet, except nine galleys (including the sacred ship), with which Conon contrived to escape to Cyprus, where he took refuge with Evagoras. This was one of the most masterly strokes of generalship that ever was performed in ancient, or perhaps even in modern times ; for by it Lysander, in the space of an hour, put an end to a war, that had already lasted twenty-seven years, and but for him would probably have lasted much longer.

The number of prisoners amounted to three thousand, and the fate of these is a shocking proof of the barbarous manners of the age ; for it cannot be denied that, with all their attainments in eloquence and poetry, and the other arts that depend upon the imagination, the Greeks

and Romans were greatly inferior to the moderns, not
merely in their knowledge of nature, but in civility,
politeness, and in every thing that tends to humanize
the mind of man. The fact is, these unhappy men were
instantly put to death, though this was said to be only
by way of retaliation: for that the Athenians had caused
to be thrown down a precipice all the men that were
taken in two Lacedæmonian galleys, and had likewise
made a decree for cutting off the thumb of the right
hand of all the prisoners of war, in order to disable
them from handling the pike, and that they might be
fit only to serve at the oar. Philocles, the chief author
both of this barbarous act and this severe decree, was
now called upon to show what he could urge in his
defence, when he haughtily replied—"Accuse not
people of crimes who have no judges, but as you are
victors, use your right, and do by us as we had done
by you if we had conquered." The only person that
was saved out of the whole number was Adamantus,
who had opposed the decree.

The Athenians were no sooner informed of the entire
defeat of their army, than they were overwhelmed with
consternation. They already thought they saw Lysander at their gates, nor was it long before he came there.
But before he did so, he commanded all the Athenians,
that were scattered up and down in different parts of
Greece, to take shelter in Athens on pain of death.
This he did with a design so to crowd the city, that he
might be able soon to reduce it by famine. And indeed, in a little time, he actually so reduced it. For
Agis and Pausanias, the two kings of Sparta, having
besieged it by land, and Lysander himself blocking it
up by sea, the wretched Athenians, after undergoing
the most intolerable hardships, were driven to such
extremity, that they sent deputies to Agis, with offers
of abandoning all their possessions, their city and port
only excepted. The haughty Lacedæmonians referred
their deputies to the state itself, and when these sup-
pliants made known their commission to the Ephori,
they were ordered to depart, and come again with
other proposals, if they expected peace.

H

At length Theramenes, an Athenian, undertook to manage the treaty with Lysander; and, after a conference which lasted three months, he received full powers to treat at Lacedæmon. When he, attended by nine others, arrived before the Ephori, some of the confederates represented the necessity of destroying Athens entirely, without listening to any further proposals. But the Lacedæmonians told them that they would not consent to the destruction of a city, which had preserved the general independence of Greece in the most critical juncture; and they therefore agreed to a peace upon these conditions: that the long walls and fortifications of the Pyræus should be demolished; that they should deliver up all their ships but twelve; that they should restore their exiles; that they should make a league offensive and defensive with the Lacedæmonians, and serve them in all their expeditions both by sea and land.

Theramenes, being returned with the articles to Athens, was asked, why he acted in a manner so contrary to the intentions of Themistocles, and gave those walls into the hands of the Lacedæmonians, which he built in defiance of them? "I have my eye," said he, "upon Themistocles' design; he raised these walls for the preservation of the city, and I for the very same reason would have them destroyed; for if walls only secure a city, Sparta, which has none, is in a very bad condition." Such an answer would not have satisfied the Athenians at any other time; but, being now reduced to the last extremity, it did not admit of a long debate whether they should accept the treaty. At last Lysander, coming to the Pyræus, demolished the walls with great solemnity and all the insulting triumphs of music; and thus was a period put to the famous Peloponnesian war, the longest, the most expensive, and the most bloody, in which Greece had ever been engaged.

It would be unpardonable in us not to pay that tribute of gratitude and respect, which is due to the memory of those exalted geniuses, whose labours adorned the nations of their own time, and have polished and humanized all succeeding ages. Wars and political contests serve but to depopulate the earth, or to fill the minds of men with animosity and hate; while the labours of the historian, the fancies of the poet, and the discoveries of the philosopher enlighten the understanding, meliorate the heart, and teach us fortitude and resignation. Such peaceful and improving arts well deserve our notice. More especially does the cultivation of them in Greece deserve our attention, as many of the writers of that country were renowned for military and political, as well as literary, accomplishments.

Of Homer it is unnecessary to say much, his merit being well known. It is not probable, that he was the first of the Grecian poets. There seem to have been authors prior to him, from whom he has borrowed in the execution of his Iliad; but as he was the first poet of note, it was not unnatural to place him at the head of all ancient bards. Seven different places contended for the honour of giving him birth, but Smyrna seems to have the best claim. He is supposed to have been born about two hundred and forty years after the destruction of Troy.

Hesiod was either cotemporary with Homer, or lived immediately after him. Their works will not bear a comparison. Homer is stately and sublime, while Hesiod is plain and agreeable. But when we say so, we do not mean to detract in the least from the reputation of Hesiod. To write with ease and propriety was all he aimed at, and this he certainly attained.

About the beginning of the war which preceded the peace concluded between the Athenians and Lacedæmonians for fifty years, died Æschylus, the Athenian dramatic writer. He has the same claim to the title of *father of tragedy*, which Homer has to that of *epic poetry*. For though he was not the first who attempted that sort of composition, yet he was the first who reduced it to any kind of regularity or method. In the days of Solon, Thespis made a considerable improvement, by introducing a single person, whose business was to relieve the chorus, by the recital of some extraordinary adventure. It was Æschylus who exchanged the cart of Thespis for a theatre: who introduced a variety of performers, each taking a part in the representation of some great action, and dressed in a manner suited to his character. The style of Æschylus is pompous, and sometimes sublime, but far from being harmonious. He is frequently too so very obscure, that it is no easy matter to find out his meaning. The chief object of his pieces is *terror;* and, to do him justice, it must be acknowledged, that few dramatic writers have surpassed him in exciting that passion.

During that period, in which Greece was so much distracted by the Peloponnesian war, there flourished Sophocles, Euripides, Aristophanes, &c. among the poets; Herodotus and Thucydides among the historians; and Socrates among the philosophers.

Sophocles had applied so intensely to the study of tragedy, when a young man, that his first piece was judged not inferior to the very best of those of Æschylus. Both these poets were stately in their manner, but Æschylus was the more sublime. That advantage, however, was more than counterbalanced by the versatility of Sophocles' genius, and by his superior perspicuity and éloquence. He was also more successful than his master in his appeal to the passions; and though he did not harrow up the breast by *terror*, he softened it more by *pity*, and acquired, of course, the reputation of being a more amiable and polite writer. Sophocles was likewise much more happy than his predecessor in the conduct of his plots. He made them more interesting by being more artful. He also contrived to make the performances of the chorus bear a relation to the main action, and so rendered the whole entire. He wrote a hundred and twenty tragedies, of which seven only remain. He lived to the age of eighty-five, and then is said to have died of joy for the success of his last piece, as Æschylus is reported to have done of grief for being foiled by him in his first.

Euripides, the rival of Sophocles, aimed not at the lofty strains of Æschylus, or of his great competitor. He is more sententious and moral than either of them, and seemed to have as strong a desire to instruct mankind, as to obtain their applause. Correctness and elegance were the qualities of style which he appears to have admired. He is less artful and magnificent than Sophocles, but then he is more natural and more useful. We have already mentioned a circumstance much to his honour, the emancipation of many of the Athenians who were made prisoners at Syracuse, because they were able to repeat some of his beautiful verses.

While Tragedy was improving in the hands of Sophocles and Euripides, Comedy was advancing under the guidance of Eupolis, Cratinus, and Aristophanes. But the most distinguished of this kind was Aristophanes. At the same time that he entertained the Athenians with his pleasantry, he lashed them with his satire. True it is, he did not possess much of that fine raillery, which has given so smooth, and yet so sharp an edge to modern comedy: but then he had fire and strength; and as he introduced his characters by their real names, occupations, &c. his performances were often more relished, and, very probably, more useful than those of the tragedians.

As to History, Herodotus is considered as the father of that species of composition in Greece. He wrote the history of the wars between the Greeks and Persians, and gave a detail of the affairs of almost all other nations, from the reign of Cyrus to that of Xerxes. His work consists of nine books. It is clothed in the Ionic dialect, and is a perfect model of simplicity and elegance.

Thucydides is esteemed a more able writer than even Herodotus. He wants, indeed, that native elegance for which his predecessor is admired, but then he is more judicious and energetic. He wrote the history of the Peloponnesian war.

Of Socrates, Plato, Aristotle, Demosthenes, and other illustrious Grecian writers and philosophers, mention is made in the different parts of this work. There is a circumstance that merits our attention here—the discovery of the *Metonic*, or *golden number*, by Meton. That philosopher flourished a little before the commencement of the Peloponnesian war, and was much esteemed by the Athenians. Pindar was a native of Thebes, and contemporary with Meton.

CHAPTER X.

FROM THE DEMOLITION OF THE ATHENIAN POWER TO THE
DEATH OF SOCRATES.

THOUGH the Lacedæmonians would not consent to the
entire destruction of Athens, as they would not be
guilty, they said, of putting out one of the eyes of
Greece, yet they not only reduced it to the lowest
condition in point of political consequence, but even
altered the form of its government; for they compelled
the people to abolish the democracy, and submit to the
government of thirty men, who were commonly known
by the name of the Thirty Tyrants. The Greeks, indeed, were sufficiently disposed to give that name to
men of virtuous characters; but these rulers of Athens,
who were the mere creatures of Lysander, appear to
have deserved, in every respect, the most opprobrious
appellation. Instead of compiling and publishing a
more perfect body of laws, which was the pretence for
their being chosen, they began to exercise their power
of life and death; and though they appointed a senate,
and other magistrates, they made no farther use of
them than to confirm their own authority, and see
their commands executed. At first, it is true, they proceeded with some caution, and condemned only the
most profligate sort of citizens, viz. such as lived by
informing and giving evidence against their neighbours; but this was only to blind the eyes of the populace; their real design was to make themselves absolute: and as they well knew, that this could not be
done without a foreign power, they next contrived to
have a guard sent them from Sparta. This guard was
commanded by one Callibius, whom they soon won
over to their designs; and from this time forward they
proceeded to act without control, filling the city with
the blood of those, who, on account of their riches,
interests, or good qualities, were most likely to oppose
them.

One of their first acts of cruelty was to procure the
death of Alcibiades, who had taken refuge in the dominions of Persia. This man, though driven from his

country, did not cease to interest himself in its welfare, and the tyrants dreading, that, by his popularity at Athens, where he was still much beloved, he would thwart all their schemes, entreated the Lacedæmonians to rid them of so formidable an opponent. This request the Lacedæmonians had the meanness to comply with; and accordingly wrote to Pharnabasus, the Persian governor for that purpose; and he, in his turn, was no less base and unprincipled, for, without having received any personal injury from Alcibiades, he readily promised to take him out of the way. The manner of this great man's death did not disgrace the high character for courage he had maintained during life. The assassins sent against him were afraid to attack him openly. They, therefore, surrounded the house in which he was, and set it on fire. Alcibiades forced his way through the flames, sword in hand, and drove the barbarians before him, not one of whom had the courage to oppose him; but all of them discharging their darts and javelins upon him from a distance, he at last fell covered with wounds, and instantly expired. Timandra, his mistress, took up his body, and having covered and adorned it with the finest robes she had, she made as magnificent a funeral for it as her present circumstances would allow. To what we have already said of Alcibiades, it may not be improper to add, that his great popularity, wherever he resided, was principally owing to the extreme versatility of his genius, and the surprising facility with which he accommodated himself to the manners and customs of different people; for in this respect no man ever exceeded, or perhaps even equalled him. Plutarch says, that at Sparta he was hardy, frugal, and reserved; in Ionia, luxurious, indolent and gay; and when transacting affairs with the king of Persia's lieutenants, he surpassed even these men themselves in pomp and magnificence.

The tyrants, though eased of their apprehensions from this quarter, began to dread an opposition from another, that is, from the general body of the people, whom they well knew to be dissatisfied with their conduct; and they therefore invested three thousand citizens with some part of their power, and by their assistance kept the rest in awe. Encouraged now by such an accession of strength, they soon proceeded to still greater extremities than any they had hitherto ventured on; they agreed to single out every one his man, to put him to death, and seize their estates for the maintenance of their guard. Theramenes, one of their number, was the only man that was struck with horror at their proceedings: Critias, therefore, the principal author of this detestable resolution, thought it necessary to take him out of the way, and he accordingly accused him to the senate of endeavouring to subvert the government. Sentence of death was immediately passed upon him, and he was obliged to drink the juice of hemlock, the usual mode of execution at that time in Athens. Socrates, whose disciple he had been, was the only person of the senate who ventured to appear in his defence; he made an attempt to rescue him out of the hands of the officer of justice, and, after his execution, went about as it were in defiance of the thirty, exhorting and animating the senators and citizens against them.

The tyrants thus freed from the opposition of a colleague, whose presence alone was a continual reproach to them, set no longer any bounds to their cruelty and rapacity. Nothing was now heard of but imprisonments, confiscations, and murders; every one trembled for himself or his friends; and amidst the general consternation which had seized the citizens on account of their personal danger, all hope seems to have been lost of recovering public liberty.

The Lacedæmonians, not content with supporting the Thirty Tyrants in the exercise of their cruelty, were unwilling to let any of the Athenians escape from their hands. They published an edict to prohibit the cities of Greece from giving them refuge, decreed that such of them as fled should be delivered up to the thirty, and condemned all those who contravened this edict to pay a fine of five talents. Two cities only, Megara and Thebes, rejected with disdain so unjust an ordinance. The latter went still farther, and published a decree,

that every house and city of Bœotia should be open and
free for any Athenian that desired protection; and that
whoever did not assist a fugitive Athenian who was
seized, should be ·fined a talent.   Thrasybulus, a man
of an admirable character, who had long deplored the
miseries of his country, was now the first to relieve it.
At Thebes he held a consultation with his fellow citizens, and the result was, that some attempt, with whatever danger it might be attended, should certainly be
made for restoring the public liberty.   Accordingly,
with a party of thirty men only, as Nepos says, but as
Xenophon more probably relates, of near seventy, he
seized upon Phyle, a strong castle on the frontiers of
Attica.   This enterprise alarmed the tyrants, who immediately marched out of Athens with their three thousand followers, and their Spartan guard, and attempted
the recovery of the place, but were repulsed with loss.
Finding they could not carry it by a sudden assault,
they resolved upon a siege; but not being sufficiently
provided for that purpose, and a great snow falling in
the night, they were forced to retire the next day into
the city, leaving only part of their guard to prevent
any farther incursions into the country.

   Encouraged by this success, Thrasybulus no longer
kept upon the defensive, but marching out of Phyle
by night at the head of a thousand men, made himself
master of Pyræus.   The thirty flew thither with their
troops, and a battle sufficiently warm ensued; but as
the soldiers, on one side, fought with spirit and ardour
for their liberty, and, on the other, with indolence and
neglect for the power of their oppressors, the victory
was not long doubtful, but followed the better cause;
the tyrants were overthrown; Critias was killed upon
the spot; and, as the rest of the army were taking to
flight, Thrasybulus cried out, "Wherefore do you fly
from me as from a victor, rather than assist me as the
avenger of your liberty? We are not enemies but fellow
citizens; neither have we declared war against the city,
but against the Thirty Tyrants." He entreated them
to remember, that they had the same origin, country,
laws, and religion; he exhorted them to pity their

exiled brethren, to restore to them their country, and resume their liberty themselves. This discourse had the desired effect. The army, upon their return to Athens, expelled the thirty, and substituted ten persons to govern in their room, but whose conduct proved no better than that of their predecessors.

Though the 'government was thus altered, and the thirty deprived of their power, they still had hopes of being reinstated in their former authority, and sent deputies to Sparta to demand aid. Lysander was for granting it to them; but Pausanias, who then reigned in Sparta, moved with compassion at the deplorable condition of the Athenians, favoured them in private, and obtained a peace for them: it was sealed with the blood of the tyrants, who having taken arms to restore themselves to power, were put to the sword, and Athens left in full possession of its liberty. Thrasybulus then proposed an amnesty, by which the citizens engaged upon oath that all past actions should be buried in oblivion. The government was reestablished upon its ancient footing, the laws recovered their former vigour, the magistrates were elected with the usual ceremonies, and democracy was once more restored to this unfortunate people. Xenophon says, that this intestine commotion consumed as many in eight months, as the Peloponnesian war had done in ten years.

From Europe we must now pass over into Asia, which was the scene of the next great action in which the Greeks were concerned. This was no other than the famous expedition of Cyrus, the younger son of Darius Nothus, late king of Persia, who had long entertained hopes of being one day able to dethrone his elder brother, Artaxerxes. He had, indeed, made several attempts for this purpose already, and had as often been pardoned by his brother, at the earnest entreaty of their mother Parysatis. Artaxerxes carried his generosity to a still greater, and even to an imprudent length; for he bestowed upon Cyrus the absolute command of all those provinces that had been left him by the will of his father. Cyrus no sooner found himself in this exalted situation, than he began to use every art for the

accomplishment of his ambitious project; and with this
view he engaged in his service a body of thirteen thousand Greeks under the command of Clearchus, an able
Lacedæmonian officer, who had been banished his native
country, and for some time resided at the court of Cyrus.
These were joined by a great number of Persians from
the provinces which Cyrus himself commanded, as well
as from those under the government of Tissaphernes,
where several cities had revolted in his favour. The
common Grecians, however, were entire strangers to
the purpose for which they were enlisted, nor was any
one let into Cyrus's design but Clearchus himself.
When the troops, therefore, began their march, and
had advanced as far as Tarsus, the Greeks refused to
proceed any farther, rightly suspecting that they were
intended against the king, and loudly exclaiming that
they had not entered into the service upon that condition. Clearchus had need of all his dexterity and
address to stifle this commotion in its birth. At first
he made use of authority and force; but finding these
had little effect, he desisted from an open opposition
to the sentiments of the soldiers: he even affected to
enter into their views, and to support them with his
approbation and credit. By this artful evasion he
appeased the tumult, and made the men easy for the
present; and they chose him and some others for their
deputies. Cyrus, whom he had secretly apprized of
every thing, made answer, that he was going to attack
Abrocomas, his enemy, at twelve days' march from
thence, upon the Euphrates. When this answer was
reported to them, though they plainly saw against
whom they were going, they resolved to proceed, and
only demanded an augmentation of their pay. Cyrus,
instead of one daric a month to each soldier, promised
to give them one and a half. And the more to ingratiate himself, when he was told, that two officers had
deserted from the army, and was advised to pursue and
put them to death, he publicly declared, that it should
never be said he had detained any one person in his
service against his will; and he therefore ordered their
wives and children, who had been left as hostages in

his army, to be sent after them. A conduct so wise, and apparently generous, had a surprising effect in gaining the affections of the soldiers, and made even those his firm adherents who before were adverse to his cause.

As Cyrus advanced by long marches, he received intelligence from all quarters, that the king did not intend to come to a battle with him directly, but had resolved to wait in the interior parts of Persia till all his forces were assembled; and that, to stop his progress, he had ordered an intrenchment to be thrown up on the plains of Babylon, with a ditch of five fathoms broad, and three deep, extending the length of twelve parasangs, or leagues, from the Euphrates to the wall of Media. Between the Euphrates and the ditch, a way had been left of twenty feet in breadth, by which Cyrus passed with his whole army, having reviewed it the day before. The king had neglected to dispute this pass with him, and suffered him to continue his march towards Babylon.

As Cyrus expected to engage every moment, he took care to proceed in order of battle, giving the command of the right wing of the Greeks to Clearchus, and that of the left to Menon. At length he discovered his brother's army, amounting to twelve hundred thousand men, besides a select body of six thousand horse, approaching and preparing to attack him.

The place where the battle was fought was called Cunaxa, about twenty-five leagues from Babylon. Cyrus getting on horseback, with his javelin in his hand, commanded the troops to stand to their arms, and proceed in order of battle. The enemy, in the meantime, who were headed by Artaxerxes in person, advanced slowly and in good order. This sight extremely surprised the Greeks, who expected to have found nothing but tumult and confusion in so great a multitude, and to have seen them rushing on with strange and hideous outcries.

The armies were not distant above four or five hundred paces, when the Greeks began to sing the hymn of battle, and to march on softly at first, and with silence.

When they came near the enemy, they set up great cries, striking their darts upon their shields to frighten the horse; and then moving altogether, they sprung forward upon the barbarians with all their force, who did not wait their charge, but took to their heels, and fled universally, except Tissaphernes, who stood his ground with a small part of his troops.

Cyrus saw with pleasure the enemy routed by the Greeks, and was proclaimed king by those around him; but he did not give himself up to vain joy, nor as yet reckoned himself sure of the victory. He perceived that Artaxerxes was wheeling his right wing to attack him in flank, and marched directly against him with six hundred horse. Discovering his brother, he cried out, with eyes sparkling with rage, "I see him!" and spurred against him, followed only by his principal officers: for his troops had quitted their ranks, to pursue the fugitives; which was a capital blunder. The battle then became, in some measure, a single combat between Artaxerxes and Cyrus; and the two brothers were seen transported with rage and fury, endeavouring, like Eteocles and Polynices, to plunge their swords into each other's hearts, to assure themselves of the throne by the death of their rival.

Cyrus having forced his way through those who were drawn up before his brother, joined him, and killed his horse, that fell with him to the ground: he rose, and was remounted upon another, when Cyrus attacked him again, gave him a second wound, and was preparing to give him a third, in hopes that it would prove his last. The king, like a lion wounded by the huntsman, was only more furious from the smart, and sprung forward, impetuously pushing his horse against Cyrus, who running headlong, and without regard to his person, threw himself into the midst of a flight of darts aimed at him from all sides, and received a wound from the king's javelin, at the same time that all the rest discharged upon him. Cyrus fell dead; some say by the wound given him by the king; others affirm, that he was killed by a Carian soldier, to whom, as a reward, Artaxerxes granted the privilege of bearing a golden cock on the point of his spear at the head of the army. The prin-

pal officers of his court, resolving not to survive so
good a master, were all killed around him; a certain
proof, says Xenophon, that he well knew how to choose
his friends, and that he was truly beloved by them.
Ariæus, who ought to have been the firmest of all his
adherents, fled with his right wing, as soon as he heard
of his death.

Artaxerxes, after having caused the head and right
hand of his brother to be cut off, pursued the enemy
into their camp. Ariæus had not stopped there, but
having passed through it, continued his retreat to the
place where the army had encamped the day before,
which was about four leagues distant.

Tissaphernes, after the defeat of the greatest part of
his left wing by the Greeks, led on the rest against
them, and by the side of the river, passed through the
light-armed infantry of the Greeks, who opened to give
him a passage, and made their discharges upon him as
he passed, without losing a man. They were commanded by Episthenes of Amphipolis, who was esteemed
an able captain. Tissaphernes kept on without returning to the charge, because he perceived he was too
weak, and went forward to Cyrus's camp, where he
found the king, who was plundering it, but had not
been able to force the quarter defended by the Greeks,
who saved their baggage.

The Greeks on their side, and Artaxerxes on his,
who did not know what had passed elsewhere, believed
each of them that they had gained the victory: the first,
because they had put the enemy to flight, and pursued
them; and the king, because he had killed his brother,
beat the troops he had fought, and plundered their
camp. The matter was soon cleared up on both sides.
Tissaphernes, upon his arrival at the camp, informed
the king, that the Greeks had defeated his left wing,
and pursued it to a great distance; and the Greeks,
on their side, learnt, that the king, in pursuing Cyrus's
left, had penetrated into the camp. Upon this advice,
the king rallied his troops, and marched in quest of the
enemy, and Clearchus, being returned from pursuing
the Persians, advanced to oppose him.

The two armies were very soon near each other,

.when, after several movements on both sides, in order to gain the advantage of the ground, they at last came to a battle, and the Greeks routed the barbarians with the same facility as before. They even pursued them to a hill at a considerable distance, where the enemy ventured to halt, and were preparing to attack them a second time, when the Persians, dreading another overthrow, betook themselves again to flight in the utmost disorder.

As it was almost night, the Greeks laid down their arms to rest themselves, much surprised that neither Cyrus, or any from him, appeared; and imagining, that he was either engaged in the pursuit of the enemy, or was making himself master of some important place (for they were still ignorant of his death, and the defeat of the left wing of the army,) they determined to return to their camp, and found the greatest part of their baggage taken, with all the provisions, and four hundred waggons laden with corn and wine, which Cyrus had expressly caused to be carried along with the army for the Greeks, in case of any pressing necessity. They passed the night in the camp, the greatest part of them without any refreshment, concluding that Cyrus was alive and victorious. But when they heard of his death, they sent to Ariæus, as conqueror and commander in chief, to offer him the Persian crown. Meanwhile the king also considering himself as conqueror, sent to them to surrender their arms and implore his mercy; representing to them at the same time, that as they were in the heart of his dominions, surrounded with vast rivers and numberless nations, it would be impossible for them to escape his vengeance, and therefore they had no other choice left but to submit to the present necessity.

Upon debating among themselves what answer they should return, Proxenus desired to know of the heralds, upon what terms the king demanded their arms: if as a conqueror, it was in his power to take them; if upon any other footing, what would he give them in return? He was seconded by Xenophon, who said, that they had nothing left but their arms and their liberty, and that they could not preserve the one without the other. Clearchus observed to the same effect, that if the king was disposed to be their friend, they should be better able to serve him with their arms than without; if their enemy, they should have need of them for their defence. Some, indeed, spoke a milder language; that as they had served Cyrus faithfully, they would also serve Artaxerxes, if he would employ them; and provided he would, at the same time, put them in possession of Egypt. At last it was agreed, that they should remain in their present situation, without either advancing or retreating; and that if they did either, it should be looked upon as a declaration of war; so that the treaty seems to have been managed in such a manner as to avoid giving a direct answer, and merely to amuse the king and gain time.

While this affair was in agitation, they received Arisæus's answer, that there were too many great men in Persia to let him quietly possess the throne; for which reason he intended to set out early the next morning on his return to Greece; and that, if they had a mind to accompany him, they must join him that night in his camp; which they accordingly all did, except Milthocytus, a Thracian, who went over with a party of three hundred men and forty horse to the king. The rest, in conjunction with Arisæus's forces, decamped by break of day, and continued their march until sunset, when they discovered from the neighbouring villages that the king was in pursuit of them.

Clearchus, who had the command of the Greeks, ordered his men to halt, and prepared for an engagement. The king of Persia, intimidated by so resolute a conduct, sent heralds, not to demand their surrender, but to propose terms of accommodation. When Clearchus was informed of their arrival, he ordered his attendants to bid them wait, and to tell them that he was not yet at leisure to hear them. He purposely put on an air of haughtiness and grandeur, to denote his intrepidity, and, at the same time, to show the fine appearance and good condition of his troops. When he advanced with the most showy of his officers, expressly

chosen for the purpose, and had heard what the heralds
had to say, he made answer, that they must begin with
giving battle, because his men being in want of provisions, they had no time to lose. The heralds having
carried back this message to their master, returned
immediately; which showed that the king, or whoever
spoke in his name, was not far off. They said they had
orders to conduct them to villages where they would
find plenty of provisions, and conducted them thither
accordingly.

. After three days' stay, Tissaphernes arrived, and insinuated to them the good offices he had done them
with his master. Clearchus vindicated himself and his
men, by alleging, that they were engaged in this expedition without knowing the enemy against whom they
were to fight; that they were free from all engagements,
and would commit no act of hostility against the Persian
king, if he would allow them to return quietly. Tissaphernes assured them that they should meet with no obstruction: on the contrary, that they should be supplied
with all kinds of provisions on their march; and, the
more effectually to ensure their safety, that he himself
would accompany them on the way. But this satrap's
duplicity was equal to his cruelty: for the barbarian
army always encamping at about a league's distance
from the Grecian, left some room for suspicion; and
when they were arrived on the banks of the river Za-
batus, Tissaphernes pretended that some of Clearchus's
principal officers had endeavoured to sow jealousies
between the two armies; and that if he would bring
them to his tent the next day, he would point out the
persons he had in his eye. Clearchus was so weak as
to agree to this proposal; and accordingly he, together
with Menon, Proxenes, Agis, and Socrates, went to the
Persian general's tent, where they had no sooner arrived,
than, on a signal given, they were instantly seized,
their attendants put to the sword, and themselves, after
being sent bound to the king, were beheaded in his
presence.

The consternation of the Greeks, upon being informed
of this massacre of their generals, may be more easily

1

conceived than described. They were now near two thousand miles from home, surrounded with great rivers, extensive forests, and inimical nations, without any supplies of provisions. In this forlorn condition, they were almost overwhelmed with despair, and could think of taking neither refreshment nor repose : but they recovered some faint hopes, when they began to reflect upon the abilities of Xenophon, a young Athenian, who had accompanied Proxenes into Asia, and had hitherto served as a volunteer in the army. This was that Xenophon afterwards so famous as an historian; and his conduct seemed equal to his eloquence, in which he surpassed all the rest of mankind. This young soldier went to some of the Greek officers in the middle of the night, and represented to them that they had no time to lose; that it was of the last importance to prevent the bad designs of the enemy; that, however small their number, they would render themselves formidable, if they behaved with boldness and resolution; that valour, and not multitudes, determines the event of battles; and that it was necessary, above all things to nominate generals immediately, because an army without commanders is like a body without a soul. A council was immediately held, at which a hundred officers were present; and Xenophon being desired to speak, explained at large the reasons he had at first but slightly touched upon; and, by his advice, commanders were appointed. They were, Timasion for Clearchus, Xanthicles for Socrates, Cleanor for Agis, Philesius for Menon, and Xenophon for Proxenes.

Before break of day they assembled the army. The generals made speeches to animate the men, and Xenophon among the rest. "Fellow soldiers," said he, " the loss of so many brave men by vile treachery, and the being abandoned by our friends, is very deplorable; but we must not sink under our misfortunes; and, if we cannot conquer, let us resolve rather to perish gloriously, than fall into the hands of barbarians, who would inflict upon us the greatest miseries : let us call to mind the glorious battles of Platæa, Thermopylæ, Salamis, and many others, wherein our ancestors,

through with a small number, have fought and defeated
the innumerable armies of the Persians, and thereby
rendered the name alone of Greeks for ever formidable.
It is to their invincible valour we owe the honour we
possess, of acknowledging no masters upon earth but
the gods, nor any happiness but what consists with
liberty. Those gods, the avengers of perjury, and wit-
nesses of the enemy's treason, will be favourable to us;
and as they are offended by the violation of treaties,
and take pleasure in humbling the proud and exalting
the humble, they will also follow us to battle, and combat
for us. For the rest, fellow soldiers, we have no refuge
but in victory, which must be our hope, and will make
us ample amends for whatever it costs us to attain it.
And I should think, if it were your opinion, that, for
the making a more ready and less difficult retreat, it
would be proper to rid ourselves of all the useless
baggage, and to keep only what is absolutely necessary
in our march." All the soldiers that moment lifted up
their hands, to signify their approbation of what had
been said, and without loss of time set fire to their tents
and baggage; such of them as had too much equipage
giving it to others who had too little, and destroying
the rest.

The van was led by Cherisophus the Spartan general, and Xenophon, with Timasion, brought up the rear.
They directed their march towards the heads of the
great rivers, in order to pass them where they were
fordable. But they had not advanced far before they
were overtaken by a party of the enemy's archers and
slingers, commanded by Mithridates, which galled their
rear, and wounded several of them, who being heavy-
armed and without cavalry, could make no resistance.
To prevent the like inconvenience, Xenophon furnished
two hundred Rhodians with slings, and mounted fifty
more of his men upon baggage horses: so that when
Mithridates came up with them a second time, and
with a much greater body, he was repulsed with loss,
and the Greeks made good their retreat to the city of
Larissa, on the banks of the Tigris. From thence they
marched to another desolate city, called Mepaila; and

about four leagues from that place, Tissaphernes came
up to them with his whole army, but after several skirmishes was obliged to retire. They afterwards met
with some obstruction in passing an eminence which
the enemy had seized; but from this they soon found
means to dislodge them, and descended into the plain
on the other side.

Their difficulties, however, seemed to multiply as
they advanced; for they were now hemmed in on the
one hand by the river Tigris, and on the other by almost
impassable mountains, inhabited by the Carduci, a fierce
and warlike people, who, as Xenophon says, had, in
these dangerous passes, entirely destroyed an army of a
hundred and twenty thousand Persians. But as they
had no boats to cross the river, and as the road through
the mountains led into the rich plains of Armenia, they
resolved to pursue their march that way. The Carduci
soon took the alarm; but not being prepared to oppose
the Greeks in a body, they possessed themselves of the
tops of the rocks and mountains, and from thence annoyed them with darts and great stones, which they
threw down upon them as they passed through the
defiles, where they were likewise attacked by several
other parties: and though their loss was not considerable, yet, what with storms and famine, beside seven
days' tedious march, and being continually forced to
fight their way, they underwent here much greater
hardships than any they had hitherto suffered.

Not far from the foot of the mountain, they met with
a fresh obstruction. The river Centrites, about two
hundred feet in breadth, presented itself before them.
Twice did they attempt to cross it; at first without
success, on account of the depth of the water; but the
second time they were more fortunate, and at length
got to the other side.

They now proceeded with less interruption; passed
the Tigris near its source, and arrived at the little river
Teleboa, which is the boundary of the Western Armenia. This province was governed by Tiribasus, a great
favourite of the king, and who had the honour to help
him to mount on horseback when at court. He offered

to let the army pass, and to furnish the men with the
necessary provisions, provided they abstained from all
acts of hostility; and this proposal was accepted and
ratified on both sides. Tiribasus, however, kept a flying camp at a small distance from the army. There
fell, at the same time, a great quantity of snow, which put
the troops to some inconvenience; and they learnt from
a prisoner, that Tiribasus intended to attack them in
a defile of the mountains, through which they must
necessarily pass. They took care, however, to prevent
him, by seizing that post, after having routed the enemy.
After some days' march through the desert, they passed
the Euphrates near its head, not having the water above
their middle.

They were afterwards incommoded by a north wind,
which blew in their faces, and prevented respiration,
so that it was thought necessary to sacrifice to the wind;
upon which, we are told, it began to abate. They proceeded through the snow five or six feet deep, which
killed several servants and beasts of burden, besides
thirty soldiers. They made fires in the night, for they
found plenty of wood. All the next day they continued
their march through the snow, when many of them,
from long fasting, followed with languor or fainting,
fell down upon the ground through weakness and want
of spirits; but when something had been given them to
eat, they found themselves relieved, and resumed their
march.

After a march of seven days, they arrived at the river
Araxes, otherwise called the Phasus, which is about
one hundred feet in breadth. Two days after they
discovered the Phasians, the Chalybes, and the Taochi-
ans, who had seized the pass of the mountains, to prevent
their descending into the plain. Xenophon, however,
observed, that they defended only the ordinary passage;
and by his advice, therefore, a party was sent to take
possession of the heights which commanded that passage; by which means the enemy were soon dislodged,
and the road effectually cleared. Thus, after a march
of twelve or fifteen days more, they arrived at a very
high mountain, called Tecqua, from whence they des-

cried the sea. The first who perceived it raised great shouts of joy for a considerable time, which made Xenophon imagine the vanguard was attacked, and he therefore advanced to support it with the utmost expedition. As he approached nearer, the cry of *The sea! the sea!* was distinctly heard, and the alarm changed into joy and exultation: and when they came to the top, nothing was heard but a confused noise of the whole army crying out together, *The sea! the sea!* whilst they could not refrain from tears, nor from embracing their generals and officers: and then without waiting for orders, they heaped up a pile of stones, and erected a trophy with broken bucklers and other arms.

From thence they advanced to the mountains of Colchis, one of which was higher than the rest, and of that the people of the country had taken possession. As the ground in this pass was extremely unequal, the Greeks marched in files, instead of line of battle; and attacking the enemy with great spirit, they soon put them to flight, and descended into the plain on the other side of the mountains. Here a very singular accident befell them, which at first threw them into some consternation: for finding a number of bee-hives in the place, and eating greedily of the honey, they were suddenly seized with violent vomitings and fluxes; so that those who were least ill seemed like drunken men, and the rest either furiously mad or dying. The earth was strewed with their bodies as after a defeat; not one of them, however, died, and the distemper ceased the next day about the same hour it began. The third or fourth day the soldiers got up, but in that condition which people are usually in after taking a violent medicine.

Two days after, the army arrived near Trebisond, a Greek colony of Sinopians, situated upon the Euxine, or Black Sea, in the province of Colchis. Here they lay encamped for thirty days, and acquitted themselves of the vows they had made to Jupiter, Hercules, and the other deities, to obtain a happy return into their own country. They also celebrated the games of horse and foot races, and wrestling and boxing, or the pancratians; the whole attended with the greatest joy and solemnity. Here Xenophon formed a project of settling them in those parts, and founding a Grecian colony, which was approved of by some; but his enemies representing it to the army as only a more honourable way of abandoning them, and to the inhabitants as a design to subdue and enslave the country, he was obliged to give over the enterprise. The noise of it, however, had this good effect, that the natives did what they could, in a friendly manner, to hasten their departure, advising to go by sea as the safest way, and furnished them with a sufficient number of transports for that purpose.

Accordingly, they set sail with a fair wind, and the next day got into the harbour of Sinope, where Cherisophus met them with some galleys; but instead of the money he had promised to pay them, he only told them they should receive their arrears as soon as they got out of the Euxine Sea. This answer gave them so much disgust, that they resolved to put themselves under one general: and they desired Xenophon, in the most pressing and affectionate terms, to accept of that command, which he modestly declined, and procured the appointment to fall upon Cherisophus. But he did not enjoy it above six or seven days; for they were no sooner arrived at Heraclea, than they deposed him for refusing to extort a sum of money from the inhabitants of that city; and as this was a Greek colony, Xenophon likewise refused to have any concern in the affair: so that the army, being disappointed in their hopes of plunder, broke out into a mutiny, and divided into three bodies. In a little time, however, they were happily reunited, and encamped at the port of Calpe, where they settled the command as before, substituting Neon in the room of Cherisophus, who died here, and making it death for any one hereafter to propose the dividing of the army. But being straitened for provisions, they were obliged to disperse themselves up and down the country, where Pharnabazus's horse, being joined by the inhabitants, cut five hundred of them in pieces: the rest escaping to a hill were rescued and

brought off by Xenophon, who led them first to Chry-
sopolis of Chalcedon, and afterwards to Byzantium.

From thence he conducted them to Salmydessa, to
enable Seuthes, prince of Thrace, to recover his father's
dominions, of which his enemies had deprived him.
This prince had made great promises to Xenophon
and his men, if they would assist him in this important
undertaking; but when they had done him the service
he wanted, he was so far from keeping his word, that
he did not even give them the pay agreed on. Xenophon reproached him severely with his breach of faith.
Which, however, he attributed to the ill advice of his
minister Heraclides, who thought to make his court to
his master, by saving him a sum of money at the expense
of every thing that ought to be dear to a prince.

In the meantime, Charminus and Polynices arrived
as ambassadors from Lacedæmon, with advice, that the
republic had declared war against Tissaphernes and
Pharnabazus; that Thimbron had already embarked
with the troops; and that the Spartans would give a
daric a month to every soldier, two to each officer, and
four to the colonels, who should engage in the service.
Xenophon accepted the offer, and having obtained from
Seuthes, by the mediation of the ambassadors, part of
the pay due to him, he went by sea to Lampsachus with
the army, which amounted still, after all its losses, to
about six thousand men. From thence he advanced to
Pergamus, a city in the province of Troas. Having
met, near Parthenia, a great nobleman returning into
Persia, he took him, his wife and children, with all
their equipage, and by that means was enabled to dis-
tribute among the soldiers very handsome gratuities,
and to make them ample amends for all the losses they
had sustained. Thimbron at length arrived, and having
assumed the command of the troops, and united them
with his own, he marched against Tissaphernes and
Pharnabazus.

Such was the end of Cyrus's expedition. Xenophon,
who himself has written a most elegant history of it,
computes, from the first setting out of that prince's
army from the city of Ephesus, to their arrival at the

place where the battle was fought, five hundred and
thirty parasangs, or leagues, and fourscore and thirteen
days' march; and in their retreat from the field of battle
to Corcyra, a city upon the coast of the Euxine, or
Black Sea, six hundred and twenty parasangs, or leagues,
and one hundred and twenty days' march: and, adding
both together, he says, the way going and coming, was
eleven hundred and fifty-five parasangs, or leagues, and
two hundred and fifteen days' march; and that the whole
time the army took to perform that journey, including
the days of rest, was fifteen months.

We come now to an affair of a more private and
domestic, but not of a less interesting nature; we mean
the death of Socrates, one of the most amiable and
exalted characters that ever appeared in the world,
either in. ancient or modern times. We have already
seen this great man, who was the son of a stone-cutter
at Athens, emerging from the obscurity of his birth,
and giving examples of courage, moderation, and wisdom; we have seen him saving the life of Alcibiades in
battle, refusing to concur in the edict which unjustly
doomed the six Athenian generals to death, withstanding
the proceedings of the Thirty Tyrants; and, in a word,
expressing his detestation of every thing which he
deemed inconsistent with the principles of honour and
justice. Possessed, as he always was, of the most unbounded philanthropy, he was ready to forgive those
vices in others, from which he himself was in a great
measure free. He seemed, says Libanus, the common
father of the republic; so attentive was he to the
happiness and welfare of every individual of the state.
But knowing how difficult it is to reform the old, and
to make people change those principles which from
their earliest infancy they have been accustomed to
hold sacred, he applied himself chiefly to the instruction of youth, in order to sow the seeds of virtue in a
soil more likely to produce the fruits of it. He had,
however, no open school like the rest of the philosophers, nor set times for his lessons; he had no benches
prepared, nor ever mounted a professor's chair; he was
the philosopher of all times and seasons; he taught in

all places, and upon all occasions—in walking, conversation, at meals, in the army, in the midst of the camp, and in the public assemblies of the people.

Such was the man whom a faction in the city had long devoted to destruction: he had been, for many years before his death, the object of their satire and ridicule. Aristophanes, the comic poet, was engaged to expose him upon the stage. He composed a play, called The Clouds, in which he introduced the philosopher in a basket, uttering the most ridiculous absurdities. Socrates, who was present at the exhibition of his own character, seemed not to feel the least emotion; and as some strangers' were present who desired to know the original for whom the play was intended, he rose from his seat, and showed himself during the whole representation. This was the first blow struck at him, and it was not till twenty years after that Melitus appeared in a more formal manner as his accuser, and entered a regular process against him. The two chief crimes of which he accused him were, that he did not admit the gods acknowledged by the republic, and introduced new divinities; and that he corrupted the youth of Athens: and he therefore concluded with inferring, that sentence of death ought to be passed upon him.

The second charge was evidently groundless. How far the first was founded in truth, we cannot, at this distance of time, pretend to determine. It is not likely, indeed, that amidst so much zeal and superstition as then prevailed in Athens, he would venture openly to oppose the received religion; but it is very probable, from the discourses he frequently held with his friends, that in his heart he despised and laughed at their monstrous opinions and ridiculous mysteries, as having no other foundation than the fables of the poets; and that he had attained to the notion of the one true God, the creator and preserver of the universe.

As soon as the conspiracy broke out, the friends of Socrates prepared for his defence. Lysias, the most able orator of his time, brought him an elaborate discourse of his own composing, in which he vindicated the conduct of Socrates with great force of reasoning, and interspersed the whole with tender and pathetic strokes, capable of moving the most obdurate hearts. Socrates read it with pleasure, and approved of it very much; but as it was more conformable to the rules of rhetoric, than the sentiments and fortitude of a philosopher, he told him plainly that it did not suit him. Lysias asked him, how it was possible for it to be well done, and not to suit him? In the same manner, said he, using, according to his custom, a vulgar comparison, that an excellent workman might bring me magnificent apparel, or shoes embroidered with gold, to which nothing would be wanting on his part, but which, however, would not suit me. He persisted, therefore, inflexibly in the resolution not to demean himself, by begging suffrages in the low abject manner common at that time. He employed neither artifice nor the glitter of eloquence; he had recourse to no entreaties; he brought neither his wife nor children to incline the judges in his favour by their sighs and tears. Nevertheless, though he refused to make use of any other voice but his own in his defence, or to appear before his judges in the submissive posture of a suppliant, he did not behave in that manner out of pride, or contempt of the tribunal: it was from a noble and intrepid assurance, resulting from greatness of soul, and a consciousness of his own innocence; so that his defence had nothing weak or timorous in it: his discourse was bold, manly, generous, without passion, without emotion, full of the noble sentiments of a philosopher, with no other ornament than that of truth, and brightened throughout with the character and language of innocence. Plato, who was present, transcribed it afterwards, and, without any addition, formed from it the work which he calls The Apology of Socrates, one of the most masterly compositions of antiquity. I shall here make an extract from it.

Upon the day appointed, the proceedings began in the usual form; the parties appeared before the judges, and Melitus spoke: the worse his cause, and the less provided it was with proofs, the more occasion had he

for art and address to cover its weakness; he omitted
nothing that might render the adverse party odious;
and instead of reasons, which he could not produce,
he substituted the glitter of a pompous declamation.
Socrates, in observing that he could not tell what impression the discourse of his accuser had made upon
the judges, owns, that, for his own part, he scarce knew
how it had affected himself. Melitus had given such
artful colouring and likelihood to his arguments, though
there was not one word of truth in all he had advanced.

"I am accused," said he, "of corrupting the youth,
and of instilling dangerous maxims into them, as well
in regard to the worship of the gods, as the rules of
government. You know, Athenians, that I never made
it my profession to teach; nor can envy, however
violent against me, reproach me with ever having sold
my instructions. I have an undeniable evidence for me
in this respect, which is my poverty. Always equally
ready to communicate my thoughts to the rich and
poor, and to give them leisure to question or answer
me, I lend myself to every one who is desirous of becoming virtuous; and if, amongst those who hear me,
there are any that prove either good or bad, neither
the virtues of the one, nor the vices of the other, to
which I have not contributed, are to be ascribed to me.
My whole employment is to persuade the young and
old against too much love for the body, for riches, and
all other precarious things, of whatever nature they be,
and against too little regard for the soul, which ought
to be the object of their affections. For I incessantly
urge upon you, that virtue does not proceed from riches,
but, on the contrary, riches from virtue; and that all
the other goods of human life, as well public as private,
have their source in the same principle.

"If to speak in this manner be to corrupt youth, I
confess, Athenians, that I am guilty, and deserve to be
punished. If what I say be not true, it is most easy to
convict me of falsehood. I see here a great number of
my disciples; they have only to appear. But, perhaps,
their regard for a master who has instructed them,
will prevent them from declaring against me: at least

their fathers, brothers, and uncles, cannot, as good relations and good citizens, dispense with their standing forth against me, and demanding vengeance upon the corrupter of their sons, brothers, and nephews. But these are the persons who take upon them my defence, and interest themselves in the success of my cause.

"Pass on me, Athenians, what sentence you please; but I can neither repent nor change my conduct: I must not abandon nor suspend a function which God himself has imposed on me. Now he has charged me with the care of instructing my fellow citizens. If after having faithfully kept all the posts wherein I was placed by our generals at Potidæa, Amphipolis, and Delium, the fear of death should at this time make me abandon that in which the Divine Providence has placed me, by commanding me to pass my life in the study of philosophy, for the instruction of myself and others, this would be a most criminal desertion indeed, and make me highly worthy of being cited before this tribunal as an impious man, who does not believe the gods.

"Should you resolve to acquit me; for the future, I should not hesitate to make answer: Athenians, I honour and love you; but I shall choose rather to obey God than you; and to my latest breath shall never renounce my philosophy, nor cease to exhort and reprove you according to my custom, by saying to each of you, when you come in my way, 'My good friend, and citizen of the most famous city in the world for wisdom and valour, are you not ashamed to have no other thought than that of amassing wealth and acquiring glory, credit, and dignities, whilst you neglect the treasures of prudence, truth, and wisdom, and take no pains in rendering your soul as good and perfect as it is capable of being?'

"I am reproached with abject fear and meanness of spirit, for being so busy in imparting my advice to every one in private, and for having always avoided to be present in your assemblies, to give my counsels to my country. I think I have sufficiently proved my courage and fortitude, both in the field, where I have borne arms with you, and in the senate, where I opposed the unjust sentence you pronounced against the ten

captains, who had not taken up and interred the bodies
of those who were killed or drowned in the sea-fight
near the island of Arginusæ; and when, upon more
than one occasion, I opposed the violent and cruel
orders of the Thirty Tyrants.

"What is it then that has prevented me from appearing in your assemblies? It is that demon, that voice
divine, which you have so often heard me mention, and
Melitus has taken so much pains to ridicule. That
spirit has attached itself to me from my infancy: it is a
voice which I never hear, but when it would prevent
me from persisting in something I have resolved on;
for it never exhorts me to undertake any thing: it is
the same being that has always opposed me when I
would have intermeddled in the affairs of the republic,
and that with the greatest reason; for I should have
been amongst the dead long ago, had I been concerned
in the measures of the state, without effecting any thing
to the advantage of my country.

"Do not take it ill, I beseech you, if I speak my
thoughts without disguise, and with truth and freedom.
Every man, who would generously oppose a whole
people, either amongst us or elsewhere, and who inflexibly applies himself to prevent the violation of the
laws, and the commission of iniquity in a government,
will never do so long with impunity. It is absolutely
necessary for him, who would contend for justice, if
he has any thoughts of living, to remain in a private
station, and never to have any concern in public affairs.

"For the rest, Athenians, if, in the extreme danger
I am now in, I do not imitate the behaviour of those,
who upon less emergencies have implored and suppli-
cated their judges with tears, and have brought forth
their children, relations, and friends, it is not through
pride and obstinacy, or any contempt for you, but solely
for your honour, and for that of the whole city. You
should know, that there are amongst our citizens those
who do not regard death as an evil, and who give that
name only to injustice and infamy. At my age, and
with the reputation, true or false, which I have, would
it be consistent for me, after all the lessons I have given

upon the contempt of death, to be afraid of it myself, and to belie, in my last action, all the principles and sentiments of my past life?

"But without speaking of my fame, which I should extremely injure by such a conduct, I do not think it allowable to entreat a judge, nor to be absolved by supplications. He ought to be persuaded and convinced. The judge does not sit upon the bench to show favour by violating the laws, but to do justice in conforming to them. He does not swear to discharge with impunity whom he pleases, but to do justice where it is due. We ought not, therefore, to accustom you to perjury, nor you to suffer yourselves to be accustomed to it; for, in so doing, both the one and the other of us equally injure justice and religion, and both are criminals.

"Do not, therefore, expect from me, Athenians, that I should have recourse amongst you to means which I believe to be neither honest nor lawful, especially upon this occasion, wherein I am accused of impiety by Melitus; for if I should influence you by my prayers, and thereby induce you to violate your oaths, it would be undeniably evident, that I teach you not to believe in the gods; and, even in defending and justifying myself, should furnish my adversaries with arms against me, and prove that I believe no divinity. But I am very far from such bad thoughts: I am more convinced of the existence of God than my accusers; and so convinced, that I abandon myself to God and you, that you may judge of me as you may deem best for yourselves."

Socrates pronounced this discourse with a firm and intrepid tone: his air, his action, his visage, expressed nothing of the accused; he seemed the master of his judges, from the assurance and greatness of soul with which he spoke, without, however, losing any thing of the modesty natural to him. But how slight soever the proofs were against him, the faction was powerful enough to find him guilty. By his first sentence, however, he was only convicted of the crimes laid to his charge: but when, by his answer, he seemed to appeal from their tribunal to that of justice and posterity; when, instead of confessing himself guilty, he demanded rewards and honours from the state, the judges were so highly offended, that they condemned him to drink the juice of hemlock, the usual method of execution at that time in Athens.

Socrates received this sentence with the utmost composure. Apollodorus, one of his disciples, breaking out into invectives and lamentations that his master should die *innocent*: "What," replied Socrates with a smile, "would you have me die *guilty*? Melitus and Anytus may kill, but they cannot hurt me."

After his sentence, he still continued with the same serene and intrepid aspect, with which he had long enforced virtue, and kept tyrants in awe. When he entered the prison, which now became the residence of probity and virtue, his friends followed him thither, and continued to visit him during the interval between his condemnation and death, which lasted for thirty days. This long delay was owing to the following circumstance: the Athenians sent every year a ship to the isle of Delos, to offer certain sacrifices; and it was not permitted to put any person to death in the city, from the time that the priest of Apollo had crowned the poop of this vessel as a signal of her departure, till she returned home: so that sentence having been passed upon Socrates the day after this ceremony was performed, it became necessary to defer the execution of it till the ship should arrive at Athens.

In this long interval, death had sufficient opportunities to present itself before his eyes in all its terrors, and to put his fortitude to proof, not only by the severe rigour of a dungeon, and the irons upon his legs, but by the continual prospect and cruel expectation of an event at which nature always recoils. In this sad condition, he did not cease to enjoy that profound tranquillity of mind, which his friends had always admired in him. He entertained them with the same cheerfulness he had always preserved; and Crito says, that the evening before his death, he slept as quietly as at any other time. He composed also a hymn in honour of

Apollo and Diana, and turned one of Æsop's fables into verse.

So little, indeed, was he apprehensive of death, that he absolutely refused to escape from prison, when it was in his power. For the day before, or the same day that the ship arrived, Crito, his intimate friend, came to him, and told him, that it now depended upon himself to quit the prison; that the jailer was gained; that he would find the doors open; and that he might, if he pleased, enjoy a safe retreat in Thessaly. Socrates laughed at this proposal, and asked him, whether he knew any place out of Attica where people did not die? Crito urged every argument he could think of to induce him to accept of his proffered deliverance. Socrates heard him with great attention, commended his zeal, and thanked him for his kindness. But, before he would give into his opinion, he was for examining whether it was just for him to depart out of prison without the consent of the Athenians. The question therefore here was, whether a man condemned to die, though unjustly, could, without a crime, elude the execution of the sentence that had been passed upon him. Socrates held that he could not; and, therefore, nobly refused to escape out of prison. He reverenced the laws of his country, and resolved to obey them in all things, even in death itself.

At length the fatal ship returned to Athens, which was as it were the signal for the death of Socrates. The next day all his friends, except Plato, who was sick, repaired to the prison early in the morning. The jailer desired them to wait a little, because the eleven magistrates, who had the superintendence of the prisons, were at that time acquainting the prisoner, that he was to die the same day. Presently after they entered, and found Socrates, whose chains had been taken off, sitting by Xantippe his wife, who held one of his children in her arms. As soon as she perceived them, setting up great cries, sobbing, and tearing her face and hair, she made the prison resound with her lamentations, exclaiming, "Oh, my dear Socrates! your friends are come to

see you this day for the last time!" He desired she might
be taken away, and she was immediately carried home.

Socrates passed the rest of the day in conversing
with his friends, with great cheerfulness, upon one of
the most important topics that can engage the attention
of the human mind, and one at the same time the best
adapted to the occasion: it was upon the immortality
of the soul. What gave rise to this conversation was
a question introduced in a manner by chance. Whether a true philosopher ought not to desire, and take
pains to die? This proposition, taken too literally, im-
plies an opinion, that a philosopher may kill himself.
Socrates shows, that nothing can be more unjust than
this notion; and that man appertaining to God, who
formed and placed him with his own hand in the post
he occupies, cannot abandon it without his permission,
nor depart from life without his order. What is it
then that can induce a philosopher to be desirous to
die? It can be only the hope of that happiness which
he expects in another life; and that hope can be founded
only upon the belief of the soul's immortality,

Socrates employed the last day of his life in enter-
taining his friends upon this great and important subject; from which conversation Plato's admirable dia-
logue, entitled the Phædon, is wholly taken. He ex-
plains to his friends all the arguments for believing
the soul immortal, and refutes all the objections against
it, which are very nearly the same that are made at
this day.

When Socrates had done speaking, Crito begged he
would give him, and the rest of his friends, his last
instructions with regard to his children, and other
affairs, that, by executing them, they might have the
consolation of showing their respect for his memory.
" I shall recommend nothing to you this day," replied
Socrates, " more than I have already done, which is to
take care of yourselves; you cannot give me and my
family a greater satisfaction." Crito having asked him
afterwards in what manner he would wish to be buried:
"As you please," said Socrates, " if you can lay hold of
me, and I escape not out of your hands." At the same

time, looking on his friends with a smile, "I can never," added he, "persuade Crito, that Socrates is he who converses with you, and arranges the several parts of his discourse; for he always imagines that I am what he is going to see dead in a little time: he confounds me with my carcass, and therefore asks me how I would be interred." On finishing these words, he rose up, and went to bathe himself in a chamber adjoining. After he came out of the bath, his children were brought to him; for he had three, two very little, and the other grown up. He spoke to them for some time, gave his orders to the women who took care of them, and then dismissed them. Being returned into his chamber, he laid himself down upon his bed.

The servant of the eleven entered at the same instant, and having informed him that the time for drinking the juice of hemlock was come (which was at sunset) the servant was so deeply afflicted, that he turned his back, and fell a weeping. "See," said Socrates, "the good heart of this man; since my imprisonment he has often come to see me, and to converse with me; he is more worthy than all his fellows; how heartily the poor man weeps for me!" The fatal cup was now brought. Socrates asked what it was necessary for him to do? "Nothing more," replied the servant, "than, as soon as you have drunk off the whole draught, to walk about till you find your legs grow weary, and afterwards lie down upon your bed." He took the cup without any emotion, or change in his colour or countenance; and regarding the man with a steady and assured look: "Well," said he, "what say you of this drink, may one make a libation of it?" Upon being told there was only enough for one dose: "at least," continued he, "we may say our prayers to the gods, as it is our duty, and implore them to make our exit from this world, and our last stage happy, which is what I most ardently beg of them." After having spoke these words, he kept silence for some time, and then drank off the whole draught, with an amazing tranquillity, and serenity of aspect not to be expressed or hardly even conceived.

Until then his friends had been able, though with great difficulty, to refrain from tears; but after he had drunk the potion, they were no longer masters of themselves, but wept abundantly. Apollodorus in particular, who had been in tears almost during the whole day, began then to make such loud and bitter lamentations as pierced the hearts of all that were present. Socrates alone remained unmoved, and even reproved his friends, though with his usual mildness and goodnature. "What are you doing?" said he to them: "I wonder at you! Oh! what is become of your virtue? Was it not for this I sent away the women, that they might not fall into these weaknesses; for I have always heard you say that we ought to die peaceably, and blessing the gods. Be at ease, I beg you, and show more constancy and resolution." He then obliged them to restrain their tears.

In the meantime he kept walking to and fro; and when he found his legs grow weary, he lay down upon his back, as he had been directed. The poison then operated more and more. When Socrates found it begin to gain upon the heart, uncovering his face, which had been covered, no doubt, to prevent any thing from disturbing him in his last moments, "Crito," said he, "we owe a cock to Æsculapius; discharge that vow for me, and pray do not forget it." Soon after which he breathed his last. Crito went to his body, and closed his mouth and eyes.—Such was the end of Socrates, in the first year of the ninety-fifth olympiad, and the seventieth of his age.

It was not till some time after the death of this great man, that the people of Athens perceived their mistake, and began to repent of it; but their hatred against him being at length extinguished, their prejudices cured, and time having given them an opportunity for reflection, the notorious injustice of the sentence appeared in all its horrors. Nothing was heard throughout the city but discourses in favour of Socrates. The academy, the lyceum, private houses, public walks, and market-places, seemed still to reecho the sound of his loved voice. "Here," said they, "he formed our youth, and taught our children to love their country, and to honour their parents. In this place he gave us his admirable lessons, and sometimes bestowed on us seasonable reproaches, to engage us more warmly in the pursuit of virtue. Alas! how have we rewarded him for such important services!" All Athens was plunged into the deepest affliction. The schools were shut up, and the public exercises suspended. The accusers were called to account for the innocent blood they had caused to be shed. Melitus was condemned to die, and the rest banished. Plutarch observes, that all those who had any share in this odious transaction were held in such detestation among the citizens, that no one would give them fire, answer them any question, or go into the same bath with them; and they had the place cleaned where they bathed, lest they should be polluted by touching it; which drove them at last to such despair, that many of them killed themselves.

The Athenians, not content with having punished his accusers, caused a statue of brass to be erected to him, of the workmanship of the celebrated Lysippus, and placed it in one of the most conspicuous parts of their city. They carried their respect to a still higher degree, even to a religious veneration. They dedicated a chapel to him, as to a hero and a demigod, and gave it the name of The Chapel of Socrates.

CHAPTER XI.

FROM THE DEATH OF SOCRATES TO THE DEATH OF EPAMINONDAS.

AFTER the destruction of the Athenian power by Lysander, the Spartans were the next state that took the lead in the affairs of Greece, and the Eleans were the first that felt the weight of their resentment, for having refused to admit them to the Olympic games in common with the rest of the Greeks. About the same time, Agesilaus, being chosen king of Sparta, was sent into Asia with an army, under pretence of freeing the Grecian cities in that quarter. He gained a signal victory over Tissaphernes, near the river Pactolus, where he forced the enemy's camp, and found considerable plunder. The Persian monarch, afraid to oppose him openly in the field, endeavoured to subvert his interest among the Grecian states by power of money; and in this he was but too successful. The first whom he gained over to his side, were the Thebans, and these were soon after followed by the Athenians, who gladly seized this opportunity of throwing off the Spartan yoke. In a little time, the Argives, Corinthians, Eubœans, and other states, acceded to the confederacy; so that the Spartans were obliged to recall Agesilaus out of Persia, where he was carrying on the war, in order to oppose the powerful combination that was now forming against them. But before his arrival, they were forced to come to an engagement with the enemy near Sicyon, where, though the Spartan allies were at first routed, yet they themselves, by their single valour, in the end gained the victory, with the loss of no more than eight men.

This advantage, however, was in some measure counterbalanced by a loss at sea, which the Spartans sustained near Cnidus. Conon, the Athenian general, being appointed to command the Persian fleet against them, took fifty of their ships, and pursued the rest into port. Agesilaus, on the other hand, obtained a considerable victory over the Athenians and their allies, upon the plains of Coronea. Thus was the war carried on by furious but undecisive engagements, till at length all parties growing equally weary of a quarrel, in which none of them were any great gainers, a peace was concluded in the second year of the ninety-eighth olympiad; and from the many stipulations in favour of Persia, Plutarch terms this peace, the ruin and reproach of Greece.

The Spartans, being thus freed from all fears of a foreign foe, began to spread the terror of their name among the petty states of Greece. They compelled the Mantineans to throw down their walls; they obliged the Corinthians to withdraw their garrison from Argos; they reduced the Olynthians to subjection; and interfering in the domestic quarrels of the Thebans, they placed a garrison of their own in the citadel of Thebes. The Thebans, after submitting to this yoke for four years, at last threw it off by the following stratagem. A correspondence having been established between the Theban exiles at Athens, and such of their country-men as were well affected to them in Thebes, a plan was laid for surprising the governors and the garrison. The two principal exiles that conducted this plot, were Pelopidas and Melon. Charon, a man of the first con-sequence in the city, joined in the conspiracy, and offered his house for the reception of the exiles, when they should arrive; and Phyllidas, secretary to the governors, managed the correspondence between the exiles and the citizens, and promised to admit the former into the town.

Matters being thus previously concerted, Pelopidas and Melon, with ten associates, dressed themselves like peasants, and beat about the fields with dogs and hunt-ing-poles, as if in search of game. Having thus passed unsuspected, and conveyed themselves into the city, they met at Charon's house, where they were soon after joined by thirty-six more of their confederates. To render the execution of the plot the more easy and more complete, Phyllidas had that day contrived to give a grand entertainment to the two governors, Archias and Philip. The associates, therefore, now divided themselves into two bands. One of these, led by Charon and Melon, were to attack the governors and their company; and accordingly having put on women's clothes over their armour, with pine and poplar over their heads, to shade their faces, they took the opportunity when the guests were well heated with wine, to enter the room, and immediately stabbed Ar-chias and Philip, with such others of the company as were pointed out to them by Phyllidas. In the mean-time, Pelopidas and Damoclides attacked Leontidas, another adherent of the Spartans, who was at home and in bed. But this man made a desperate resistance; for taking up his sword, he met them at his chamber-door, and slew Cephisodorus, who was the first that set upon him : but after a long and violent struggle, he was at last overcome by Pelopidas, who killed him on the spot. His friend and neighbour, Hypates, soon after met with the same fate ; and the two bands then reuniting, sent an account of their success to the other exiles at Athens, and entreated them to hasten their return to Thebes.

The work, however, was yet but half done. The garrison, together with such of the citizens as favoured the Spartan cause, had taken refuge in the citadel ; and till these were reduced, Thebes could not be said to be free. But a party of five thousand foot, and two thousand horse, arriving next morning from Athens, and several bodies of troops coming in at the same time from different parts of Bœotia, Pelopidas soon found himself at the head of so powerful an army, that he compelled the garrison to surrender at discretion.

The Spartans, though mortified, were by no means dispirited with this reverse of fortune. They sent an army of near twenty thousand men, under Agesilaus, to reestablish their power at Thebes. The name of the general alone struck terror into the enemy, who were afraid to meet him in the open field, and they therefore took possession of a hill in the neighbourhood of the city. Agesilaus sent a party to provoke them to come down, and give him battle ; and when he saw they declined this, he drew out his whole army in order to attack them. But Chabrias, who commanded the Theban mercenaries, ordered his men to present themselves, and keep their ranks close together, with their shields laid down at their feet, their spears advanced, one leg forward, and the knee upon the half bend. Agesilaus finding them prepared in this manner to receive him, and that they stood as it were in defiance of him, thought fit to withdraw his army, and contented himself with ravaging the country. This was looked upon as an extraordinary stratagem ; and Chabrias valued himself so much upon it, that he procured his statue to be erected in that posture.

The Spartans had hitherto been deemed unequalled in military prowess ; but they now began to be rivalled, and even excelled, in that noble quality, by the Thebans. This particularly appeared in the battle of Tegyra. Pelopidas, the Theban general, had resolved to attack Orchomenus, which was garrisoned by the Spartans, and he therefore marched against it with a small party of three hundred foot, and forty horse; but hearing that a large body of Spartans were hastening to its relief, he thought it best to retire. In this retreat he fell in with this reinforcement near Tegyra, and finding it impossible to avoid a battle, he resolutely prepared to engage. After a violent struggle, which was maintained with equal bravery on both sides, Gorgoleon and Theopompus, the two Spartan generals, fell; and this so intimidated their men, that they immediately retired on either hand, and opened a way for the Thebans to pass. But a safe retreat could not satisfy Pelopidas. Encouraged by his late success, he drew up his men afresh, and renewed the battle; and after committing a most terrible havock among the enemy, he put them to an entire rout.

This was the most signal disgrace the Spartans had ever met with. They had never before been known to yield even to an equal number : but here they were beat by a force not one-third of their own. It must be acknowledged, however, that these three hundred foot were the flower of the Theban army. They were distinguished by the name of *The sacred band.* They were as remarkable for their fidelity to each other, as for their strength and courage; they were linked together by the bonds of common friendship, and were sworn to stand by each other to the very last extremity. Thus united they became invincible, and generally turned the scale of victory in their favour for a number of years ; till at length they were cut down as one man by the Macedonian phalanx under Philip.

Pelopidas was not the only nor even the greatest general that Thebes produced. Epaminondas, his contemporary and colleague in command, was every way his equal, and, if possible, his superior. These two great men lived in the strictest intimacy and friendship ; and the only cause of rivalship between them was, which of

them should distinguish himself most in promoting the
interest, or advancing the glory of their native country.
Epaminondas had spent the earlier part of his life in the
study of philosophy, remote from the management of
public affairs, either of a civil or military nature, in
neither of which he would ever engage, until he was
overcome by the importunities of his countrymen, who
thought they perceived in him, amidst all his diffidence
and self-denial, the seeds of many great and excellent
qualities. Nor were they deceived in their opinion;
for when he was placed, as it were by force, and against
his will, at the head of an army, he showed the world,
that an application to the polite arts, so far from dis-
qualifying a man for a public station, only renders him
capable of filling it with more distinguished lustre.

Under these two excellent generals, therefore, Thebes
was able not only to maintain its own independence,
but even to threaten the rest of Greece with subjection;
and it was probably the apprehension of this last event,
that had made the Athenians break off their alliance
with the Thebans, and join in a confederacy with the
Spartans against their former allies. · The Spartans
had long considered themselves as the umpires and
arbitrators of Greece, and could ill bear a rival in this
boasted preeminence. They, therefore, resolved to
humble the pride of Thebes, and with this view their
general, Cleombrotus, marched towards the frontiers
of Bœotia with a numerous army. But in order to
give an air of justice to their hostilities, they first sent
to demand of the Thebans, that they should restore the
cities they had seized to their liberties; that they should
rebuild those they had demolished, and make reparation
for all the wrongs they had done. To this it was replied, "That the Thebans were accountable to none
but heaven for their conduct." Nothing now remained
on either side, but to prepare for action. Epaminondas
immediately raised all the troops he could, and began
his march; his army did not amount to six thousand
men, and the enemy had above four times that number.
As several bad omens were urged to prevent his setting
out, he replied only by repeating a verse from Homer,

importing, that there is but one good omen to fight for one's country. However, to reassure the soldiers (by nature superstitious) and whom he perceived to be discouraged, he instructed several persons to come from different places, and report auguries and omens in his favour, which revived the spirit and hopes of his troops.

Epaminondas had wisely taken care to secure a pass, which would have shortened Cleombrotus's march considerably. The latter, after having taken a large compass, arrived at Leuctra, a small town of Bœotia, between Platæa and Thespia. Both parties consulted whether they should give battle; which Cleombrotus resolved to do by the advice of his officers, who said, that if he declined fighting with such a superiority of troops, it would confirm the current report, that he secretly favoured the Thebans. And these last, on their side, had an essential reason for hastening a battle before the arrival of the troops, which the enemy daily expected. However, the six generals, who formed the council of war, being equally divided in their sentiments, the seventh, who was Pelopidas, came in very good time to join the three that were for fighting : and his opinion carrying the question, it was at last determined to engage.

The two armies, as we have already said, were very unequal in number. The Lacedæmonians amounted to twenty-four thousand foot, and sixteen hundred horse. The Thebans had only six thousand foot and four hundred horse; but all of them choice troops, animated by the love of glory, and resolved either to conquer or die. The Lacedæmonian cavalry, composed of men picked up by chance, without valour, and ill-disciplined, were as much inferior to their enemies in courage, as superior in number. The infantry could not be depended on, except the Lacedæmonians; the allies having engaged in the war with reluctance, because they did not approve the motive of it, and being besides dissatisfied with the Spartans. The ability of the generals alone supplied the place of great armies, especially that of the Theban commander, who was the most accomplished soldier of his time; and he was nobly supported by Pelopidas, who was then at the head of The sacred band.

Upon the day of battle, the two armies drew up on a plain. Cleombrotus was upon the right, at the head of the Lacedæmonians, in whom he most confided, and whose files were twelve feet deep. The left wing, consisting of the allies, was commanded by Archidamus, the son of Agesilaus. Epaminondas took post in the left of his army, and was opposed to Cleombrotus, whom he was determined to attack, convinced that if once he could break the Lacedæmonian phalanx, the rest of the army would soon be put to flight.

The action began with the cavalry, which were posted on both sides in the front of the left wing. As the Thebans were better mounted, and braver troops than the Lacedæmonian horse, the latter were soon broke, and driven upon the infantry, which they put into some confusion. Epaminondas following his horse close, marched swiftly up to Cleombrotus, and fell upon his phalanx with all the weight of his heavy battalion. The latter, to make a diversion, detached a body of troops, with orders to take Epaminondas in flank, and to surround him. Pelopidas, upon sight of that movement, advanced with incredible speed and boldness, at the head of the sacred band, to prevent the enemy's design, and flanked Cleombrotus himself; who, by that sudden and unexpected attack, was put into disorder. The battle was very fierce and obstinate; and while Cleombrotus could act, the victory continued in suspense, and declared for neither party. But when he fell dead with his wounds, the Thebans, to complete the victory, and the Lacedæmonians, to avoid the shame of abandoning the body of their king, redoubled their efforts, and a great slaughter ensued on both sides. The Spartans fought with so much fury about the body, that at length they gained their point, and carried it off. Animated by so glorious an advantage, they proposed to return to the charge, which would perhaps have proved successful had the allies seconded their ardour: but these last, seeing the Lacedæmonian phalanx broken, and believing all lost, especially when they heard that the king was dead, took to flight, and drew the rest of the army after them. The Thebans remained masters of the field, erected a trophy, and permitted the enemy to bury their dead.

The Lacedæmonians had never received such a terrible blow. The most bloody defeat, till then, had scarce ever cost them more than four or five hundred of their citizens. Here they lost four thousand men, of whom one thousand were Lacedæmonians, and four hundred Spartans, out of seven hundred who were in the battle. The Thebans had only three hundred men killed, among whom were four of their citizens.

It is remarkable, that when the news of this defeat was brought to Sparta, the Ephori would not suffer the public games, which were then celebrating, to be interrupted. Whether this proceeded from an affectation of indifference, as if they wished to represent their loss as but trifling, and were desirous of concealing the real greatness of it from the people; or that luxury and dissipation had then made a considerable progress even in Sparta itself; it is difficult, at this distance of time, to determine. Next day, however, the loss of each particular family being known, the fathers and relations of those who had fallen in battle, went to the temples to thank the gods, and congratulated each other upon their glory and good fortune, whilst the relations of those who had escaped were overwhelmed with grief and affliction.

But there was another point to be determined with regard to these last. They were, by the law, to be degraded from all honour, and rendered infamous; insomuch that it was a disgrace to intermarry with them: they were to appear publicly in mean and dirty habits, with patched and party-coloured garments, and to go half shaved; and whoever met them in the streets, might insult and beat them, without their daring to make any resistance. This was so severe a law, and such numbers had on this occasion incurred the penalties of it, many of whom were of great families and interest, that they apprehended the execution of it might excite some public commotion ; besides that these citizens, such as they were, could very ill be spared at this time, when they wanted to recruit the army.   Under this difficulty, they gave Agesilaus a power even over the laws, to dispense with them, to abrogate them, or to enact such new ones as the present emergency required. He would not abolish or alter the law.   He only made a public declaration, that it should lie dormant for that single day, but revive and be in full force again on the morrow ; and by that expedient, he saved the citizens from infamy.

It was not long before the Spartans felt the consequences of this dreadful overthrow.   Numbers of Greek cities, that had hitherto remained neuter, now declared in favour of the Thebans, and increased their army to the amount of seventy thousand men.   With this mighty force Epaminondas entered Laconia, and overran the the open country.   He did not, however, attempt any thing against Sparta itself ; but he reinstated the Arcadians in all their ancient rights and privileges, of which they had been deprived by the Spartans, and he enabled them to build a new city, which, from the name of the old one, was called Messenia.

So jealous were the ancient Greeks of every the least encroachment on their liberty, that no action, however great or meritorious in other respects, was sufficient to atone for it.   This was signally exemplified in the case of Pelopidas and Epaminondas, who upon their return home, instead of being received as heroes and conquerors, were summoned as criminals before a court of justice, to answer for their conduct in having retained their command four months beyond the time limited by law.   This offence was capital by the laws of Thebes ; and those who stood up for the constitution were zealous for having it adhered to on the present occasion. Pelopidas was the first cited before the tribunal.   He defended himself with less strength and greatness of mind, than was expected from a man of his character, by nature warm and fiery.   That valour, which was haughty and intrepid in fight, forsook him before his judges.   His air and discourse, which had something timid and low in it, denoted a man who was afraid of death, and did not in the least incline the judges in his favour, who nevertheless, acquitted him, though not without difficulty.

Epaminondas, on the contrary, appeared with all the confidence of conscious innocence. Instead of justifying himself, he enumerated his actions: he related, in haughty terms, in what manner he had ravaged Laconia, reestablished Messenia, and delivered the Arcadians. He concluded with saying, that he should die with pleasure, if the Thebans would relinquish the sole glory of those actions to him, and declare that he had done them by his own authority, and without their participation. All the voices were in his favour, and he returned from his trial as he used to do from battle, with glory and universal applause. Such dignity has true valour, that it in a manner seizes the admiration of mankind by force. This bold and manly deportment had so good an effect, that his enemies declined any further prosecution: and he and his colleague were honourably acquitted. His enemies, however, jealous of his glory, were determined to mortify him, and with this view, procured him to be elected the city scavenger; but he accepted the place with thanks, and declared, that, instead of thinking himself disgraced by the office, he would render it honourable by his manner of discharging it.

In the meantime the Spartans, struck with consternation at their late defeat, applied to the Athenians for succour; and that people, notwithstanding their jealousy of their old rivals, engaged to assist them with all their forces. They likewise had recourse to the Persian king for the same purpose; but Pelopidas, undertaking an embassy to the court of that prince, prevailed upon him to remain neuter.

Soon after Pelopidas was sent with an army against Alexander, king of Pheræ, one of the most blood-thirsty tyrants that ever existed, and who had, for some time, given great disturbance to the whole country of Thessaly. This savage had caused several people to be buried alive, and others to be dressed in bears' and boars' skins, and then baited them with dogs, or shot at them for diversion. This monster, however, Pelopidas compelled to submission, and even endeavoured, by mild usage, to reform the natural brutality of his temper; but, Alexander, instead of being grateful for the salutary counsels that were given him, resolved to take the first opportunity of being revenged on his benefactor. Nor was it long before such an occasion offered; for Pelopidas being appointed ambassador to Alexander, was treacherously seized upon, and made prisoner, contrary to all the laws of nations and humanity. It was in vain that the Thebans complained of this violation of laws: it was in vain they sent a powerful army, but headed by indifferent generals, to revenge the insult: their army returned without effect, and Alexander treated his prisoner with great severity. It was reserved for Epaminondas to bring the tyrant to reason. Entering Thessalia at the head of a powerful army, his name spread such terror, that the tyrant offered terms of submission, and delivered up Pelopidas from prison.

Pelopidas was scarce set at liberty, when he resolved to punish the tyrant for his perfidy and breach of faith. He led a body of troops against him to a place called Cynocephalus, where a bloody battle ensued, in which the Thebans were victorious, but Pelopidas was unfortunately slain; and his countrymen considered those successes as very dearly earned, which were purchased at the expense of his life. His death was equally lamented by the Thebans and Thessalonians, who begged and obtained the honour of performing his funeral rites, which were very grand and magnificent. Alexander himself was soon after killed by his wife Thebe, and her three brothers, who, long shocked at his cruelties, had resolved to rid the world of such a monster. It is said, that his whole palace was every night filled with guards, except his bed-chamber, which was an upper room, guarded by a dog, and ascended by a ladder. Thebe allured away the dog, and covered the steps of the ladder with wool, to prevent noise; and then her three brothers ascending, one of them seized him by the feet, and another by the hair, and the third stabbed him to the heart.

In the meantime, the war between the Thebans and Spartans was carried on with unabated vigour. The Theban troops were commanded by their favourite general Epaminondas; Agesilaus, the only man in Greece then capable of opposing him, was at the head of the Spartans. The first attempt of Epaminondas in this campaign showed his great abilities, and his skill in the art of war. Hearing that Agesilaus had begun his march for Mantinea, and had left but few citizens to defend Sparta at home, he marched directly thither by night, with a design to take the city by surprise, as it had neither walls nor troops to protect it. But luckily Agesilaus had got scent of his design, and dispatched one of his horse to apprize the city of its danger; soon after which he himself arrived with a powerful succour: and he had scarce entered the town, when the Thebans were seen crossing the Eurotas, and advancing against the city. Epaminondas, finding that his design was discovered, thought it below his character to retire without making some attempt. He therefore employed valour instead of stratagem, and attacking the city at several quarters, penetrated as far as the public place, and made himself master of that part of Sparta, which lay upon the hither side of the river. Agesilaus exerted himself with greater activity than could have been expected from one of his years. He saw well that it was not now a time, as before, to spare himself, and to act only upon the defensive; but that he had need of all his courage and intrepidity to repel such an assailant. His son, Archidamus, at the head of the Spartan youth, behaved with incredible bravery wherever the danger was greatest; and, with his small troop, stopped the enemy, and made head against them on all sides.

A Spartan youth, named Isadas, filled not only his countrymen, but even the enemy, with admiration of his valour. He had a beautiful face, an elegant shape, an advantageous stature, and was just in the prime of youth; he had neither armour nor clothes upon his body, which shone with oil. Upon the first alarm he

L

ran out of his house with a spear in one hand, and a
sword in the other, and rushing into the thickest of the
enemy, he bore down all before him, laying numbers
dead at his feet, without himself receiving the least
wound.   Whether the enemy were confounded at the
sight, as thinking him something more than human, or
whether, says Plutarch, the gods took pleasure in preserving him on account of his extraordinary valour,
remains a question.   His gallantry, however, was so
much admired, that the Ephori decreed him a garland ;
but they afterwards fined him a thousand drachmas, for
having gone out to battle without armour.

   Epaminondas, having failed in his design upon Sparta,
was determined to strike some other blow that might
compensate for his miscarriage.   Hearing therefore,
that, in order to protect Sparta, all the troops had
been withdrawn from Mantinea, he resolved to march
thither without delay.   But as he intended to attack
the.-town, he dispatched a troop of horse, to view
its situation, and to clear the fields of stragglers.—
A little, however, before they reached Mantinea, an
army of six thousand Athenian auxiliaries arrived by
sea ; who, without allowing either themselves or their
horses any refreshment, rushed out of the city, and
attacked and defeated the Theban horse.   In the meantime, Epaminondas was advancing with his whole army,
with the enemy close upon his rear.   Finding it impossible to accomplish his purpose, before he was overtaken,
he determined to halt and give them battle.   He had
now got within a short way of the town, which has had
the honour of giving its name to the conflict of that day ;
a conflict the most splendid, and the best contested that
is to be found in the history of Greece, or perhaps
in that of any other country.   The Greeks had never
fought among themselves with more numerous armies :
the Lacedæmonians amounted to above twenty thousand
foot, and two thousand horse ; the Thebans to thirty
thousand foot, and three thousand horse.

   Epaminondas marched in the same order of battle in
which he intended to fight, that he might not be obliged,
when he came up with the enemy, to lose, in disposing

of his army, a precious time which cannot be recovered. He did not march directly, and with his front to the enemy, but in a column upon the hills, with his left wing foremost, as if he did not intend to fight that day. When he was over against them, at a quarter of a league's distance, he made the troops halt, and lay down their arms, as if he designed to encamp there. The enemy, in effect, were deceived by this step; and reckoning no longer upon a battle, they quitted their arms, dispersed themselves about the camp, and suffered that ardour to cool, which the near approach of a battle is wont to kindle in the hearts of soldiers.

Epaminondas took advantage of this supine conduct of the enemy. By suddenly wheeling his troops to the right, he changed his column into a line; and having drawn out his choice troops, he made them double their files upon the front of his left wing, in order to add to its strength, and enable it to attack in a point the Lacedæmonian phalanx, which, by the movement he had made, faced it directly. He ordered the centre and right wing of his army to move very slow, and to halt before they came up with the enemy, that he might not hazard the event of the battle upon troops of which he had no great opinion.

He expected to decide the victory with that body of chosen troops which he commanded in person, and which he had disposed in a column to attack the enemy in the form of a wedge. He was persuaded, that if he could penetrate the Lacedæmonian phalanx, in which the enemy's chief strength lay, he should find it no difficult matter to rout the rest of the army, by charging upon the right and left with his victorious troops.

To prevent the Athenians in the left wing from coming to the support of their right against his intended attack, he made a detachment of his horse and foot advance out of the line, and posted them upon a rising ground, in readiness to flank the Athenians, if they should venture to advance to sustain their right.

After having drawn up his army in this manner, he moved on to charge the enemy with the whole weight of his column. They were greatly surprised when they saw Epaminondas advancing towards them in this order, and immediately flew to their arms, bridled their horses, and made all the haste they could to their ranks.

While Epaminondas was marching against the enemy, the cavalry, that covered his flank on the left, the best at that time in Greece, consisting entirely of Thebans and Thessalians, had orders to attack the enemy's horse. The contest here was violent, but not long. The Lacedæmonian horse were soon repulsed, and obliged to take refuge behind their infantry. In the meantime, Epaminondas, with his body of foot, had charged the Lacedæmonian phalanx. The troops fought on both sides with incredible ardour, both the Thebans and Lacedæmonians being resolved to perish, rather than yield the glory of arms to their rivals. They began fighting with their spears; but these being soon broken in the fury of the combat, they charged each other sword in hand. The resistance was equally obstinate, and the slaughter very great on both sides. Despising danger, and desirous only of distinguishing themselves by the gallantry of their conduct, the men chose rather to die in their ranks, than lose a step of their ground.

This terrible slaughter having continued for some time, without the victory inclining to either side, Epaminondas, to turn the scale in his own favour, determined to make an extraordinary effort in person, without regard to the danger of his own life. He formed, therefore, a troop of the bravest and most resolute about him; and putting himself at the head of them, made a vigorous charge upon the enemy, where the fight was hottest, and wounded the general of the Lacedæmonians with the first javelin he threw. The troops by his example, having wounded or killed all that stood in their way, broke and penetrated the phalanx. The Lacedæmonians, dismayed by the presence of Epaminondas, and overpowered by the weight of that intrepid party, were obliged to give ground. The bulk of the Theban army, animated by their general's example and success, drove back the enemy upon their right and left, and made great havock among them. But some troops of the Spartans, perceiving that Epaminondas was carried away by his ardour, suddenly rallied, and returning to the charge, overwhelmed him with a shower of javelins. While he kept off part of those darts, shunned some of them, fenced off others, and was fighting with the most heroic valour, a Spartan, named Callicrates, gave him a mortal wound with a javelin in his breast, across his cuirass. The wood of the javelin being broke off, and the iron head remaining in the wound, the torment was intolerable, and he fell immediately. The battle began around him with redoubled fury; the one side exerting their utmost efforts to take him alive, and the other to save him. The Thebans at last gained their point, and carried him off, after having put the enemy to flight.

After several different movements, and alternate losses and advantages, the troops on both sides stood still, and rested upon their arms; and the trumpets of the two armies, as if by mutual consent sounded the retreat at the same time. Each party pretended to the victory, and erected a trophy; the Thebans, because they had defeated the right wing, and remained masters of the field; the Athenians, because they had cut the general's detachment in pieces: and from this point of honour, both sides at first refused to ask leave to bury their dead; which, with the ancients, was confessing their defeat. The Lacedæmonians, however, sent first to demand that permission; after which the rest had no thoughts but of paying the last duties to the slain.

In the meantime, Epaminondas had been carried into the camp. The surgeons, after having examined the wound, declared, that he would expire as soon as the head of the dart was drawn out of it. These words filled all that were present with the deepest affliction, who were inconsolable on seeing so great a man upon the point of expiring. For him, the only concern he expressed was about his arms, and the fate of the battle. When they showed him his shield, and assured him that the Thebans had gained the victory, turning towards his friends with a calm and serene air, "All then is well," said he; and soon after, upon drawing the head of the javelin out of his body, he expired in the arms of victory.

As the glory of Thebes rose with Epaminondas, so it fell with him; and he is, perhaps, the only instance of

one man's being able to inspire his countrymen with a
love of military fame, without having had a predecessor,
or leaving an imitator of his example.

The battle of Mantinea was followed by a peace,
which was ratified by all the states of Greece, except
Sparta; the conditions of it were, that every state should
retain what they possessed, and hold it independent of
any other power. Nothing remarkable happened for
some time after this, except an expedition of Agesilaus
into Egypt, whither he went to assist Tachos, who had
usurped the throne of that kingdom. Upon his arrival
in Egypt, every one was eager to see a man who had
acquired so splendid a reputation. Accordingly great
multitudes of people flocked to the place where he was;
but how much were they surprised, when, instead of
an elegant, portly figure, they found a little old man,
lying on the grass, with his clothes thread-bare, and
his hair uncombed! They were still more astonished,
upon their offering him presents of perfumes, and other
Egyptian luxuries: "Give these things," said he, "to
my helots; Spartan freemen know not how to use
them." Being ill used by Tachos, whom he found
very ungrateful, he joined Nectanebus, his nephew, and
raised him to the throne: and when he, in his turn,
was opposed by another competitor, Agesilaus found
means to defeat all the attempts of this last, and left
Nectanebus in possession of the supreme power. As a
reward for his services, he received a present of two
hundred and thirty talents of silver; and was treated,
besides, with every mark of gratitude and respect. In
returning home he was driven into the haven of Menelaus, which lies upon the coast of Africa, where he was
attacked with an acute disease, and carried off, being
then upwards of eighty years of age, forty of which he
had been king.

The character of Agesilaus was a compound of very
different and even opposite qualities. He was of a
little stature, and lame of a leg; and, indeed, he was
so fully convinced of the meanness of his appearance,
that he would never suffer any statue of him to be
erected during his life; and he strictly prohibited the
Spartans from erecting any after his death. He always

paid the utmost deference to the senate and the Ephori, by which means he had it in his power to execute all his designs without any opposition. A rigid observer of the old Spartan plainness and frugality, he was capable of enduring the greatest labour and fatigue. The love of his children was a distinguished feature in his character. One day, when a friend found him riding with them on a hobby-horse, and expressed some surprise, "Don't," said he, "say one word of this, till you yourself become a father." His generosity to his enemies was only exceeded by his partiality to his friends; of the latter of which he gave a remarkable proof in his request to Idrieus, prince of Caria, in favour of Nicias: "If Nicias," said he, "be innocent, acquit him on his own account; if guilty, acquit him on mine; in any event, acquit him." He had a very singular way of deceiving his enemies. When about to enter upon a march, he took care to publish the true account of his intended rout, and time of marching; by which he generally had the pleasure of hearing, that they had moved on a different day, and taken a different road from that which they wished to take. So high was his reputation both for courage and conduct, that the Spartans appointed him not only their general, but likewise their admiral; a mark of honour never conferred upon any one before.

Of all the Greeks, the Athenians were the most remarkable for their love of the polite arts, and particularly for their attachment to the stage. This last passion, indeed, they now carried to such an extravagant length, that, according to Plutarch, it cost more to represent some of the famous pieces of Sophocles and Euripides, than it had done to carry on the war against the barbarians. And, in order to support this charge, they seized upon the fund which had been set apart for the war, with a prohibition, upon pain of death, ever to advise the applying of it to any other purpose. They not only reversed this decree, but went as far the other way, making it death to propose the restoring this fund to the uses for which it had been originally raised. It is not to be supposed that the other states of Greece would pay much respect to a people that were thus immersed in luxury and dissipation; and accordingly many of those who had hitherto been in alliance with the Athenians now commenced hostilities against them [A. J. C. 358]. This war, however, which was soon terminated, was not attended with any remarkable event, except that Chabrias, the Athenian general, at the siege of Chio, preferred his honour to his life, and chose to perish in his vessel rather than abandon her. In the mean time, a power was growing up in Greece, hitherto unobserved, but now too conspicuous and formidable to be overlooked in the general picture; this was that of the Macedonians, a people hitherto obscure, and in a manner barbarous; and who, though warlike and hardy, had never yet presumed to intermeddle in the affairs of Greece: but now several circumstances concurred to raise them from that obscurity, and to involve them in measures which, by degrees, wrought a thorough change in the state of Greece. It will be necessary, therefore, to begin with a short account of their power and origin before we enter into a detail of that conspicuous part which they afterwards performed on the theatre of the world.

CHAPTER XII.

FROM THE BIRTH TO THE DEATH OF PHILIP, KING OF MACEDON.

THE first king who is mentioned, with any degree of certainty, to have reigned in Macedonia, was Caranus, by birth an Argive, and said to be the sixteenth in descent from Hercules. It was upon this foundation, that Philip afterwards grounded his pretensions to be of the race of Hercules, and assumed to himself divine honours. Caranus is commonly supposed to have led forth a body of his countrymen, by the advice of the oracle, into those parts where he settled, and to have made himself king. Caranus having, according to the general account, reigned twenty-eight years, the succession was continued after him to the times we are now treating of. But there is very little worth notice recorded of these kings, who were generally employed in defending themselves against the incursions of their neighbours. And as to their domestic affairs, they were remarkable only for the frequent murders and usurpations which happened in the royal family.

Amyntas, the father of Philip, left two elder sons, Alexander and Perdiccas, both of whom possessed the throne in their turn. The second of these left a son, named Amyntas, who, while yet an infant, succeeded his father; but the state of public affairs requiring a prince of mature years, Amyntas was soon deposed, and his uncle Philip advanced in his room.

Philip began his reign in the twenty-fourth year of his age, and the first year of the hundred and fifth olympiad. He had received a considerable part of his education at Thebes, whither he had been carried, in his youth, as a hostage; and he there acquired, under Epaminondas, that intimate acquaintance with the art of war, as it was then conducted, which he afterwards displayed so signally during the whole course of his reign. He had now, indeed, occasion for all his activity and address, for he was surrounded with almost as many enemies as he had neighbours. The Illyrians, who had seized a part of his dominions, were preparing to attack him with a great army; the Pæonians were making daily incursions into his territories: and he had, at the same time, the misfortune to have two pretenders to his crown; Pausanias, the Lacedæmonian, who was supported by the Thracians; and Argæus, whom the Athenians had undertaken to assist.

Under these circumstances, with so many enemies on his hands at once, and that before he was well settled on the throne, his first care was to make sure of his own people, to gain their affections, and to raise their spirits; for they were very much disheartened, having lost above four thousand men in a battle they had lately fought with the Illyrians. He succeeded in these points by his dexterity and address, and still more by the force of his eloquence, of which he was a great master. His next step was to train and exercise them, and reform

their discipline; and it was at this time that he instituted the famous Macedonian phalanx, which did so
much execution.   It was an improvement upon the
ancient method of fighting among the Grecians, who
generally drew upon their foot so close, as to stand the
shock of the enemy without being broken.

The complete phalanx was thought to contain above
sixteen thousand men; though it was also taken in
general for any company or party of soldiers, and frequently for the whole body of foot. But this of Philip's
invention is described by Polybius to be an oblong
square, consisting of eight thousand pike-men, sixteen
deep, and five hundred in front; the men standing so
close together, that the pikes of the fifth rank were
extended three feet beyond the line of the front.   The
rest, whose distance from the front made their pikes
useless, rested upon the shoulders of those who stood
before them, and so locking them together in file,
pressed forward to support and push on the former
ranks, by which means the assault was rendered more
violent, and almost irresistible.

Philip, having settled his affairs at home, and com-
promised all differences with such of his enemies as
lay nearest to him, turned his arms against the Athenians, who were marched up to Methone to assist
Argæus. He gave them battle, and defeated them;
and the death of Argæus, who was killed in the action,
put an end to that dispute: for he permitted the Athenians, when they were in his power, to return home.
This instance of his moderation gained so far upon
them, that they soon after concluded a peace with him;
which yet he observed no longer than was necessary
for securing the other part of his dominions.

Accordingly he marched northward, and subdued
first the Pæonians, and afterwards the Illyrians, the
latter of whom he likewise compelled to restore all
the conquests they had made in Macedonia.   He next
made himself master of Amphipolis, which lay upon
the river Strymon, and was the key of his dominions
on that quarter.   This place he had seized in the
beginning of his reign, but afterwards abandoned it in

compliment to the Athenians, to whom it originally belonged; but now, being less apprehensive of the displeasure of that people, he made an entire conquest of it, and added it to his dominions. The Athenians, however, themselves, he always treated with great respect, whenever they fell into his hands, as he particularly did upon his taking possession of Pydna and Potidæa; for this last place being garrisoned by the Athenians, he sent them home safe with many marks of civility.

Proceeding still in his encroachments upon his neighbours, he seized the city of Crenides, which had been built only two years before, and he now called it Philippi, from his own name. It was here that he discovered a gold mine which every year produced a hundred and forty-four thousand pounds sterling. This, which was an immense sum for that age, was much more serviceable than fleets and armies in fighting his battles; and he seldom failed to make use of it in every negotiation. It is said that, consulting the oracle of Delphos concerning the success of an intended expedition, he received for answer, "That with silver spears he should conquer all things." He took the hint, and, by his success, verified the prediction of the oracle: indeed he was less proud of the success of a battle, than of a negotiation; well knowing that his soldiers and generals shared in the former, whereas the honour of the latter was all his own.

But a larger field was now opening to his ambition. The mutual divisions of the states of Greece were at no time wholly cemented, and they now broke out upon a very particular occasion. The first cause of the rupture (which was afterwards called *The sacred war*) arose from the Phocians having ploughed up a piece of ground belonging to the temple of Apollo at Delphos. Against this all the neighbouring states exclaimed as a sacrilege: they were cited before the council of the Amphictyons, who had the care of sacred matters; and they were cast, and fined in a very heavy sum. This the Phocians were unable to pay: they refused to submit to the decree; they alleged, that the care and patronage of the temple anciently belonged to them; and to prove this, they quoted a precedent from Homer.

Philomelus, one of their citizens, had the chief hand in exciting them to take up arms, he raised their ardour, and was appointed their general. He first applied himself to the Spartans, who had likewise been fined by the Amphictyons for having seized the Cadmea after the battle of Leuctra. For this reason they were very well disposed to join him, but did not yet think proper to declare themselves openly: nevertheless they encouraged him secretly, and supplied him with money; by which means he raised troops, and, without much difficulty, got possession of the temple. The principal opposition he met with in the neighbourhood was from the Locrians; but having defeated them, he erased the decree of the Amphictyons, which was inscribed on the pillars of the temple. Willing, however, to give a colour to his proceedings, he thought it convenient to consult the oracle, and to procure an answer in his favour. But when he applied to the priestess for that purpose, she refused to officiate, until being intimidated by his threats, she told him, the god left him at liberty to act as he pleased; which he looked upon as a good answer, and as such took care to publish it.

The Amphictyons meeting a second time, a resolution was taken to declare war against the Phocians. Most of the states of Greece engaged in this quarrel, and espoused the cause of the one party or the other. The Thebans, the Locrians, the Thessalians, and several other neighbouring states declared in favour of the god; whilst Athens, Sparta, and some other cities of Peloponnesus joined with the Phocians. This war, which lasted for some time, was not remarkable for any thing else, except that which distinguishes, or rather disgraces, all religious wars; I mean, the cruelties exercised by both parties. The Thebans, having taken some prisoners, condemned them all to die, as sacrilegious wretches; and the Phocians in their turn, by way of reprisal, inflicted the same punishment on their captives. Nay, Philomelus their leader, being attacked on an eminence, and finding it impossible to escape, threw himself headlong from a rock, rather than fall alive into the hands of his enemies. He was ~ceeded by Oenomarchus.

Philip did not choose to interfere in this quarrel, which it was rather his interest to encourage than suppress; being well pleased to see the different states of Greece weaken one another, and thus render them all an easier prey to him when he should be at leisure to attack them.

It was just on the conclusion of this sacred war that *Alexander the Great* was born. In his earlier years he had several masters to teach him music, and other superficial accomplishments: but when he grew up, his father wrote to Aristotle, the most celebrated philosopher of his time, begging he would come and undertake the education of his son, and inspire him with those sentiments of magnanimity and justice, which every great man ought to possess, and which no other person was so capable of inculcating. He added, "I return thanks to the gods, not so much for having given me a son, as for having given him to me in the age in which Aristotle lives."

Being desirous of reducing Thrace under his dominion, he determined to make himself master of Methone, which obstructed his designs in that quarter. He accordingly besieged it, obliged it to surrender, and levelled it with the ground. He lost one of his eyes before this place by a very singular accident. Aster of Amphipolis had offered him his services, telling him that he was so excellent a marksman, that he could bring down birds in their most rapid flight. "Well," said Philip, "I will take you into my service, when I make war upon starlings;" which answer stung the archer to the quick. He immediately threw himself into the town, and let fly an arrow, on which was written, "To Philip's right eye." This carried a most cruel proof of his skill as an archer, for he hit Philip in the right eye; and that prince sent him back the same arrow, with this inscription, "If Philip takes the city, he will hang up Aster;" and accordingly he was as good as his word.

After this Philip marched to the relief of the Thessalians, who had implored his assistance against their tyrant Lycophron, the successor of Alexander of Pheræ.

This man, after having acted the part of a deliverer for some time, renewed all the cruelties and barbarities of his predecessor; and, being supported by a large body of Phocians under Oenomarchus, he thought himself secure from all opposition. Philip, however, attacked him boldly; routed his army; killed six thousand men upon the field of battle; and three thousand Phocians, who were taken prisoners, were by his order thrown into the sea, as sacrilegious wretches, the professed enemies of religion.

Having thus freed the Thessalians, he resolved to carry his arms into Phocis, and with this view was going to take possession of Thermopylæ, the key of Greece, and especially of Attica on that side: but the Athenians, being informed of his intention, took care to be beforehand with him, and sent a body of troops to occupy that pass; and Philip, being unwilling to come as yet to an open rupture with them, thought proper for the present to relinquish his design. The Athenians were roused to this exertion of spirit by the persuasion of Demosthenes, the celebrated orator, who, from the beginning, foresaw the ambitious views of Philip, and the power he had of carrying them into effect.

This illustrious orator and statesman, whom we shall hereafter find acting so considerable a part in the course of this history, was born in the last year of the ninety-ninth olympiad. He was the son not of a mean and obscure mechanic, as Juvenal has represented him, but of an eminent Athenian citizen, who had raised a considerable fortune by the making of arms. At the age of seven years he lost his father; and, to add to this misfortune, the guardians to whom he was intrusted wasted and embezzled a considerable part of his inheritance. The first specimen he gave of his abilities as a speaker was, in pleading against these corrupt guardians; though here the goodness of his cause was of more avail than the force of his eloquence; for his early attempts were unpromising, and soon convinced him of the necessity of a graceful and manly pronunciation. In this respect, indeed, he laboured under impediments that, at first sight, might appear to be altogether unsurmountable. He had a stammering in his speech; but this he corrected by pronouncing orations with pebbles in his mouth. He had a weak and effeminate voice; but this he strengthened by repeating speeches or verses when he was out of breath either with running, or with walking up hill. He had an awkward and ungraceful gesture; but this he regulated and improved by declaiming privately before a lookingglass. And conscious of the natural aversion of the human mind to submit to severe study, he compelled himself, as it were, to perform this part of his duty; for having built a closet under ground for the express purpose of his improvement, he sometimes confined himself there for two or three months together; and, in order to cut off all possibility of his coming abroad, shaved one half of his head, while he left the other unshaved.

But even all these preparations would not have been sufficient, had it not been for the salutary advice and instructions of the player, Satyrus. This man, having one day met Demosthenes overwhelmed with shame and confusion on account of his having been hissed in a public assembly of the people, for his awkward and uncouth delivery, desired him to repeat some verses of Sophocles, which he accordingly did: the other repeated them after him, but with such a different tone and accent as fully convinced him that he knew very little of elocution. But by the instructions of Satyrus, and his own perseverance, he at last attained to such perfection in the art of delivery, that he surpassed all his cotemporaries as much in this as he did in the more noble and sublime parts of his profession. In a word, he soon began to be looked upon as the standard of true eloquence; insomuch that people flocked from all parts of Greece to hear him, and none of his countrymen have been put in competition with him; nor, even among the Romans, any but Cicero. And though it has been made a question by the ancient writers, to which of the two they should give the preference, they have not ventured to decide it, but have contented themselves with describing their different

beauties, and showing that they were both perfect in
their kind.

His eloquence was grave and austere, like his temper; masculine and sublime, bold, forcible, and impetuous; abounding with metaphors, apostrophes, and interrogations; which, with his solemn way of invoking and appealing to the gods, the planets, the elements, and the manes of those who fell at Salamis and Marathon, had such a wonderful effect upon his hearers that they thought him inspired. In a word, the councils and conduct of his countrymen were so much under his control, and he had it so much in his power to lead them into any measures he thought proper to recommend, that Philip used to say, he was more afraid of him than of all the fleets and armies of the Athenians, and that he had no enemy but Demosthenes.

Philip, not choosing to attack the Athenians at present, turned his arms against their allies, particularly the Olynthians, whom he easily subdued, notwithstanding the reinforcement sent them from Athens; and having taken their city, he plundered it, and sold the inhabitants among the rest of the spoil. His two bastard brothers, who were among the captives, he put to death, as he had formerly done the other. Justin says, that the protection which the Olynthians had given his brothers was the plea which he used for attacking them.

In the mean time, the Thebans being unable alone to terminate the war, which they had so long carried on against the Phocians, addressed themselves to Philip, and solicited his assistance. This he readily granted them, being glad of so plausible a pretext for interfering in the affairs of Greece; and desiring, at the same time, to acquire the character of a religious prince; which he knew he should easily do, by waging war against those who were convicted of sacrilege. And in order to prevent the Athenians from thwarting his design by sending aid to the Phocians, he took care to amuse them with proposals of peace; which had so good an effect, that they actually sent ten ambassadors, among whom were Æschines and Demosthenes, into Macedon, to carry on the treaty. All of these, however, Philip found means to corrupt, except Demosthenes: and he thus continued to protract the negotiation until he had marched into Phocis, and compelled the enemy, by the terror of his name, to surrender at discretion.

As to the allies of the Phocians, and particularly eight thousand mercenaries from Peloponnesus, he allowed them to return home without molestation, but the Phocians themselves were left entirely at his mercy. As this, however, was an affair in which the Greeks in general were concerned, he did not think proper to act in it by his own private authority, but referred it to the Amphictyons, whom he caused to be assembled for that purpose. But they were so much under his influence, that they served only to give a sanction to his determination. They decreed, that all the cities of Phocis should be demolished; that they who had fled, as being principally concerned in the sacrilege, should be stigmatized as accursed, and proscribed as outlaws; that they who remained in the towns should be dispersed in villages, and obliged to pay out of their lands a yearly tribute of sixty talents, until the whole of what had been taken out of the temple should be restored (for it is to be observed, that Philomelus, their first leader, had plundered the temple). To add to their punishment, they were adjudged to lose their seat in the council of the Amphictyons, in which they had a double voice. This Philip got transferred to himself, which was a very material point, and may be looked upon as the principal step towards his gaining that authority which he afterwards exercised in the affairs of Greece. At the same time he gained, in conjunction with the Thebans, the superintendency of the Pythian games, which the Corinthians had forfeited for their having taken part with the Phocians. Philip having in this manner accomplished his professed design, did not think it prudent as yet to disclose his secret views of ambition, and he therefore returned in triumph into his own country.

It was about this time that he performed an act of private justice, which, in the eye of a philosopher, ennobles his character more than all his public victories.

M

A certain soldier in the Macedonian army had, in many instances, distinguished himself by extraordinary acts of valour, and had received many marks of Philip's favour and approbation. On some occasion he embarked on board a vessel, which was wrecked in a violent storm, and he himself cast on the shore naked and helpless, and scarcely with any signs of life. A Macedonian, whose lands were contiguous to the sea, came opportunely to be witness of his distress, and, with all possible tenderness, flew to the relief of the unhappy stranger. He bore him to his house, laid him in his own bed, revived, cherished, comforted, and for forty days supplied him freely with all the necessaries and conveniences which his languishing condition could require. The soldier, thus happily rescued from death, was incessant in the warmest expressions of gratitude to his benefactor, and assured him of his interest with the king, and of his power and resolution of obtaining for him, from the royal bounty, the noble returns which such extraordinary benevolence deserved. He was now completely recovered, and his kind host supplied him with money to pursue his journey. Some time after, he presented himself before the king; he recounted his misfortunes, magnified his services, and, having looked with an eye of envy on the possessions of the man who had preserved his life, was so abandoned to every sense of gratitude, as to request the king to bestow upon him the house and lands where he had been so kindly and tenderly entertained. Unhappily Philip, without examination, inconsiderately granted his infamous request; and this soldier now returned to his preserver, and repaid his kindness by driving him from his settlement, and taking immediate possession of all the fruits of his honest industry. The poor man, stung with this instance of unparalleled ingratitude, boldly determined to seek relief; and, in a letter addressed to Philip, represented his own and the soldier's conduct, in a lively and affecting manner. The king was instantly fired with indignation; he ordered that justice should be done without delay; that the possessions should be immediately restored to the man, whose.

charitable offices had been thus horribly repaid; and, having seized the soldier, caused these words to be branded on his forehead, *The Ungrateful Guest*—a character infamous in every age, and among all nations, but particularly among the Greeks, who, from the earliest times, were most scrupulously observant of the laws of hospitality.

The next military operation which Philip undertook was against the Chersonese. This peninsula had for many years belonged to the Athenians; and though Cotys, as king of the country, had lately wrested it from them, and left it to his son Chersopleptes, yet he being unable to defend himself against Philip, restored it to its former masters, and reserved only to himself the capital city, Cardia. But the Cardians, afraid of falling back under the dominion of the Athenians, implored the protection of Philip, which he readily granted them. Diopithes, who was the chief of the Athenian colony lately sent to the Chersonese, considered this proceeding of Philip as an act of hostility against Athens; and he therefore, by way of retaliation, invaded the maritime parts of Thrace, which Philip had lately conquered. Philip sent a letter to Athens, complaining of this conduct of Diopithes, which he represented as an infraction of the peace; and his creatures there were at great pains to show that his complaints were well founded, and that Diopithes had acted very improperly: but Demosthenes, in a speech which he made upon the occasion, and which may be considered as the foundation of all the other orations that go by the name of Philippics, proved that Diopithes had done no more than his duty; and that, instead of incurring the censure, he ought to receive the thanks of his country.

Philip, however, was no way intimidated by the wordy resistance of his eloquent antagonist; but proceeding still to extend his influence among the different states of Greece, he offered his protection to the Messenians and Argives, who had been oppressed by the Spartans; and these being soon after joined by the Thebans, formed altogether a very powerful confede-

racy. The natural balance against it was a union between Athens and Sparta, which the Spartans pressed
with great eagerness, and Philip and the Thebans did
all they could to prevent. But Demosthenes, exerting
himself with great spirit, roused up the Athenians, and
put them so far on their guard, that, without coming
to an open rupture with Philip, they obliged him for
the present to remain quiet.

Quiet, however, he could not long continue. His
restless and enterprising spirit was ever at work. He
had long fixed his eye upon the island of Euboea, as
being very conveniently situated for favouring the
design he had formed against Greece; and he now
contrived, upon pretence of an invitation from some
of the inhabitants, to send a body of troops thither;
by which means he possessed himself of several strong
places, dismantled Porthmos, and established three
tyrants, or kings, over the country. The Athenians
were conjured, in this distressful situation, by Plutarch
of Eretria, to come to the relief of the inhabitants;
and they accordingly despatched a few troops thither
under the command of Phocion, a general of whom
great hopes were entertained, and whose conduct justified the high opinion the public had of him.

This man would have done honour to the earliest
and most uncorrupt times of the Athenian state. His
manners were formed in the academy, according to the
rules of the purest and most rigid virtue. It is said,
that no one ever saw him laugh, or weep, or deviate in
the least from the most settled gravity and composure.
He learned the art of war under Chabrias, and frequently moderated the excesses and corrected the
errors of that general: his humanity he admired and
imitated, and taught him to exercise it in a more liberal and extensive manner. When he had received his
directions to sail with twenty ships, to collect the con-
tributions of the allies and dependent cities, "Why this
force?" said Phocion; "for if I am to meet them as
enemies, it is insufficient; if as friends and allies, a
single vessel will serve." He bore the hardships of a
military life with so much ease, that if ever he appeared

warmly clothed, the soldiers at once pronounced it the sign of a cold season. His outward appearance was forbidding, and his enemies taking advantage of this circumstance, sometimes reproached him with his supercilious aspect; and one day, when Chares did so, and the Athenians seemed pleased with the sarcasm, Phocion quickly replied, "The sternness of my countenance never made any of you sad, but the mirth of these sneerers has cost you many a tear." In popular assemblies, his lively, close, and natural manner of speaking seemed, as it were, the echo of the simplicity and integrity of his mind; and had frequently a greater effect, than even the dignity and energy of Demosthenes, who called him the pruning-hook of his periods. He studied only good sense and plain reasoning, and despised every adventitious ornament. He was sensible of the depravity of his countrymen, and ever treated them with the utmost severity. He defied their censures; and so far did he affect to despise their applause, that once, when his sentiments extorted their approbation, he turned about in surprise, and asked a friend, "If any thing weak or impertinent had escaped him?" His fondness for pacific measures arose from a thorough persuasion of the degeneracy of his countrymen. He saw the designs of Philip, but imagined that the state was too corrupted to give him any effectual opposition; so that he was, according to Demosthenes in his third Philippic, of the number of those men, who gave up the interests of the republic, not ignorantly or corruptly, but from a melancholy conviction of the indispensable necessity of yielding to the fatality of the times, and of submitting to an event which could not be avoided. He was, of consequence, ever of the party opposite to Demosthenes; and having been taught, by experience, to suspect the popular leaders, considered his earnestness to rouse the Athenians to arms, only as an artifice to embroil the state, and by that means to gain an ascendant in the public assemblies. "Phocion," said Demosthenes, "the people in some mad fit will sacrifice you to their fury." "Yes," replied he, "and you will be their victim, if ever they come to their senses." Yet they often prevailed on him to act against his judgment, though never to speak against his conscience. He never refused or declined the command, whatever might be his opinion of the expedition. Forty-five times was he chosen to lead their armies, generally in his absence, and ever without the least application. They knew his merit ; and, in the hour of danger forgot that severity with which he usually treated their inclinations and opinions.

It was to him the Athenians gave the command of the forces they sent to the assistance of Plutarch. But this traitor repaid his benefactors with ingratitude ; he set up his standard against them, and endeavoured openly to repulse the very army he had requested. Phocion, however, was not at a loss how to behave to such a renegado ; he pursued his enterprise, won a battle, and drove Plutarch from Eretria.

Philip, disappointed in his designs upon Euboea, endeavoured to distress the Athenians in another quarter. He well knew that they had most of their supplies of corn from Thrace ; and he, therefore, resolved to shut up the ports of that country against them, and particularly to make himself master of Perinthus and Byzantium. Unwilling, however, still to break with them entirely, he took care to amuse them with professions of his regard, and of his extreme reluctance to give them the least offence. Nay, he wrote them a letter upon the present occasion, in which he strongly insinuated, that they, and not he, were the violators of the peace. "In the times of great enmity," says he, "the most you did was to fit out ships of war against me, and to seize and sell the merchants that come to trade in my dominions ; but now you carry your hatred and injustice to such prodigious lengths, as even to send ambassadors to the king of Persia, to make him declare against me."

This letter gave such of the orators, as were in Philip's interest, a fine opportunity of justifying his conduct. Demosthenes alone stood firm, and still continued to expose his artful designs ; and in order to remove the first impressions which the perusal of this letter might make, he immediately ascended the tribunal, and from thence harangued the people with all the thunder of his eloquence. He told them, the letter was written in a style not suitable to the people of Athens; that it was a plain declaration of war against them; that Philip had long since made the same declaration by his actions; and that, by the peace he had concluded with them, he meant nothing more than a bare cessation of arms, and to fall upon them afresh when they were more unprepared. From thence he proceeded to his usual topic, of reproving them for their sloth, and suffering themselves to be deluded by their orators, who were in Philip's pay. "Convinced of these truths," continued he, "O Athenians, and strongly persuaded that we can no longer say with propriety that we enjoy peace (for Philip has now declared war against us by his letter, as he has long since done by his conduct) you ought not to spare either the public treasure, or the possessions of private persons, but, when occasion shall require, haste to your respective standards, and set abler generals at your head, than those you have hitherto employed: for no one among you ought to imagine, that the same men who have ruined your affairs, will have abilities to restore them to their former happy situation. Think how infamous it is, that a man from Macedon should contemn dangers to such a degree; that, merely to aggrandize his empire, he should rush into the midst of combats, and return from battle covered with wounds; and that the Athenians, whose hereditary right it is to obey no man, but to impose law on others, sword in hand; that the Athenians, I say, merely through dejection of spirit and indolence, should degenerate from the glory of their ancestors, and abandon the interest of their country!"

Though Phocion seldom agreed with Demosthenes in any thing, he heartily assented to what he had now said. He further urged the incapacity of the generals already chosen; and these being rejected, he himself was appointed to command the troops that were to go against Philip, who was still besieging Byzantium.

Phocion's conduct, on this occasion, did not detract from the high character he had already acquired; and

he was nobly supported by his officers and soldiers,
who had an entire confidence in his gallantry and good
fortune.   He obliged Philip to give over the siege ;
he drove him out of the Hellespont; he took some of
his ships; he recovered many fortresses which he had
seized; and having made several descents upon different
parts of his territories, he plundered all the open country, till a body of forces assembling to oppose him, he
thought proper to retire.

Philip having met with so severe a check in Greece,
turned his arms against the Scythians, whom he easily
defeated; but, in his return from Scythia, he was
obliged to come to an engagement with the Triballi,
when he received a wound in his thigh, and had his
horse killed under him.   Alexander, who accompanied
him in this expedition, immediately flew to his father's
relief, and covering him with his shield, killed or put
to flight all who attacked him.

The Athenians considered the siege of Byzantium as
an open declaration of war; and therefore, in order to
retaliate upon Philip, they blocked up his ports by sea,
and put an entire stop to his commerce.   Philip at first
endeavoured to appease them by offering them terms
of peace, which Phocion, with his usual moderation,
advised them to accept, but Demosthenes persuaded
them to reject with indignation.   Philip, therefore,
began to form new alliances against them, particularly
with the Thebans and Thessalians; but knowing how
difficult it would be to persuade these powers to act
directly against Athens, merely on account of his personal quarrels, he took care to supply them with a more
plausible pretext for embracing such a measure.   He
found means, by his artifice and intrigues, to sow dissensions between the Locrians of Amphissa and their
capital city.   They were accused of impiety, in having
ploughed up a spot of sacred ground which lay near the
temple of Apollo, in the same manner as the Phocians
had done upon a former occasion.   This spar , which
at first might easily have been extinguished, Æschines,
the most celebrated orator of his time next to Demosthenes, and who was entirely in the interest of Philip,

contrived to blow up into a flame; and, by his advice, a resolution was taken to send a solemn deputation to Philip, inviting him to assist Apollo and the Amphictyons, and to repel the outrages of the impious Amphissæans; and further to declare, that he was constituted, by the Greeks, a member of the council of Amphictyons, and general and commander of their forces, with full and unlimited powers.

This was the very station which Philip had long aspired to, and now thought himself supremely happy in having attained. Most of the inferior states of Greece approved of the conduct of the Amphictyons, in giving the command of their forces to a man, so eminent and illustrious for his piety, and so capable of executing the vengeance of heaven. The Athenians and Spartans, however, considered the matter in a very different light. They saw, that while Philip openly affected to vindicate the honour of Apollo, he was secretly promoting the views of his own ambition; and that, under pretence of aiding one part of the Greeks against the other, he was in reality forging chains for the whole. Nor was it long before their suspicion was justified by the event; for Philip had no sooner assembled his forces, than instead of marching, as he had promised, against the irreverent Locrians, he made himself master of Elatea, a capital city of Phocis, which was very conveniently situated for awing the Thebans, of whom he began to grow jealous, and for opening to him a way into the heart of Attica. By so extraordinary and unexpected a step he fairly threw off the mask, and bade defiance, as it were, to the whole body of Grecians.

The news of this transaction quickly spread into the neighbouring countries, and, wherever it came, filled the minds of the people with terror and consternation. They now plainly perceived the designs of Philip, which his artifice and their own stupidity had hitherto concealed from their eyes: but they were at a loss to know what steps they ought to take, in order to render them abortive. Nay, even the Athenians themselves, though they had long apprehended some such event, were as much confounded and alarmed as their neighbours.

For when they met in a general assembly, in order to deliberate upon the present critical situation of affairs, and the herald, as usual, demanded with a loud voice, " Which among them would ascend the tribunal," not one of them had the courage to rise or open his mouth; till at last Demosthenes, animated with the greatness of the approaching danger, and fired with that noble spirit of indignation, which he had ever cherished and avowed against the insidious designs of Philip, arose, and addressed the people in the following terms: " Athenians! permit me to explain the circumstances of that state which Philip has seized upon. Those of its citizens, whom his gold could corrupt, or his artifice deceive, are all at his devotion. What then is his design? By drawing up his forces, and displaying his powers on the borders of Thebes, he hopes to inspire his adherents with courage and assurance, and to terrify and controul his adversaries, that fear or force may drive them into those measures which they have hitherto opposed. If then we are resolved, in this conjuncture, to cherish the remembrance of every act of unkindness which the Thebans have done to Athens; if we regard them with suspicion, as men who have ranged themselves on the side of our enemy; in the first place we shall act agreeably to Philip's warmest wishes, and then I am apprehensive, that the party, who now oppose him, may be brought over to his interest; the whole city submit unanimously to his direction; and Thebes and Macedon fall, with their united force, on Attica. Grant due attention to what I now propose, let it be calmly weighed without dispute or cavil, and I doubt not but my counsels may direct you to the best and most salutary measures, and dispel the dangers now impending over the state. What then do I recommend? First, shake off that terror which hath possessed your minds; and, instead of fearing for yourselves, let the Thebans be the objects of your apprehensions: they are more immediately affected: they are the first to feel the dangers. In the next place, all those of the age for military service, both infantry and cavalry, should march instantly to Eleusis, that Greece may see

that you also are assembled in arms; and your friends
in Thebes be emboldened to assert their rights, when
they are assured, that as they, who have sold their
country to the Macedonians, have a force at Elatea to
support them, so you are ready to assist the men who
bravely contend for liberty. In the last place, I recommend to you to nominate ten ambassadors, who, with
the generals, may have full authority to determine the
time, and all other circumstances of this march. When
these ambassadors arrive at Thebes, how are they to
conduct this great affair? This is a point worthy of
your most serious attention. Make no demands on the
Thebans; at this conjuncture it would be dishonour-
able: assure them that your assistance is ready for their
acceptance, as you are deeply concerned for their danger, and have been so happy as to foresee and to guard
against it. If they approve of your sentiments, and
embrace your overtures, we shall effect one great purpose, and act with a dignity worthy of our state. But
should it happen that we are not so successful, whatever
misfortunes may befall them, to themselves alone they
shall be imputed; while your conduct shall appear, in
no one instance, inconsistent with the honour and renown of Athens."

This speech, dictated by the feelings of a patriotic
heart, and delivered with all that fire and vehemence
for which the orator was so remarkable, immediately
produced the desired effect. The Athenians determined
to follow the advice that had been now given them;
they appointed Demosthenes himself to head the embassy to be sent to Thebes; and they resolved to fit
out a fleet of two hundred sail, to cruise near to Thermopylæ.

Upon his arrival at Thebes, Demosthenes found himself opposed by one Python, a man of considerable
abilities, whom Philip had purposely sent thither to
counteract the designs of the Athenian orator. This,
however, he was not able to effect. The masculine
eloquence of Demosthenes carried all before it, and
inspired the Thebans with so strong a passion for liberty,
that they resolved to join their forces with those of the

Athenians, in preventing the further progress of the Macedonian arms.

Philip, disconcerted by the union of two such powerful states, sent ambassadors to the Athenians, requesting them to desist from their warlike preparations; but finding them determined to adhere to their engagements with Thebes, he endeavoured to intimidate both them and their allies with omens and predictions, which he took care to procure from the priestess of Apollo. Demosthenes, however, persuaded them to pay no regard to these ridiculous oracles. He told them, the priestess Philipized, thereby insinuating, that it was Philip's money that inspired her, and that opened her mouth, and made her draw from Apollo whatever answers she thought proper. He bade the Thebans remember their Epaminondas, and the Athenians their Pericles, who considered these oracles and predictions as idle scarecrows, and consulted only their reason. The Athenian army set out immediately, and marched to Eleusis; and the Thebans, surprised at the diligence of their confederates, joined them and waited the approach of the enemy.

Philip, conscious of his own abilities, and at the same time convinced of the extreme weakness of those who commanded the allied army, determined to bring on a general engagement as soon as possible; and with this view advanced into the plain of Chæronea, a place rendered famous by the event of this important contest. His army amounted to about thirty-two thousand men; that of the confederates did not exceed thirty thousand.

On the eve of the day on which this decisive battle was fought. Diogenes, the cynic, who had long looked with equal contempt on either party, was led by curiosity to visit the camps, as an unconcerned spectator. In the Macedonian camp, where his person and character were not known, he was stopped by the guards, and conducted to Philip's tent. The king asked him sternly whether he came as a spy: "Yes," said Diogenes, "I am come to spy upon your folly and ambition, in thus setting your life and kingdom to the hazard of an hour."

And now the fatal morning appeared which was for
ever to decide the cause of liberty and the empire of
Greece. Before the rising of the sun both armies were
ranged in order of battle. The Thebans, with the
sacred band in front, occupied the right wing of the
confederate Greeks; the Athenians, commanded by
Lysicles and Chares, formed the left; and the Corinthians and Peloponnesians were posted in the centre.
On the left of the Macedonian army stood Alexander,
at the head of a chosen body of noble Macedonians,
supported by the famous cavalry of Thessaly. In the
centre were placed those Greeks who had united with
Philip, and on whose courage he could least depend;
while the king himself commanded on the right, where
his renowned phalanx stood, to oppose the impetuosity
with which the Athenians were well known to begin
their onset.

The charge began on each side with all the courage
and violence which ambition, revenge, the love of glory,
and the love of liberty, could excite in the several
combatants. Alexander, at the head of the Macedonian
nobles, first fell, with all the fury of youthful courage,
on the sacred band of Thebes; which sustained the
attack with a bravery and vigour worthy its former
fame. The gallant youths who composed this body, not
being timely, or duly supported by their countrymen,
bore up for a while against the torrent of the enemy;
till at length, oppressed and overpowered by superior
numbers, without yielding or turning their backs on
their assailants, they sunk down on that ground where
they had been originally stationed, each by the side of
his darling friend, raising up a bulwark by their bodies
against the progress of the enemy. But the young
prince and his forces, in all the enthusiastic ardour of
valour, animated by success, pushed on through all the
carnage, and over all the heaps of slain, and fell furiously
on the main body of the Thebans, where they were
opposed with obstinate and deliberate courage, and the
contest was, for some time, supported with equal resolution on both sides.

In the meantime, the Athenians, on the left wing,

fought with a spirit and intrepidity worthy of the character which they boasted, and of the cause by which they were animated. Many gallant efforts were made by either party, and success was for some time doubtful; till at length part of the centre, and the right wing of the Macedonians (except the phalanx) yielded to the impetuous attack of the Athenians, and fled with some precipitation. Happy had it been that day for Greece, if the conduct and abilities of the Grecian generals had been equal to the valour of their soldiers! But those brave champions of liberty were led on by the despicable creatures of intrigue and cabal. Transported by the advantage now obtained, the presumptuous Lysicles cried out, "Come on, my gallant countrymen; the victory is ours; let us pursue these cowards, and drive them back to Macedon: and thus, instead of improving the happy opportunity, by charging the phalanx in flank, and so breaking this formidable body, the Athenians wildly and precipitately pressed forward, in pursuit of the flying enemy, themselves in all the tumult and disorder of a rout.

Philip saw this fatal error with all the contempt of a skilful general, and the secret exultation arising from the assurance of approaching victory. He coolly observed to those officers that stood round him, that the Athenians knew not how to conquer; and ordered his phalanx to change its position, and, by a sudden evolution, to gain possession of an adjacent eminence. From thence they marched deliberately down, firm and collected, and fell, with their united force, on the Athenians, now confident of success, and blind to their danger. The shock was irresistible; they were at once overwhelmed, many of them lay crushed by the weight of the enemy, and expiring of their wounds; while the rest escaped from the dreadful slaughter, by a shameful and precipitate flight; bearing down, and hurrying along with them, those troops which had been stationed for their support. And here it was, that the great orator and statesman, who had excited his countrymen to make this glorious struggle in defence of their liberty, tarnished all the honours he had acquired in the senate by his pusillanimity in the field. He took to flight the very first onset; and throwing away his shield, on which were inscribed these words, *To Good Fortune*, he appeared among the foremost in the general rout. The ridicule and malice of his enemies related, or perhaps invented, another shameful circumstance; that being impeded in his flight by some brambles, his imagination was so possessed by the presence of the enemy, that he loudly cried out for quarter.

While Philip was thus triumphant on his side, Alexander continued the conflict on the other wing, and at length broke the Thebans, in spite of all their acts of valour, who now fled from the field, and were pursued with great carnage. The centre of the confederates was thus totally abandoned to the fury of a victorious enemy. But enough of slaughter had already been made: more than one thousand of the Athenians lay dead on the field of battle, two thousand were made prisoners, and the loss of the Thebans was not inferior. Philip, therefore, determined to conclude his important victory by an act of apparent clemency, which his policy and ambition really dictated. He gave orders that the Greeks should be spared, carefully locking up in his own breast the design he had formed against their liberties, and hoping one day to march at their head to accomplish the conquest of the Persian monarchy.

Philip's behaviour, upon obtaining this victory, is differently represented by different historians. Some say, that he expressed his joy in so extravagant and even ludicrous a manner, as to extort from Demades, one of the Athenian prisoners, the following severe reprimand :—" Fortune," said that orator to him " has given you the part of Agamemnon, but you are acting that of Thersites." Justin, however, represents his conduct in a more amiable and engaging light. He says, that he was at great pains to dissemble his joy; that he affected extreme modesty, and the utmost compassion for the prisoners; that he was not even seen to laugh; that he would have no sacrifice, no crowns, no perfumes; that he forbade all kinds of sports; and did nothing that might make him appear to the conquerors to be elated, nor to the conquered to be insolent. Certain it is, that·

he immediately concluded a peace with the Athenians;
and though he treated the Thebans, as unfaithful allies,
with greater severity, yet, after compelling them to
pay a ransom for their prisoners, and a large sum of
money for leave to bury their dead, and after placing
a garrison in their citadel, he agreed to make a peace
with them also.

It is said that Isocrates, the celebrated rhetorician,
was so deeply affected when he heard of the loss of
Chæronea, that unable to survive the disgrace which
that event had brought upon his country, he hastened
his end by abstaining from all kind of food : he was then
in the ninety-eighth year of his age.

Lysicles, who had the chief command of the Athenians in this engagement, and by whose misconduct the
battle had been lost, was soon after summoned before
an assembly of the people, and was condemned to die
at the instance of Lycurgus, who had great credit and
influence in the city, but was a severe judge, and a
most bitter accuser. "You, Lysicles," said he, "were
general of the army; a thousand citizens were slain,
two thousand taken prisoners; a trophy has been
erected to the dishonour of this city, and all Greece
is enslaved. You had the command when all these
things happened; and yet you dare to live, and view
the light of the sun, and blush not to appear publicly
in the forum; you, Lysicles, who are born the monument of your country's shame." This Lycurgus, who
did not disgrace the name which he bore, was one of
the first orators of the age, and was still more remarkable for the integrity of his life than the force of his
eloquence. For, after having managed the public
treasure for the space of twelve years, he caused an
exact register of every thing he had done during his
whole administration to be fixed up on a pillar, that
every body might see it, and censure it if they pleased.
Nay, he carried this point so far, that, in his last illness,
he ordered himself to be carried to the senate-house,
to give a public account of all his actions ; and, after
having refuted one who accused him there, he went
home and died. Though naturally grave and even
austere in his temper, he was a great encourager of the

stage; and, as a proof of his regard for dramatic writers, he erected the statues of Æschylus, Sophocles, and Euripides.

Chares, who was probably as guilty as Lysicles, appears to have escaped merely through the insignificance of his character. Indeed, his abilities were so contemptible, that, according to Timotheus, "he was much fitter to carry the general's baggage, than to be a general himself."

Many people thought, that Demosthenes might, on account of his speeches, be considered as the real cause of the terrible blow which Athens had now sustained, and that upon him therefore would certainly fall the principal weight of the natural resentment. But in this they were disappointed. The Athenians were so fully convinced of his integrity and patriotism, that, at the very moment they were smarting under the wound they had just received, they submitted entirely to his counsels and direction. Indeed, he appears to have been highly deserving of all the confidence they reposed in him. For being appointed, at this time, to supply the city with provisions, and to repair the walls, he executed the latter commission with so much generosity, that as the public treasure was unequal to the expense, he made up the deficiency out of his own private fortune.

It was for this instance of public spirit, that his friend Ctesiphon proposed in an assembly of the people, that a crown of gold should be bestowed upon him; and this gave rise to the celebrated contest between Æschines and Demosthenes, one of the most remarkable that is to be found in history. Æschines, the declared rival of Demosthenes, not only in eloquence but in politics, brought an accusation against Ctesiphon for the proposal he had made in favour of his friend, who naturally defended the equity of the measure, in which he thought his own honour so essentially concerned.

No cause ever excited so much curiosity, or was pleaded with so much ability. People flocked to it from all parts, and they had good reason for so doing; for what sight could be nobler, than a conflict between

two orators, each of them excellent in his way, both
formed by nature, improved by art, and animated by
perpetual dissensions, and an implacable animosity
against each other. The juncture seemed to favour
Æschines very much; for the Macedonian party, whom
he always befriended, was very powerful in Athens,
especially since the ruin of Thebes. Nevertheless, he
lost his cause, and was justly sentenced to banishment
for his rash accusation. He thereupon went and settled
himself at Rhodes, where he opened a school of eloquence, the fame and glory of which continued for
many ages. He began his lectures with the two orations that had occasioned his banishment. Great encomiums were passed upon that of Æschines; but when
he repeated the speech of Demosthenes, the plaudits
and acclamations were redoubled. And it was then he
uttered these words, so highly praiseworthy in the
mouth of a rival: "Alas! what unbounded applauses
would you have bestowed on this speech, had you heard
Demosthenes deliver it himself."

Demosthenes, thus become victor, made a good use
of his conquest. For the instant Æschines left Athens,
in order to embark for Rhodes, Demosthenes ran after
him, and forced him to accept of a purse of money.
On this occasion, Æschines cried out, "How will it be
possible for me not to regret a country, in which I leave
an enemy more generous, than I can hope to find friends
in any other part of the world?"

In the meantime, Philip had his ambition pleased,
but not satisfied, with his last victory. The sovereignty
of Greece, even if he had acquired it, he always considered but as a secondary object, and only as the means
of preparing his way for the conquest of Persia, which
he had long planned in his mind, and hoped to be able
one day to accomplish. But this he knew he could not
do without the assistance of the Greeks, which, however, he thought he could the more easily procure for
such an undertaking, as they had long burned with an
ardent desire of revenging upon Persia the injuries
they had received from it, and of working the total
destruction of that empire. Philip, therefore, now

proposing to lead them to such a glorious gratification of their revenge, they readily chose him generalissimo of their forces; and he, accordingly, began to make preparations for invading the dominions of the Persian monarch.

But while Philip was thus successful in his public undertakings, the violent dissensions that reigned in his family destroyed all his private peace, and at last brought him to an untimely end. He had married Olympias, the daughter of the king of Epirus, and the early part of their union was crowned with happiness; but as she was naturally of a peevish and vindictive disposition, a coldness at first, and afterwards a rooted aversion took place between them. This was probably hastened by the passion which Philip had conceived for Cleopatra, niece to Attalus, one of his principal officers. In a word, his love to this lady, and his aversion to Olympias, grew at last so strong, that he resolved to espouse the former, after having divorced the latter. In vain did Alexander his son remonstrate, that by divorcing Olympias, and engaging in a second marriage, he exposed him to the danger of contending with a number of competitors for the crown, and rendered his succession precarious. " My son," said the king, " if I create you a number of competitors, you will have the glorious opportunity of exerting yourself to surpass them all in merit: thus shall their rivalship only render you more worthy of the throne."

His marriage with Cleopatra was now declared in form, and celebrated with all the pomp and magnificence which the occasion required. The young prince, however dissatisfied, was yet obliged to attend on these solemnities, and sat in silent indignation at that feast which proclaimed the disgrace of his mother. In such circumstances, his youthful and impetuous mind could not fail to take fire at any the least shadow of insult. Attalus, uncle to the new queen, was so unguarded as, in the midst of the entertainment, to call aloud upon the Macedonian nobles, to pour out their libations to the gods, that they might grant the king the happy fruits of the present nuptials, and legitimate heirs to his throne. "Wretch!" cried Alexander, with his eyes sparkling with that indignation which he had till now suppressed, "dost thou then call me bastard?" And instantly darted his goblet at Attalus, who returned the outrage with double violence. Clamour and confusion arose, and the king, in a sudden fit of rage, snatched his sword, and flew directly towards his son. His precipitation, his lameness, (for he had been wounded in the battle with the Triballi) and the quantity of wine in which he had indulged, happily disappointed his rash purpose: he stumbled and fell on the floor, while Alexander, with an unpardonable insolence, cried out, "Behold, ye Macedonians! this is the king who is preparing to lead you into Asia; see, where, in passing from one table to another, he is fallen to the ground."

Philip, however, did not lose sight of the conquest of Asia. Full of the mighty project, he consulted the gods, to know what would be the event of it; and the priestess replied, "The victim is already crowned, his end draws nigh, and he will soon be sacrificed." Philip interpreted this oracle in his own favour; though the ambiguity of it might have made him suspect its meaning, and that it was as applicable to some other event as to the conquest of Asia. The fact is, it soon after appeared that it was more applicable to himself than to the Persian monarch. For while he was celebrating the nuptials of his daughter Cleopatra with Alexander, king of Epirus, and brother to his queen Olympias, he was suddenly stabbed in the height of the solemnity, and in the midst of his guards, by one Pausanias, a noble Macedonian, whom Attalus, his favourite general, had cruelly abused; and who having repeatedly demanded reparation of the king in vain, at last turned the edge of his resentment from the author of his wrong to his sovereign himself, and took this dreadful method of satiating his revenge.

Olympias is supposed to have instigated Pausanias to this desperate act. Certain it is, that when his dead body (for he was instantly despatched by the guards) was hung up on a gibbet, it appeared next morning crowned with a golden diadem; a mark of respect, which no one could have ventured to show to it but Olympias. In a few days after she took a further occasion of publishing her triumph and exultation in her husband's fall, by paying the same funeral honours to Pausanias, that were paid to Philip: both bodies were burned on the same pile, and the ashes of both deposited in the same tomb. She is even said to have prevailed on the Macedonians to pay annual honours to Pausanias; as if she feared, that the share which he had in the death of Philip should not be known to the whole world. She consecrated to Apollo the dagger which had been the instrument of the fatal deed, inscribed with the name of Myrtalis, the name which she bore when their loves first began.

Thus died Philip, a prince possessed of great abilities both in peace and war, but much fonder of gaining his ends by dexterity and address than by force of arms. The news of his death was a joyful surprise in Greece, and particularly at Athens, where the people crowned themselves with garlands, and decreed a crown to Pausanias. They sacrificed to the gods for their deliverance, and sung songs of triumph, as if Philip had been slain by them in battle. But this excess of joy very ill became them, because it was altogether inconsistent with their late behaviour to that prince; for when he was chosen generalissimo of the Greeks, and still more when he celebrated the nuptials of his daughter, the Athenians were the most forward and the most fulsome in their compliments to him, and carried their adulation so far, as almost to exalt him to the rank of a god.

CHAPTER XIII.

FROM THE BIRTH OF ALEXANDER TO HIS SETTING OUT FOR ASIA.

ALEXANDER, the son of Philip, ascended the throne upon the death of his father, and took possession of a kingdom rendered flourishing and powerful by the policy of the preceding reign.

He came into the world the very day the celebrated temple of Diana at Ephesus was burnt, which gave occasion to Hegesias the historian to say, " that it was no wonder the temple was burnt, as Diana was that day employed at the delivery of Olympias, to facilitate the birth of Alexander."

The passion, by which Alexander was most powerfully actuated, even in his tender years, was ambition, and a love of glory, but not of every kind of glory. Philip, like a sophist, valued himself upon his eloquence, and the beauty of his style ; and had the vanity to have engraved, on his coins, the several victories he had won in the chariot-race at the Olympic games. But it was not after such empty honours that his son aspired. When his friends one day asked him, Whether he would contend at these games? "Yes," said he, " I readily will, provided I may have kings to contend with me."

Every time news was brought him that his father had taken some city, or gained some great battle, Alexander, so far from sharing in the general joy, used to say, in a plaintive tone of voice, to the young persons that were brought up with him, "Friends, my father will possess himself of every thing, and leave nothing for me to do."

Some ambassadors from the king of Persia having one day arrived at court in his father's absence, and Alexander being obliged to entertain them, he not only charmed them with the politeness of his behaviour, but he filled them with astonishment at his good common sense and the sagacity of his remarks. For, instead of asking them questions about such trifling circumstances as are commonly the objects of curiosity to people of his years; such as the so much boasted gardens suspended in the air ; the riches and magnificence of the palace and court of the king of Persia, which excited the admiration of the whole world ; the famous golden plantain-tree; and that golden vine, the grapes of which were emeralds, carbuncles, rubies, and all sorts of precious stones, under which the Persian monarch was said frequently to give audience—instead,

I say, of asking such frivolous questions as these, Alexander inquired, Which was the road to Upper Asia? what was the distance of the several places? in what the real strength of the king of Persia consisted? in what part of the battle he fought? how he behaved towards his enemies? and in what manner he governed his subjects? The ambassadors, surprised to see him discover a sagacity so greatly beyond his years, could not help exclaiming, "This young prince is great, and ours is rich; that man must be extremely insignificant who has no other merit than his riches!"

So ripe a judgment in this young prince was as much owing to the good education which had been given him, as to the strength of his natural parts. Several preceptors, as we have already observed, were employed to teach him music and other superficial accomplishments; but the tutor, from whom he received all his real and useful knowledge, was Aristotle, the most famous and most learned philosopher of the age: it was he that was entrusted with the chief care of Alexander's education. One of the reasons which prompted Philip to give him a master of so much eminence and merit, was, as he himself tells us, that his son might avoid committing a great many faults, of which he himself had been guilty.

Philip was sufficiently sensible of Aristotle's merit, and he rewarded it with the liberality and munificence of a prince. He not only settled a genteel salary upon him, but he afterwards expressed his regard for him in a more public and conspicuous manner; for having formerly stormed and sacked Stagira, the native city of Aristotle, he now rebuilt it, and reinstated the inhabitants who had fled from it, or were made slaves; giving them besides a fine park in the neighbourhood, as a place for their studies and exercises. Plutarch tells us, that, even in his time, the people of Stagira showed the stone-seats of Aristotle, as also the shady walks which he used to frequent.

Alexander likewise discovered no less esteem for his master, whom he believed himself bound to love as much as if he had been his father; declaring, that he was indebted to the one for living, and to the other for living well. The progress of the pupil was equal to the care and abilities of the preceptor. He grew extremely fond of philosophy, and learned the several parts of it. But his favourite study was morality, which is properly the science of kings, because it is the knowledge of mankind, and of their duties. To this he applied himself with unwearied attention, and considered it, even at that time, as the foundation of prudence and wise policy.

Nor was Aristotle less careful to instruct him in the art of speaking, than in that of thinking and reasoning; and for this purpose he wrote his celebrated treatise on rhetoric, in the beginning of which he proves the vast advantages a prince may derive from eloquence, as it gives him the greatest ascendant over the minds of men, which he ought to acquire, as well by his wisdom as authority. Some answers and letters of Alexander, which are still extant, show that he possessed, in its greatest perfection, that strong, that manly eloquence, which abounds with sense and ideas, and which is so entirely free from superfluous expressions, that every single word has its meaning, which, properly speaking, is the eloquence of kings.

His esteem, or rather his veneration, for Homer is well known. When a golden box, enriched with precious stones, was found in the Persian camp after the battle of Arbela, and it was deliberated to what purpose it should be applied, Alexander said, that there was nothing so worthy of being put into it as Homer's Poems, which he believed to be the most perfect, and most complete production of the human mind. He admired particularly the Iliad, which he considered as a treasure of military knowledge. He always had with him that copy of it which had been revised and corrected by Aristotle, and to which he gave the name of the casket-copy; and he laid it with his sword every night under his pillow.

Fond, even to excess, of every kind of glory, he was displeased with Aristotle, his master, for having published, in his absence, certain metaphysical pieces which, he himself desired to possess exclusively of all others; and even at the time when he was employed in the conquest of Asia, and the pursuit of Darius, he wrote him a letter, which is still extant, wherein he complains upon that very account. Alexander says in it, that he had much rather surpass others in the knowledge of the sublimer sciences, than in the greatness of his power or the extent of his dominion.

He had also a taste for the whole circle of the arts, but in such a manner as became a prince; that is, he knew the value and utility of them. Music, painting, sculpture, architecture, flourished in his reign; because they found him both a judge and a generous protector, who was able to distinguish and to reward merit. But he despised certain trifling feats of dexterity, that were of no use. One day some Macedonians expressing their surprise at the ingenuity of a man, that excelled in throwing small peas through the eye of a needle, Alexander said, that he would make him a present suitable to his employment, and he accordingly sent him a basket of peas.

The first instance Alexander gave of his bold and daring spirit, was in his management of the famous horse Bucephalus, which had been brought to his father's court by Philonicus, the Thessalian, who refused to sell him for less than thirteen talents. The king went into the plains, attended by his courtiers, in order to make a trial of this horse; but they found him so very wild and unmanageable, that no one would venture to mount him. Philip, being angry that so furious and ungovernable a creature had been brought to him, gave orders for their carrying him back again. Alexander, who was present at this time, cried out, "What a noble horse we are going to lose, for want of address and boldness to back him!" Philip at first considered these words as the effect of folly and rashness, so common to young men; but as Alexander still insisted upon what he had said, and was very uneasy to see so noble a creature just going to be sent home again, his father at last gave him leave to try what he could do. The young prince, overjoyed at this per-

mission, goes up to Bucephalus, takes hold of the bridle,
and turns his head to the sun, having observed that
the thing which frightened him was his own shadow.
Alexander, therefore, first stroked him gently with his
hand, and soothed him with his voice; then seeing his
fierceness abate, he softly let fall his cloak, and spring-
ing upon his back at one leap, he first slightly tightened
the reign, without striking or vexing him; and when
he perceived that his fire was cooled, that he was no
longer so furious and violent, and that he wanted only
to move forward, he gave him the rein, and spurring
him with great vigour, animated him with his voice to
his full speed.   While this was doing, Philip and his
whole court trembled for fear, and did not once open
their lips: but when the prince, after having run his
first heat, returned with pride and triumph, at having
thus broke a horse that was deemed absolutely ungovernable, the courtiers in general burst out into acclamations of applause, while Philip, with tears of joy in
his eyes, embraced Alexander as he alighted, and said,
"My son, seek a kingdom more worthy of thee, for
Macedon is below thy merit."

Alexander, upon his accession to the throne, saw
himself surrounded with danger on every side; not
only from the barbarous nations, with whom Philip
had contended during his whole reign, and who were
impatient of the yoke he had imposed upon them; but
likewise from the Greeks themselves, who resolved to
lay hold of this opportunity to recover their liberties,
of which Philip had deprived them in reality, though
not in appearance.   The danger, indeed, from both
these quarters, was so great and so imminent, that the
more prudent among the Macedonians advised their
sovereign to ward them off by policy and address, rather
than repel them by force of arms.   But these timorous
counsels were by no means agreeable to the bold and
enterprising spirit of Alexander.   He plainly saw, that
if his enemies perceived him betraying the least symp-
tom of fear, they would be all upon him at once, would
strip him of his father's conquests, and reduce his dominions to the narrow limits of Macedon.

He therefore marched first against the barbarians; and crossing the Danube in one night, he defeated the king of the Triballi in a great battle, and struck such terror into the neighbouring nations, as obliged them for the present to remain quiet. Returning thence in a little time, he turned his arms against the Greeks, and particularly the Thebans, who, upon a false report of his death, had cut to pieces a great number of the Macedonian garrison in their citadel. To this they were chiefly instigated by the harangues of Demosthenes, who is likewise said to have invented the report of Alexander's death; and in so doing, seems not to have acted with his usual prudence: for the falsity of this report could not be long concealed, and when it was discovered, it must not only have defeated the end it was intended to serve, but must have rendered the veracity of the reporter for ever after suspicious. Alexander, however, soon convinced them that he was neither dead, nor even indisposed; for his arrival in Greece was so sudden and so unexpected, that the Thebans could scarce believe their own eyes when they saw him. Being come before their walls, he was willing to allow them time to repent; and only demanded to have Phoenix and Prothules, the two chief ringleaders of the revolt, delivered up to him; and published by sound of trumpet, a general pardon to all who should come over to him. But the Thebans, by way of insult, demanded to have Philotas and Antipater delivered to them; and invited, by proclamation, all who were solicitous for the liberty of Greece to join them in its defence.

Alexander finding it impossible to prevail upon them by gentle means, was obliged to employ more powerful arguments, and to decide the matter by force of arms. A great battle was accordingly fought, in which the Thebans behaved with a spirit and intrepidity much beyond their strength, for the enemy exceeded them vastly in numbers. But after a long and obstinate dispute, the Macedonian garrison coming down from the citadel, and attacking them in the rear, the Thebans were surrounded on all sides, the greatest part of them were cut in pieces, and the city was taken and plundered.

The calamities which they suffered on this occasion, may be more easily conceived than expressed. Some Thracians having pulled down the house of a virtuous lady of quality, Timoclea by name, carried off all her goods and treasures; and their captain having forcibly violated her chastity, inquired of her afterwards, whether she had not concealed gold and silver. Timoclea, animated by an ardent desire of revenge, said, that she had hid some; and taking him with her alone into the garden, and showing him a well, told him, that there lay her concealed treasure. The barbarian stooping down to look into the well, Timoclea, who was behind him, pushed him forward with all her might, threw him in, and afterwards killed him with great stones, which she heaped upon him. She was instantly seized by the Thracians, and being put in chains, was carried before Alexander. The prince immediately perceived by her mien, that she was a woman of quality and of a lofty spirit; for she followed those brutal wretches with an undaunted air, and without discovering the least sign of fear. Alexander asking her who she was, Timoclea replied, "I am sister to Theagenes, who fought against Philip for the liberty of Greece, and was killed in the battle of Chæronea, where he commanded." The prince, admiring her magnanimous answer, and the punishment she had inflicted on her cruel ravisher, gave orders that she should have leave to retire wherever she pleased with her children.

Alexander considered for some time with himself how he should act with regard to Thebes. His own resentment carried him to the most violent measures; and this was still farther inflamed by the representation of the Phocians, and the people of Platæa, Thespiæ, and Orchomenus, who were all of them mortal enemies to the Thebans. Transported therefore by his own furious passions, and still further instigated by their cruel advice, he unhappily adopted the most severe resolution, and the city was instantly razed to the ground. But he did not wreak his vengeance upon all the inhabitants indiscriminately. He set the priests at liberty; as also all such as had a right of hospitality with the Macedonians; the descendants of Pindar, the famous poet, who had done so much honour to Greece; and such likewise as had opposed the revolt. But all the rest, in number about thirty thousand, he sold; and upwards of six thousand had been killed in battle. The Athenians were so deeply affected on hearing of the sad catastrophe of Thebes, that they put off the celebration of the Great Mysteries, which they were about to solemnize; and they received, with the greatest humanity, all those who had escaped from the battle, and the sacking of Thebes, and made Athens their asylum.

The Athenians had not only encouraged the Thebans to set Alexander at defiance; they had even formed a league with them and the Lacedæmonians to check the progress of his arms: but his sudden arrival in Greece, and the example he had now given of the dreadful consequences of incurring his displeasure, made them begin to abate considerably of their wonted pride; and, instead of presuming to oppose his power, they judged it, for the present, the most eligible course to implore his clemency. They therefore sent a deputation to him, in which Demosthenes was included; but he had no sooner arrived at Mount Cytheron, than dreading the anger of the Macedonian prince, he quitted the embassy, and returned home.

Alexander well knew that it was the orators chiefly that kept alive the love of liberty, and the spirit of independence among the people of Athens, and consequently formed the greatest obstacle to the completion of his designs. He therefore now demanded that ten of these orators should be put into his hands. It was on this occasion, that Demosthenes related to the people the fable of the Wolves and the Dogs; in which it is supposed, that the wolves one day told the sheep, that in case they desired to be at peace with them, they must deliver up to them the dogs who were their guard. The application was easy and natural; especially with respect to the orators, who were justly compared to dogs, whose duty it is to watch, to bark, and to fight, in order to save the lives of their flock.

In this afflicting dilemma of the Athenians, who could not think of delivering up their orators to what they considered as certain death, though they had no other way to save their city, Demades, whom Alexander had honoured with his friendship, offered to undertake the embassy alone, and intercede for them. He did so, and succeeded; whether it was, that the king had already satiated his revenge, and that he was willing, by some act of clemency, to wipe out the remembrance of the cruelties he had lately committed, or perhaps was desirous of conciliating the affections of the Greeks in general, before he set out on his Asiatic expedition; certain it is, that he waved his demand with regard to the delivery of the Athenian orators, and was pacified by their sending into banishment Caridemus, who, being a native of Orsea, had been presented by the Athenians with the freedom of the city.

As for the Athenians themselves, he not only forgave them the several injuries he pretended to have received from them, but he even flattered their pride, by advising them to give particular attention to public affairs, because, in case of his death, he said, they were likely to give law to the rest of Greece. Historians relate, that many years after this expedition, he was seized with remorse for the cruel punishment he had inflicted on the Thebans; and that this softened his temper, and made him behave with greater humanity towards other nations.

Being now freed from all apprehensions of any further opposition from Greece, he summoned at Corinth an assembly of the several states and free cities of that country, in order to obtain from them the supreme command against the Persians, which had been granted to his father a little before his death. No assembly ever deliberated upon a more important subject. It was the western world deciding upon the fate of the east; and concerting methods for executing a revenge, which had been suspended for more than an age. The assembly held at this time, gave rise to events, the relation of which appears astonishing, and almost incredible; and to revolutions, which contributed to change the disposition of most things in the political world.

To accomplish such a scheme, required a prince of Alexander's bold and enterprising spirit, and a people like the Greeks, brave, hardy, and active, animated by a love of military glory, and inspired with an implacable resentment against the nation they were going to attack. The Greeks, indeed, had long wished for an opportunity to revenge upon Persia the injuries they had sustained from that empire; and they now therefore accepted with pleasure the offer of Alexander to lead them against their old and irreconcilable enemies, whose destruction they had repeatedly sworn, and whom they hoped in a little time to be able to extirpate. The Lacedæmonians were the only people that made any objections to this proposal. They said, "they had always been accustomed to point out the way to glorious deeds, and not to be directed by others." But they were obliged to submit to the prevailing sense of the assembly; and Alexander was, of course, appointed generalissimo against the Persians.

He was no sooner raised to this high rank, than he received congratulations from the philosophers, the governors of cities, and other great men; and he expected the same compliment from Diogenes of Synope, who was then at Corinth. But as Diogenes did not think proper to come to him, he went attended by his whole court, to visit that philosopher. He found him lying on the ground, and basking himself in the sun; and being surprised to see a man of so much reputation living in such extreme poverty, he naturally asked him, whether he wanted any thing? "Only," said Diogenes, "that you would stand from between me and the sun." This answer excited the contempt of all the courtiers; but the king was so struck with the philosopher's greatness of soul, that he could not help exclaiming, "Were I not Alexander, I would be Diogenes."

Before he set out for Asia, he resolved to consult the oracle of Apollo. He therefore went to Delphos, where he happened to arrive in those days which are called unlucky, that is, at a time when it was unlawful to give responses; and accordingly the priestess refused to go to the temple. But Alexander, who could not bear any contradiction to his will, took her forcibly by the arm, and as he was leading her to the temple, she cried out, "My son, thou art invincible!" Alexander, catching hold of these words as the answer of the oracle, declared that it was needless to consult the god any further, and he therefore returned to Macedon, in order to prepare for his great expedition.

Some of his friends advised him, before he embarked in this undertaking, to make choice of a consort, in order to secure himself a successor to his throne. But the king, who was of an impetuous temper, disapproved of this advice, and said, that after he had been nominated generalissimo of the Greeks, and that his father had left him so gallant an army, it would be a shame for him to lose time in celebrating his marriage, and waiting for the fruits of it; and that therefore he was determined to set out immediately.

Before he did so, however, he thought proper to settle the affairs of Macedon. He appointed Antipater to be viceroy of that kingdom, with an army of twelve thousand foot, and near the same number of horse. He then inquired into the private circumstances of his friends, giving to one an estate in land, to another a village, to a third the revenues of a town, and to a fourth the toll of an harbour. As all the revenues of his crown were already employed, or exhausted by his donations, Perdiccas said to him, "My lord, what is it you reserve for yourself?" Alexander replied, "Hope:" upon which Perdiccas said, "The same hope ought therefore to satisfy us;" and so refused very generously to accept of what the king had allotted him.

CHAPTER XIV.

FROM ALEXANDER'S ARRIVAL IN ASIA TO HIS DEATH.

ALEXANDER having taken the necessary precautions for securing the tranquillity of Macedon in his absence, set out for Asia in the beginning of the spring. His army consisted of little more than thirty thousand foot, and four or five thousand horse; but then they were all brave men, well disciplined, and enured to fatigue. They had made several campaigns under Philip, and were each of them, in case of necessity, capable of commanding: most of the officers were near threescore years of age, and the common men fifty; and when they were either assembled, or drawn up at the head of a camp, they had the appearance of a venerable senate. Parmenio commanded the infantry; Philotas, his son, had eighteen hundred horse under him; and Callas, the son of Harpalus, the same number of Thessalian cavalry. The rest of the horse, consisting of natives of the several states, were under the direction of a separate commander. And the Thracians and Phœonians, who were always in front, were headed by Cassandra. Such was the army, which was to decide the fortune, not only of Greece, but of all the eastern world. Alexander began his march along the lake Cercinum; and after passing the rivers Strymon and Hebrus, he came to the shore of the Hellespont, which he crossed in a hundred and sixty galleys, and several flat-bottomed vessels, himself steering his own galley; and upon his arrival at the opposite coast, as if to take possession of the continent, he leaped from his ship in complete armour, and expressed the greatest transports of joy.

It has frequently been thought strange, that the Persians took no step to check the progress of the Macedonians at the Hellespont, where they might certainly have been opposed with the greatest ease: especially as the former were possessed of a large and powerful fleet, and that of the latter was very-inconsiderable. Whether this proceeded from supineness and inattention, or from a contempt of the enemy, it is difficult to determine. Whatever was the cause, the event proved equally fatal to the Persians.

Alexander being arrived at Lampsacus, was going to destroy it, in order to punish the rebellion of the inhabitants; and Anaximenes, therefore, a native of the place, came to him with a view of diverting him from his cruel resolution. This man, who was a famous historian, had been very intimate with Philip his father ; and Alexander himself had a great esteem for him, having been his pupil. The king suspecting the purport of his errand, and willing to be beforehand with him, swore, that he would never grant his request. " The favour I have to desire of you," says Anaximenes, " is, that you would destroy Lampsacus." By this witty evasion, the historian saved his country.

From thence Alexander went to Troy, where he paid great honours to the memory of the heroes who had fallen there, and particularly to that of Achilles, at whose tomb he caused funeral games to be performed. He declared that he looked upon Achilles as one of the happiest of men, in having had, during his life, so faithful a friend as Patroclus, and, after his death, so famous a poet as Homer, to celebrate his actions.

When Darius was informed of Alexander's arrival in Asia, he expressed the utmost contempt for the Macedonian army, and indignation at the presumption of their general. He wrote letters to the governors of his different provinces, commanding them, if they took Alexander alive, to whip him with rods, to make prisoners of his whole army, and to send them as slaves to one of the remotest and most desert parts of his dominions. It was not long, however, before he had reason to entertain more just and more modest sentiments. Alexander being arrived on the banks of the Granicus; a river of Phrygia, found the Persians, to the number of a hundred and ten thousand men, drawn up on the other side, and ready to dispute his passage. Memnon, who commanded all the seacoast of Asia under Darius, gave it as his opinion, that the wisest course would be to lay waste the adjacent country, and thus to oblige the Macedonian army either to retreat, or to surrender at discretion for want of provisions. But this prudent advice was overruled by Arsites, a Phrygian satrap, who said, that he would never suffer the Grecians to make such havock in the territories he governed.

Nor was Alexander, on his side, without those who advised him to proceed with caution, and to refrain from crossing the river the same day on which he reached it. This, in particular, was the opinion of Parmenio, a brave and experienced officer, who observed; that the troops were already too much fatigued with their march, to be equal to the additional labour of crossing a river, especially one which was so deep, and whose banks were so craggy, and that too in the face of such an immense body of the enemy, who were perfectly fresh, and were ready to oppose him. But these arguments made no impression on Alexander, who declared, that it would be a shame for him, after crossing the Hellespont, to suffer his progress to be interrupted by a rivulet, for so he called the Granicus by way of contempt; that, on the contrary, they ought to take advantage of the terror which the suddenness of his arrival, and the boldness of his attempt had spread among the Persians, and answer the high opinion the world had conceived of his courage, and the valour of the Macedonians.

The two armies, however, continued for some time on the opposite banks of the river, the one looking out for a proper place to ford it, and the other narrowly watching their motions, and determined, if possible, to prevent their passage. At last, Alexander ordered his horse to be brought; and commanding the noblemen of his court to follow him, and behave gallantly, he caused a strong detachment to march into the river, himself following it with the right wing of his army, as Parmenio did with the left. The Persians, seeing the detachment advance, began to let fly their arrows, and march to a place where the bank was not so steep, in order to keep the Macedonians from landing. But now the horse engaged with great fury, one part endeavouring to land, and the other striving to prevent them. The Macedonians, whose cavalry were vastly inferior in number, besides the disadvantage of the ground, were overwhelmed with the showers of darts that were poured from the eminence; not to mention that the flower of the Persian horse were drawn together here, and were headed by Memnon, the ablest and most resolute of all the Persian generals. The Macedonians, therefore, at last gave way, after having performed many signal acts of valour. But Alexander coming up, restored the battle; he reinforced them with his best troops; he headed them himself; he animated them by his presence; he pushed the Persians, and at last routed them; upon which the whole army followed after, crossed the river, and attacked the enemy on all sides.

Alexander first charged the thickest part of the enemy's horse, in which the generals fought. He himself was particularly conspicuous by his shield, and the plume of feathers that overshadowed his helmet, so that he was easily distinguished from the rest of the army. The charge, therefore, was very furious about his person; and though only the horse engaged, they fought like foot, man to man, without giving way on either side. Spithridates, lieutenant-governor of Ionia, and son-in-law to Darius, distinguished himself above the rest of the generals by his superior bravery. Surrounded by forty Persian lords, all of them his relations, of experienced valour, and who never moved from his side, he carried terror wherever he came. Alexander observing in how gallant a manner he signalized himself, clapt spurs to his horse and advanced towards him. Immediately they engaged, and each having thrown a javelin, wounded the other slightly. Spithridates falls furiously sword in hand upon Alexander, who, being prepared for him, thrusts his pike into his face, and laid him dead at his feet. At that very moment, Rhœsaces, brother to that nobleman, charging him on the side, gave him a furious blow on the head with his battle axe, which beat off his plume, but went no deeper than his hair. As he was going to repeat the blow on his head, which now appeared through the broken helmet, Clytus cut off Rhœsaces's hand with one stroke of his scymitar, and by that means saved his sovereign's life. The danger to which Alexander had exposed himself, added fresh courage to his soldiers, who now performed prodigies of valour. The Persians therefore, unable any longer to sustain the assault of the Macedonians, immediately gave way, and were put to a total rout.

Alexander did not pursue them far, but, wheeling about suddenly, began in an instant to make an attack upon the foot.

The contest here was neither long nor violent; for the enemy seeing the Macedonian phalanx, which had now crossed the river, and was regularly formed, advancing against them, they immediately took to flight, all but the Grecian infantry in Darius's pay. This body of foot, retiring to a hill, demanded permission to march away unmolested; but Alexander, guided by passion rather than reason, rushed furiously into the midst of them, and had his horse killed under him by the thrust of a sword. The battle here for some time was so hot that more of the Macedonians fell in this encounter than in the preceding action; for they fought against a body of men, who were well disciplined, had been inured to war, and were actuated by despair. They were all cut to pieces, two thousand excepted, who were taken prisoners.

A great number of the Persian commanders lay dead on the spot. Arsites fled into Phrygia, where he is said to have laid violent hands on himself, for having advised his countrymen to come to an immediate engagement. In this action, twenty thousand foot, and two thousand five hundred horse were killed on the side of the barbarians; and of the Macedonians twenty-five of the royal horse were killed in the first attack. Alexander ordered Lysippus to make their statues of brass, all of which were set up in the city of Macedon, called Dia, from whence they were many years after carried to Rome by Metellus. About threescore of the other horse were killed, and near thirty foot, who, the next day, were all laid with their arms and equipage in one grave; and the king granted an exemption to their fathers and children from every kind of tribute and service.

He also took the utmost care of the wounded, visited them, and saw their wounds dressed. He inquired very particularly into their adventures, and permitted every one of them to relate his actions in the battle, and boast of his bravery. He also granted the rites of sepulture

to the principal Persians, and did not even refuse it to
such Greeks as died in the Persian service; but all
those whom he took prisoners, he put in chains, and
sent to work as slaves in Macedonia, for having fought
under the barbarian standard against their country,
contrary to the express prohibition made by Greece
on that head.

Alexander thought it his duty, and made it his pleasure, to share the honour of his victory with the Greeks.
He sent to the Athenians three hundred shields, being
part of the plunder taken from the enemy, and caused
this glorious inscription to be put upon the rest of the
spoils: "Alexander, son of Philip, with the Greeks
(the Lacedæmonians excepted), gained these spoils from
the barbarians who inhabit Asia." The greatest part of
the gold and silver plate, the purple carpets, and other
articles of Persian luxury, he sent to his mother.

The terrible defeat, which the Persians had now sustained, struck such a terror into their minds, that they
could not be brought, for a long time, to oppose Alexander in the field; and he therefore proceeded, without
interruption, to make himself master of one town after
another; some, indeed, with more, and others with less
difficulty. Sardis and Ephesus he easily reduced. The
inhabitants of the former he took under his protection,
and permitted them to be governed by their own laws;
observing to his friends, at the same time, that such as
lay the foundation of a new empire should always endeavour to have the fame of being merciful. At Ephesus
he assigned to the temple of Diana the tributes which
had been paid to the Persian kings.

He next laid siege to Miletus, and afterwards to
Halicarnassus, both of which he compelled to surrender, though not till after a sharp and obstinate resistance, as both of them were defended by Memnon, the
bravest and most experienced of all Darius's generals.
The Milesians he treated with great humanity, but
Halicarnassus he thought proper to raze to the ground.
Soon after this he restored Ada, queen of Caria, to her
kingdom, of which she had been lately dispossessed;
and she, in order to testify her gratitude, sent him

meats dressed in the most exquisite manner, and the
most excellent cooks of every kind. Alexander thanked
her for her politeness, but at the same time told her,
that he had much better cooks of his own, whom his
governor Leonidas had given him, one of whom prepared him a good dinner, and the other an excellent
supper; and these were témperance and exercise.

Advancing still further into the country, he received
the voluntary submission of several of the kings of
Lesser Asia, and, among others, that of Mithridates,
king of Pontus, who afterwards adhered to him with
unshaken fidelity, and accompanied him in his expedition. This man was the predecessor of the famous
Mithridates, who so long employed the armies of
Rome, and makes so capital a figure in the history
of that republic.

 - Next year Alexander resolved to open the campaign
very early. But, previous to his beginning his operations, he held a consultation with his principal officers,
whether he should march directly in quest of Darius,
or first subdue the other maritime provinces. The
latter opinion appeared the most prudent, as by that
means he would be freed from all apprehensions of
being molested in his rear, and would leave every
thing quiet and secure behind him. Proceeding therefore through a narrow defile near the seashore, where
the water was so high that his men were up to the
middle in passing it, he advanced to Cœlenœ, a city of
Phrygia, situated on the banks of the river Marsyas,
which the fictions of the poets have rendered so famous.
This place he immediately invested. The garrison at
first made some show of resistance, but, finding themselves unable to withstand the vigorous and repeated
assaults of the Grecians, they promised to surrender at
the end of sixty days, provided they were not relieved
within that period; and as no aid arrived within the
stipulated time, the place was delivered up according
to agreement.

From thence Alexander marched to Gordium, the
supposed residence of the celebrated king Midas. Here
he was desirous of seeing the famous chariot to which

the Gordian knot was tied. This knot, which fastened
the yoke to the beam, was tied with so much intricacy
that it was impossible to discover where the involutions
began, or where the cords terminated.· According to
an ancient tradition of the country, an oracle had declared, that the man who could untie it should possess
the empire of Asia. Alexander being firmly persuaded
that the oracle was meant for him, after many fruitless
trials, instead of attempting to untie it in the usual
manner, drew his sword and cut it in pieces, crying
out, that that was the only way to untie. The priest
hailed the omen, and declared that Alexander had fulfilled the oracle.

In the mean time Darius, who now began to be seriously alarmed for the safety of his empire, resolved to
raise an army that might enable him to stop the further
progress of the enemy. Alexander, however, still continued to advance; and having subdued Paphlagonia
and Cappadocia, he passed the straits of Cilicia, where
he might easily have been opposed by a handful of
men; but the enemy abandoned them as soon as he
approached. From thence he marched his whole army
to the city of Tarsus, where he arrived just in time to
save it from destruction, as the Persians had set fire to
it, to prevent his becoming master of the treasures it
contained. And here he gave an instance of that magnanimity and elevation of mind which formed so distinguished a part of his character. For having thrown
himself into the river Cydnus, which runs through this
city, in order to bathe, he was instantly seized with
such a violent shivering, as seemed likely in a little
time to put an end to his life. At first all his physicians
were afraid to administer the necessary medicines,
knowing they must be answerable for the consequences
that ensued. But at last one of them, whose name was
Philip, who had always attended upon Alexander from
his youth, and loved him with the utmost tenderness,
not only as his sovereign but his child, raising himself
above all prudential considerations, and being more
concerned for the life of his prince than his own safety,
offered to give him a dose, which, though violent,

would be speedy in its effects, and desired three days to prepare it. At this proposal every one trembled, except Alexander himself, who was afflicted on no other account, than because it would keep him so long from appearing at the head of his army.

In the mean time he received a letter from Parmenio, who had been left behind in Cappadocia, advising him to beware of Philip, his physician; for that Darius had bribed him by the promise, of a thousand talents, and his sister in marriage. This letter at first gave him some uneasiness, as he could not believe that Parmenio had wrote it without having received some such intelligence. But confidence in a physician, whose unshaken fidelity and attachment he had experienced from his youth, at last removed all suspicion. He therefore put the letter under his bolster without acquainting any one with the contents; and when Philip entered with the medicine, he readily took it from him, and holding the letter in one hand and the cup in the other, he delivered the former to Philip, while he himself drank off the draught without discovering the least sign of fear. This was a very singular and affecting scene; Alexander looking at Philip with all the marks of the most perfect confidence and assurance, while Philip, in perusing the letter, seemed astonished at the accusation, and called upon the gods to witness his innocence; sometimes lifting up his hands to heaven, and then throwing himself down by the bedside, and beseeching Alexander to lay aside all suspicion, and rely on his fidelity. At first the medicine worked so violently, and brought Alexander so low, as seemed to favour Parmenio's accusation; but at length it produced the desired effect, and the king in a few days recovered his wonted vigour.

Meanwhile Darius was advancing against him at the head of an immense army, of which, however, he did not know how to avail himself; for, instead of remaining in the open country, where he might have extended his forces, and surrounded the enemy, he foolishly marched into the narrow passes, where his great superiority of numbers could be of very little service. The

reason he assigned for taking this precipitate step was
that he was afraid Alexander would escape him.   But
this was a needless fear. Alexander was as desirous of
meeting him, as he was of meeting Alexander.   His
courtiers, however, encouraged him in the opinion
that Alexander was endeavouring to avoid him ; and
that if once he could bring this invader of his empire
to an engagement, he might depend upon obtaining a
complete victory.   There was one man, indeed, in his
army, who had the courage and the honesty to tell him
the truth. This was Caridemus, the Athenian, of whom
when Darius asked whether he thought him strong
enough to defeat the enemy, Caridemus replied in the
following terms : " Permit me, Sir, to speak truth now,
when only my sincerity can be of service ; your present
splendour, your prodigious numbers which have drained
the east, may be terrible indeed to your effeminate
neighbours, but can be no way dreadful to a Macedonian army.   Discipline, close combat, courage, is all
their care ; every single man among them is almost
himself a general.   These men are not to be repulsed
by the stones of slingers, or stakes burnt at the end ;
none but troops armed like themselves can stop their
career ; let therefore the gold and silver, which glitters
in your camp, be exchanged for soldiers and steel, for
weapons and for hearts that are able to defend you."
Darius, though naturally of a mild disposition, had all
his passions roused at the freedom of this man's advice ;
he ordered him at once to be executed : Caridemus all
the time crying out, that his avenger was at hand.
Darius had soon reason to repent his rashness, and experienced, when it was too late, the truth of all that
had been told him.

That prince now advanced towards the river Euphrates, but with a parade that more resembled the
triumphal entry of a sovereign into his capital after
some important victory, than the march of a warrior
who was going to put every thing to hazard of the
sword.   Over his tent was exhibited the image of the
sun in jewels, while wealth and magnificence shone in
every quarter of his army.

First they carried before him silver altars, on which lay fire, called by them sacred and eternal: and these were followed by the Magi, singing hymns after the manner of their country; they were accompanied by three hundred and sixty-five youths (equalling the number of days in a year) clothed in purple robes. Afterwards came a chariot consecrated to Jupiter, drawn by white horses, and followed by a courser of prodigious size, to whom they gave the name of the Sun's horse; and the equerries were dressed in white, each having a golden rod in his hand.

Ten chariots, adorned with sculptures in gold and silver, followed. Then marched a body of horse, composed of twelve nations, whose manners and customs were various, and all armed in a different manner. Next advanced those whom the Persians called The Immortals, amounting to ten thousand, who surpassed the rest of the barbarians in the sumptuousness of their apparel. They all wore golden collars, and were clothed in robes of gold tissue, with vestments having sleeves to them quite covered with precious stones.

Thirty paces from them, followed those called the king's relations, to the number of fifteen thousand, in habits very much resembling those of women; and more remarkable for the vain pomp of their dress, than the glitter of their arms.

Those called the Doriphori came after: they carried the king's cloak, and walked before his chariot, in which he seemed to sit as on a high throne. This chariot was enriched on both sides with images of the gods, in gold and silver; and from the middle of the yoke, which was covered with jewels, rose two statues, a cubit in height, the one representing war, the other peace, having a golden eagle, with wings extended, as ready to take flight.

But nothing could equal the magnificence of the king: he was clothed in a vest of purple, striped with silver, and over it a long robe, glittering all over with precious stones, that represented two falcons rushing from the clouds, and pecking at one another. Around his waist he wore a golden girdle, after the manner of women, whence his scymitar hung, the scabbard of which flamed all over with gems; on his head he wore a tiara, or mitre, round which was a fillet of blue mixed with white.

On each side of him walked two hundred of his nearest relations, followed by two thousand pikemen, whose pikes were adorned with silver, and tipped with gold; and lastly thirty thousand infantry, who composed the rear-guard. These were followed by the king's horses, four hundred in number, all which were led.

About one hundred or a hundred and twenty paces from thence came Sysigambis, Darius's mother, seated on a throne, and his consort on another; with the several female attendants of both queens, riding on horseback. Afterwards came fifteen large chariots, in which were the king's children, and those who had the care of their education, with a band of eunuchs, who are to this day in great esteem in the east. Then marched the concubines, to the number of three hundred and sixty, in the equipage of queens, followed by six hundred mules and three hundred camels, which carried the king's treasure, and guarded by a great body of archers. After these came the wives of the crown officers, and of the greatest lords of the court, seated also in chariots; and then the sutlers, servants, and other followers of the army. In the rear were a body of light-armed troops, with their commanders, who closed the whole march.

Such was the splendour of this pageant monarch, who, while he excited the admiration of his own barbarous subjects, inspired the Macedonians with nothing but contempt for his military skill, and a strong desire to make themselves masters of those riches of which he made so vain and pompous a display.

Alexander and Darius, being equally eager to come to an engagement, were now advancing against each other; and, after various marches and countermarches, they at last met in the neighbourhood of Issus.

The spot where the battle was fought, and which lay near this city, was bounded on one side by the

mountains, and on the other side by the sea. The
plain that was situated between them must have been
of considerable extent, as the two armies encamped in
it, and Darius's army, as we have already observed,
was vastly numerous. The river Pinarus ran through
the middle of this plain, from the mountain to the sea,
and divided it nearly into two equal parts.

Alexander drew up his army in the following order.
He posted at the extremity of the right wing, which
stood near the mountains, the Argyraspides, commanded
by Nicanor; then the phalanx of Cœnus, and afterwards
that of Perdiccas, which terminated in the centre of the
main army. On the extremity of the left wing he posted
the phalanx of Amyntas, then that of Ptolemy, and lastly
that of Meleager. Thus the famous Macedonian phalanx
was formed, which we find was composed of six distinct
bodies. Each of these were headed by able generals;
but Alexander, being always generalissimo, had consequently the command of the whole army. The horse
were placed on the two wings; the Macedonians with
the Thessalians on the right, and the Peloponnesians
with the other allies on the left. Parmenio commanded
the left wing; Alexander himself conducted the right;
while the Agrians (led on by Attalus) and some other
troops lately arrived from Greece, were destined to oppose those whom Darius had posted on the mountains.

As for Darius's army, it was drawn up in the following order. Having heard that Alexander was advancing
against him in battle array, he commanded thirty thousand horse; and twenty thousand bowmen to cross the
river Pinarus, to keep the enemy in awe, and give him
time to draw up his army on the hither side without
interruption. In the centre he posted the thirty thousand Greeks in his service, who doubtless were the
flower and chief strength of his army; and were not at
all inferior in bravery to the Macedonian phalanx, with
thirty thousand barbarians on their right, and as many
on their left. The field of battle not being able to contain a greater number, these were all that were placed
in the front line, the rest being ranged behind them,
and no doubt to a very great depth, considering the

multitude of the Persian forces. On the mountain
which lay to the left, against Alexander's right wing,
Darius posted twenty thousand men, who were so
disposed in the several windings of the mountains,
that some of them were before Alexander's army, and
others behind it.

Darius, having put his army in battle array, and
appointed commanders to the different parts of it, took
post himself in the centre, according to the custom of
the Persian monarchs. He was determined to keep on
the hither side of the river, that so, if the Macedonians
attempted to cross it, he might attack them while in
the middle of the stream, and oblige them to fight in
that disadvantageous situation.

This, however, was not sufficient to damp the spirit
nor to check the progress of Alexander. He boldly
advanced to the side of the river, and plunging into it
with great impetuosity, notwithstanding the showers
of arrows that were poured upon him by the Persians,
he soon gained the opposite shore, where, attacking
the enemy sword in hand, he threw them in a little
time into confusion. Eagerly desiring to engage
Darius, and to have the glory of killing him with his
own hand, he was just upon the point of charging that
monarch, when Oxathres, Darius's brother, observing
the danger to which he was exposed, rushed before his
chariot with the horse he commanded. This, though it
saved Darius's life, was the immediate cause of the loss
of the battle. The horses that drew his chariot became
so unruly, and shook the yoke with so much violence,
that they almost overturned the king; who seeing himself going to fall alive into the hands of his enemies,
leaped down, and mounted another chariot. The rest,
observing this, fled as fast as possible, and, throwing
down their arms, made the best of their way. Alexander received a slight wound in his thigh, but it was
not attended with any bad consequences.

In the mean time, while the Macedonians under
their king had routed the Persians under Darius, the
rest of them, who were engaged with the Greeks, met
with a stouter and more obstinate resistance; but

Alexander, having pursued the fugitives a short way, returned immediately to the field of battle, and attacking the Grecians vigorously in flank, he gave them a total and complete overthrow. The enemy now made no further resistance, but fled precipitately on all sides. Some of them struck into the high road, which led directly to Persia; others ran into woods and lonely mountains; and a small number returned to their camp, which the victorious army had already taken and plundered. In this battle sixty thousand of the Persian infantry, and ten thousand horsemen were slain; forty thousand were taken prisoners; while of Alexander's army there fell but two hundred and eighty in all.

With regard to Darius, the instant he saw his left wing broke, he was one of the first who fled in his chariot; but getting afterwards into craggy, rugged places, he mounted on horseback, throwing away his bow, shield, and royal mantle; and had it not been for the necessity Alexander was under of desisting from the pursuit, in order to return and complete the overthrow of the Greeks, he would probably have fallen alive into the hands of the conqueror.

Sysigambis, Darius's mother, and that monarch's queen (who was also his sister), were found remaining in the camp, with two of the king's daughters, his son (yet a child), and some Persian ladies; for the rest had been carried to Damascus, with part of Darius's treasure, and all such things as contributed only to the luxury and magnificence of his court. No more than three thousand talents were found in his camp; but the rest of the treasure fell afterwards into the hands of Parmenio, at the taking of the city of Damascus.

The evening after the engagement, Alexander invited his chief officers to a feast, at which himself presided, notwithstanding the wound he had that day received in battle. The festivity however had scarce begun, when they were interrupted by sad lamentations from a neighbouring tent, which at first they considered as a fresh alarm; but they were soon informed that the noise came from the tent in which the wife and mother of Darius were kept, who were expressing their sorrow for the supposed death of that monarch. A eunuch who had seen his cloak in the hands of a soldier, imagining he was killed, brought them these dreadful tidings. Alexander immediately sent Leonatus, one of his principal officers, to undeceive them; and next day he himself paid them a visit, when he did every thing in his power to comfort and solace them. He told them that no part of their former state should be withheld from them; but that they should enjoy every convenience and accommodation as in the court of Darius. Observing the infant son of Darius standing by his mother, he took him in his arms. The child, without discovering the least sign of terror, stretched out his arms to the conqueror, who, being affected with its confidence, said to Hephæstion, who attended him, "Oh! that Darius had some share, some portion of this infant's generosity." That he might prevent every suspicion of design on the chastity of Darius's consort, and at the same time remove every cause of fear or anxiety from her mind, he resolved never to visit her tent more, although she was one of the most beautiful women of her time. This moderation, so becoming in a royal conqueror, gave occasion to that noted observation of Plutarch, "That the princesses of Persia lived in an enemy's camp as if they had been in some sacred temple, unseen, unapproached, and unmolested."

Sysigambis was distinguished by extraordinary marks of Alexander's favour; Darius himself could not have treated her with greater respect than did that generous prince. He allowed her to regulate the funerals of all the Persians of the royal family who had fallen in battle; and at her intercession he pardoned several of Darius's nobles, who had justly incurred his displeasure. This magnanimous conduct has done more honour to Alexander's character than all his splendid victories. The gentleness of his manners to the suppliant captives, his chastity and continence, when he had it in his power to enforce obedience, were setting an example to heroes, which it has been the pride of many since to imitate.

The victory at Issus was soon followed by a variety

of other successes. All Phœnicia, except Tyre, the capital city, submitted to Alexander. About the same time Aristodemus, the Persian admiral, was defeated at sea, and a great part of his fleet taken. The city of Damascus too, in which Darius's treasures were deposited, surrendered to Parmenio. This place might have made a vigorous defence; but, by the treachery of the governor, it was yielded up without making the least resistance. Parmenio found in it, besides an immense sum of money and a vast quantity of plate and baggage, three hundred and twenty-nine of Darius's concubines, and a multitude of officers, whose business it was to regulate every thing relating to that monarch's entertainments.

In the mean time Darius, having travelled all night on horseback, arrived in the morning at Sochus, where he assembled the remains of his army. Dejected as he was with his late misfortune, still, however, his pride did not desert him. He wrote a letter to Alexander, in which he rather treated him as an inferior. He commanded rather than requested him to deliver up his wife, mother, and children, upon receiving a proper ransom. With regard to the empire, he would fight with him for it upon equal terms, and bring an equal number of troops into the field. To this Alexander replied, that he scorned to hold any correspondence with a man whom he had already overcome; that if he appeared before him in a suppliant posture, he would give up his wife and mother without ransom; that he knew how to conquer, and to oblige the conquered.

This proposal having produced no effect, Alexander proceeded to receive the submission of the neighbouring states and people. The Sidonians were the first that made him a tender of their allegiance, in opposition to Strato their king, who had declared in favour of Darius. Alexander dethroned him, and permitted Hephæstion (his principal favourite) to elect, in his stead, whomsoever of the Sidonians he should judge most worthy of that exalted station.

Hephæstion was quartered at the house of two brothers who were young, and of the most considerable

family in the city, and to these he offered the crown.
But they refused it, telling him that, according to the
laws of their country, no person could ascend the
throne unless he were of the blood royal. Hephæstion
admiring this greatness of soul, which could contemn
what others strive to obtain by fire and sword, "Continue," says he to them, "in this way of thinking, you
who seem sensible that it is much more glorious to
refuse a diadem than to accept it. However, name
me some person of the royal family, who may remember, when he is king, that it was you that set the
crown on his head." The brothers observing that
several, through excessive ambition, aspired to this
high station, and, to obtain it, paid a servile court to
Alexander's favourites, declared that they did not
know any person more worthy of the diadem than one
Abdolonymus, descended, though in a remote degree,
from the royal family; but who, at the same time, was
so poor that he was obliged to earn his bread by manual
labour in a garden without the city. His honesty and
integrity had reduced him, like many more, to such
extreme poverty. Wholly busied about his humble
occupation, he did not hear the clashing of the arms
which had shaken all Asia.

Hephæstion approving of their choice, the two
brothers went in quest of Abdolonymus, whom they
found weeding in his garden. When they saluted him
king, he at first began to stare at them, and thinking
they were in jest, not in earnest, asked them, whether
they were not ashamed to offer him such an insult.
But as he made a greater resistance than suited their
inclinations, they themselves washed him, and throwing
over his shoulders a purple robe, richly embroidered
with gold, they repeatedly assured him that he was
now king of Sidon, and conducted him to the palace.

The news of this was immediately spread over the
whole city. Most of the inhabitants were overjoyed
at it; but some murmured, especially the rich, who,
despising Abdolonymus's former abject state, could
not help expressing their resentment at his present
elevation. Alexander, therefore, commanded the new

elected prince to be sent for, and, after surveying him
very attentively, said, "Thy air and mien do not con-
tradict what is related of thy extraction ; but I should
be glad to know with what frame of mind thou borest
thy poverty."—"Would to the gods (replied he) that
I may bear this crown with equal patience. These
hands have procured me all I desired ; and whilst I
possessed nothing, I wanted nothing." This answer
gave Alexander a high idea of Abdolonymus's virtue ;
so that he not only presented him with the rich furni-
ture which had belonged to Strato, and part of the
Persian plunder, but likewise annexed one of the
neighbouring provinces to his dominions.

All Phœnicia, as we have already observed, was now
subdued, except Tyre, the capital city. This city was
justly entitled *the queen of the sea*, that element bringing to it the tribute of all nations. She boasted her
having first invented navigation, and taught mankind
the art of braving the winds and waves by the assistance of a frail bark. The happy situation of Tyre, at
the upper end of the Mediterranean ; the conveniency
of its ports, which were both safe and capacious ; and
the character of its inhabitants, who were industrious,
laborious, patient, and extremely courteous to strangers,
invited thither merchants from all parts of the globe ;
so that it might be considered not so much as a city
belonging to any particular nation, as the common city
of all nations, and the centre of their commerce.

Alexander thought it necessary both for his glory
and his interest to take this city. The spring was now
coming on. Tyre was at that time seated in an island
of the sea, about a quarter of a league from the continent. It was surrounded with a strong wall, a hundred
and fifty feet high, which the waves of the sea washed ;
and the Carthaginians, a colony from Tyre, a mighty
people, and sovereigns of the ocean, promised to come
to the assistance of their parent state. Encouraged,
therefore, by these favourable circumstances, the
Tyrians determined not to surrender, but to hold out
the place to the last extremity. This resolution, however imprudent, was certainly magnanimous ; but it was

soon after followed by an act, which was as blamable
as the other was praiseworthy. Alexander was desirous of gaining the place rather by treaty than by force
of arms, and with this view he sent heralds into the
town with offers of peace ; but the inhabitants were so
far from listening to his proposals, or endeavouring to
avert his resentment by any kind of concession, that
they actually killed his ambassadors, and threw their
bodies from the top of the walls into the sea. It is
easy to imagine what effect so shocking an outrage
must produce in a mind like Alexander's. He instantly
resolved to besiege the place, and not to desist till he had
made himself master of it, and razed it to the ground.

As Tyre was divided from the continent by an arm
of the sea, there was necessity for filling up the inter-
mediate space with a bank or pier, before the place
could be closely invested. This work, accordingly,
was immediately undertaken, and in a great measure
completed, when all the wood, of which it was principally composed, was unexpectedly burned by means of
a fire-ship sent in by the enemy. The damage, however, was very soon repaired, and the mole rendered
more perfect than formerly, and carried nearer to the
town, when all of a sudden a furious tempest arose,
which, undermining the stone work that supported the
wood, laid the whole at once in the bottom of the sea.

Two such disasters, following so close on the heels
of each other, would have cooled the ardour of almost
any man except Alexander ; but nothing could daunt
his invincible spirit, or make him relinquish an enterprise he had once undertaken. He therefore resolved
to prosecute the siege ; and in order to encourage his
men to second his views, he took care to inspire them
with a belief that heaven was on their side, and would
soon crown their labours with the wished-for success.
At one time he gave out, that Apollo was about to
abandon the Tyrians to their doom ; and that to prevent his flight, they had bound him to his pedestal with
a golden chain ; at another, he pretended that Hercules,
the tutelar deity of Macedon, had appeared to him,
and, having opened prospects of the most glorious kind,

had invited him to proceed to take possession of Tyre.
These favourable circumstances were announced by
the augurs, as intimations from above; and every heart
was, of consequence, cheered. The soldiers, as if but
that moment arrived before the city, now forgetting all
the toils they had undergone, and the disappointments
they had suffered, began to raise a new mole, at which
they worked incessantly.

To protect them from being annoyed by the ships of
the enemy, Alexander fitted out a fleet, with which he
not only secured his own men, but offered the Tyrians
battle; which, however, they thought proper to decline,
and withdrew all their galleys into the harbour.

The besiegers, now allowed to proceed unmolested,
went on with the work with the utmost vigour, and in
a little time completed it, and brought it close to the
walls. A general attack was therefore resolved on,
both by sea and land; and with this view the king
having manned his galleys, and joined them together
with strong cables, ordered them to approach the walls
about midnight, and attack the city with resolution.
But just as the assault was going to begin, a dreadful
storm arose, which not only shook the ships asunder,
but even shattered them in a terrible manner, so that
they were all of them obliged to be towed towards the
shore, without having made the least impression on
the city.

The Tyrians were elated with this gleam of good
fortune: but their joy was but of short duration; for
in a little time after they received intelligence from
Carthage, that they must expect no assistance from that
quarter, as the Carthaginians themselves were then
overawed by a powerful army of the Syracusans, who
had invaded their country. Reduced therefore, to the
hard necessity of depending entirely upon their own
strength and their own resources, the Tyrians sent all
their women and children to Carthage, and prepared to
encounter the very last extremities: for now the enemy
were attacking the place with greater spirit and activity
than ever. And, to do the Tyrians justice, it must be
acknowledged, that they employed a number of methods

of defence, which, considering the rude state of the art of war at that early period, were really astonishing. They warded off the darts discharged from the balistas against them, by the assistance of turning-wheels, which either broke them to pieces, or carried them another way. They deadened the violence of the stones that were hurled at them, by setting up sails and curtains made of a soft substance, which easily gave way.

To annoy the ships which advanced against their walls, they fixed grappling irons and scythes to joists or beams; then straining their catapultas (an enormous kind of crossbow) they laid those great pieces of timber upon them instead of arrows, and shot them off on a sudden at the enemy: these crushed some of their ships by their great weight, and, by means of the hooks or hanging scythes, tore others to pieces. They also had brazen shields, which they drew red hot out of the fire; and filling these with burning sand, hurled them in an instant from the top of the wall upon the enemy. There was nothing the Macedonians dreaded so much as this fatal instrument; for the moment the burning sand got to the flesh through the crevices of the armour, it penetrated to the very bone, and stuck so close that there was no pulling it off; so that the soldiers, throwing down their arms, and tearing their clothes to pieces, were in this manner exposed, naked and defenceless, to the shot of the enemy.

Alexander finding the resources and even the courage of the Tyrians increased, in proportion as the siege continued, resolved to make a last effort, and attack them at once both by sea and land, in order, if possible, to overwhelm them with the multiplicity of dangers to which they would be thus exposed. With this view, having manned his galleys with some of the bravest of his troops, he commanded them to advance against the enemy's fleet, while he himself took post at the head of his men on the mole. And now the attack began on all sides with irresistible and unremitting fury. Wherever the battering-rams had beat down any part of the wall, and the bridges were thrown out, instantly the Argyraspides mounted the breach with the utmost valour,

being led on by Admetus, one of the bravest officers in
the army, who was killed by the thrust of a spear, as
he was encouraging his soldiers.

The presence of the king, and the example he set,
fired his troops with unusual bravery. He himself
ascended one of the towers on the mole, which was of
a prodigious height, and there was exposed to the
greatest dangers he had ever yet encountered; for
being immediately known by his insignia, and the rich-
ness of his armour, he served as a mark for all the
arrows of the enemy. On this occasion he performed
wonders, killing with javelins several of those who
defended the wall; then advancing nearer to them, he
forced some with his sword, and others with his shield,
either into the city or the sea, the tower on which he
fought almost touching the wall. He soon ascended
the wall, followed by his principal officers, and possessed himself of two towers, and the space between them.
The battering-rams had already made several breaches:
the fleet had forced its way into the harbour; and some
of the Macedonians had possessed themselves of the
towers which were abandoned. The Tyrians, seeing
the enemy masters of their rampart, retired towards
an open place, called Agenor, and there stood their
ground; but Alexander, marching up with his regiment
of body-guards, killed part of them, and obliged the
rest to fly. At the same time, Tyre being taken on that
side which lay towards the harbour, a general carnage
of the citizens ensued, and none were spared, except
the few that fell into the hands of the Sidonians in
Alexander's army, who, considering the Tyrians as
countrymen, granted them protection, and carried them
privately on board their ships. The numbers that were
slaughtered on this occasion are almost incredible:
even after conquest the victor's resentment did not
subside; he ordered no less than two thousand men,
who were taken in the storm, to be nailed to crosses
along the shore. The number of prisoners amounted to
thirty thousand, and were all sold as slaves in different
parts of the world. Thus fell Tyre, that had been for
many ages the most flourishing city in the world, and

had spread the arts of commerce into the remotest regions.

While Alexander was employed in the siege of Tyre, he received a second letter from Darius, in which that monarch treated him with greater respect than before. He now gave him the title of king; he offered him ten thousand talents as a ransom for his captive mother and queen; and he promised him his daughter Statira in marriage, with all the country he had conquered as far as the river Euphrates, provided he would agree to a peace. These terms were so advantageous, that when the king debated upon them in council, Parmenio, one of his generals, could not help observing, that he would certainly accept of them, were he Alexander. "And so would I," replied the king, "were I Parmenio." But deeming it inconsistent with his dignity to listen to any proposals from a man whom he had so lately overcome, he haughtily rejected them, and scorned to accept of that as a favour which he already considered as his own by conquest.

From Tyre, Alexander marched to Jerusalem, fully determined to punish that city, for having refused to supply his army with provisions during the siege; but his resentment was mollified by a deputation of the citizens coming out to meet him, with their high priest, Jaddua, before them, dressed in white, and having a mitre on his head, on the front of which the name of God was written. The moment the king perceived the high priest, he advanced towards him with an air of the most profound respect, bowed his body, adored the august name upon his front, and saluted him who wore it with religious veneration. And when some of his courtiers expressed their surprise, that he, who was adored by every one, should adore the high priest of the Jews, "I do not," said he, "adore the high priest, but the God whose minister he is; for whilst I was at Dium, in Macedonia, my mind wholly fixed on the great design of the Persian war, as I was revolving the methods how to conquer Asia, this very man, dressed in the same robes, appeared to me in a dream, exhorted me to banish my fear, bade me cross the Hellespont boldly, and assured me that God would march at the head of my army, and give me the victory over the Persians." This speech, delivered with an air of sincerity, no doubt had its effect in encouraging the army, and establishing an opinion that his mission was from heaven.

From Jerusalem he went to Gaza, where, having met with a more obstinate resistance than he expected, he cut the whole garrison, consisting of ten thousand men, to pieces; and not satisfied with this act of cruelty, he caused holes to be bored through the heels of Bœtis, the governor, and tying him with cords to the back of his chariot, he dragged him in this manner round the walls of the city. This he did in imitation of Achilles, whom Homer describes as having dragged Hector round the walls of Troy in the same manner; but it was reading the poet to very little, or rather indeed to very bad purpose, to imitate this hero in the most unworthy part of his character.

Alexander, having left a garrison in Gaza, turned his arms towards Egypt, of which he made himself master without opposition. Here he formed the design of visiting the temple of Jupiter, which was situated in the sandy deserts of Libya, at the distance of twelve days' journey from Memphis, the capital of Egypt. His chief view in going thither, was, to get himself acknowledged the son of Jupiter, an honour he had long aspired to. In this journey he founded the city of Alexandria, which soon became one of the most capital towns in the world for commerce. Nothing could be more dreary than the desert through which he passed, nor any thing more charming, according to the fabulous accounts of the poets, than the particular spot where the temple was situated. It was a perfect paradise in the midst of an immeasurable wild. At last having reached the place, and appeared before the altar of the deity, the priest, who was no stranger to Alexander's wishes, declared him to be the son of Jupiter. The conqueror, elated with this high compliment, asked, Whether he should have success in his expedition? the priest answered, that he should be

monarch of the world. The conqueror inquired, if his
father's murderers were punished; the priest replied,
that his father Jupiter was immortal, but that the murderers of Philip had been all extirpated.

From this time forward Alexander supposed himself,
or would have it supposed by others, that he was the
son of Jupiter. Transported, however, as he was, with
the idea of being of divine origin, he never forgot the
duties of humanity, nor even those of generosity to his
female captives: for Statira, Darius's consort, dying in
child-bed about this period, he honoured her with as
grand and magnificent a funeral as she could have received, had she expired in her husband's palace. Darius was so deeply affected with this act of magnanimity
in his enemy, that, upon receiving the first intelligence
of it, he is said to have lift up his eyes to heaven, and to
have expressed himself thus: " Ye gods, the guardians
of our births, and who decree the fate of nations, grant
that I may be enabled to leave the Persian state as rich
and flourishing as I found it, that I may have it in
my power to make Alexander a proper return for his
generosity to the dearest objects of my affection. But
if the duration of this empire is near at an end, and the
greatness of Persia about to be forgotten, may none but
Alexander be permitted to sit on the throne of Cyrus."

Generous, however, as Alexander was to the wife and
mother of Darius, he still refused to listen to any terms
of accommodation from that monarch himself, who was
therefore obliged to assemble another army, in order, at
least, to make one effort more for the preservation of
his crown and empire. He accordingly exerted himself
with great spirit and activity, and in a little time
was able to raise a second army half as numerous again
as the former; and with this he now advanced towards
the Tigris, in order, if possible, to prevent Alexander
from passing that river. This, however, he was not
able to effect. Alexander passed the Tigris with greater
ease and rapidity than he had passed the Granicus;
and drawing up his army on the farther bank, he continued there encamped for two days in expectation of
the enemy. But finding that Darius was not disposed

to come in search of him, he resolved to go in quest of Darius. The minds of his men, however, were considerably damped by an eclipse of the moon, which happened about that time; for as the cause of this phenomenon was not then known, it was always supposed to be the prognostic of some great calamity. But Alexander, who was as good a politician as a soldier, immediately produced some Egyptian soothsayers, who declared, that the eclipse portended calamities not to the Greeks, but to the Persians. And having by this artful contrivance, revived the spirits of his men, he led them on to meet the enemy, and began his march at midnight.

At break of day he received intelligence, that Darius was but twenty miles distant; and at the same time a messenger arrived from that monarch with fresh proposals of peace, which were still more advantageous than the former. But Alexander rejected all his offers; proudly replying, that the world would not admit of two suns nor of two sovereigns. All hopes of accommodation, therefore, being now cut off, both sides prepared themselves for battle, equally irritated, and equally ambitious. Darius pitched his camp in a plain near the village of Gaugamela, and at some distance from the city of Arbela, from which last place the battle that ensued is usually denominated.

Alexander being informed of this, continued his march till he arrived within a few miles of the enemy. He there encamped, and having rested four days, in order to refresh his army, he set out on the evening of the fifth, with a view of attacking Darius at daybreak; but upon his arival at the mountains, where he could discover the enemy's army, he made a halt, and having assembled his general officers, he held a consultation with them, whether they should engage immediately, or pitch their camp in that place. The latter expedient was deemed the most eligible, as it would give them an opportunity of viewing the field of battle, and the manner in which the enemy were drawn up. They therefore encamped in the same order in which they marched; and in the meantime, Alexander, at the head of his light-armed infantry, and his royal regiments, marched round the plain in which the battle was to be fought.

Parmenio advised him to attack the enemy by night, and take them by surprise, as by this means he would be sure of giving them a complete overthrow; but Alexander replied, that he scorned to steal a victory, and that he was determined to fight and conquer in broad daylight. So confident, indeed, was he of success, that the night immediately preceding the action he slept more soundly than he commonly was wont to do, so that Parmenio was obliged to awake him in the morning; and upon that general's expressing some surprise at his calmness and composure on the eve of a battle, in which his whole fortune lay at stake, "How can I," replied he, "be otherwise than calm, when I see that the enemy is come to deliver himself into my hands?" So saying, he took up his arms, mounted his horse, and rode up and down the ranks, exhorting his men to behave gallantly, and, if possible, to surpass their former fame, and the glory they had already acquired.

The issue of this battle was such as might naturally be expected from the character of the combatants. On the one side was a middling army of forty thousand foot, and about seven or eight thousand horse; but these were the bravest and best disciplined troops at that time in the world: on the other was a vast and almost innumerable assemblage of men, rather than of soldiers, without order, without discipline, and consequently without any common or well directed courage. The Greeks, indeed, in Darius's pay, formed an exception to this general character of his forces; and they behaved on this, as on every other occasion, with a spirit worthy of their former fame. But nothing could resist the ardour and impetuosity of Alexander at the head of his gallant Macedonians, especially as he had taken care, with his usual address, to reinforce their native courage with the aid of superstition. For in the very heat of the action, Aristander the soothsayer, clothed in his white robes, and holding a branch of laurel in his hand, advanced into the thickest of the fight, according to the order he had received from the king, and crying out that he saw an eagle hovering over Alexander's head (a sure omen of victory) he showed, with his finger, the pretended bird to the soldiers; who relying on the veracity of the soothsayer, imagined that they saw it also, and now believing themselves invincible, they renewed the attack with greater spirit than ever, and in a little time carried all before them.

Alexander exposed himself to danger like the meanest soldier in his army. He wounded Darius's equerry with a javelin; and had not that prince saved himself by a precipitate flight, he would probably have wounded or killed him likewise. Alexander pursued the fugitives for a considerable way, but was obliged to return, in order to assist Parmenio, who commanded the left wing, and had not yet been able to break the Persian horse that opposed him. These, however, he discomfited before the arrival of Alexander, who met the enemy retiring from the field of battle, and put them almost all to the sword. And now the Persians being defeated everywhere, betook themselves to flight, and were hotly pursued by the Macedonians, who committed terrible havock among them. Alexander rode after Darius as far as Arbela, hoping every moment to overtake him; and he had almost done so, for he reached that city just as Darius had quitted it; but though the latter was thus able to save his person, he was obliged to leave his treasure behind him, which now fell into the hands of the enemy.

Such was the issue of this famous battle, which gave to Alexander the empire of Asia. The loss of the Persians on this occasion was incredible. It amounted, according to Arrian, to three hundred thousand men, besides those who were taken prisoners; whereas the loss of the Macedonians was, comparatively speaking, very inconsiderable, it not exceeding, according to the same author, twelve hundred men, and most of these were cavalry.

The dreadful defeat which Darius had now sustained struck such a terror into the neighbouring provinces, that Alexander met with little or no more opposition, in

making himself master of the whole kingdom of Persia.
Babylon surrendered to him without striking a blow;
as did also Susa; and in both these places he found
immense treasures. Leaving the mother and children
of Darius in Susa, he advanced into the country of the
Uxii, where he met with some slight resistance from
Madathes the governor; but this he soon overcame,
and pardoned Madathes at the intercession of Sysigambis, to whom that satrap was nearly related. Thence
he continued his march towards Persepolis, which he
did with the greater expedition, as he had received
intelligence from Tiridates, who commanded in that
city, that the inhabitants were preparing to plunder
Darius's treasures: but Alexander took care to prevent
them by his unexpected arrival, and distributed all the
wealth he found there, as well as in other places, among
the bravest and most deserving of his soldiers.

As he approached this city, he was met by a large
body of men, who exhibited a striking example of the
exquisite misery which human beings are sometimes
doomed to suffer. These were about four thousand
Greeks, very far advanced in years, who, having been
made prisoners of war, had undergone all the torments
which the Persian tyranny could inflict. The hands of
some had been cut off, the feet of others; and others
again had lost their noses and ears. They appeared
like so many spectres, rather than like men; speech
being almost the only thing by which they were known
to be such. Alexander could not refrain from tears at
this sight; and as they irresistibly moved him to com-
miserate their condition, he bade them with the utmost
tenderness, not to despond, and assured them, that they
should again see their wives and country. They chose,
however, to remain in a place where misfortune was
now become habitual: he therefore rewarded them
liberally for their sufferings, and commanded the governor of the province to treat them with mildness and
respect.

Alexander, upon his first entry into Persepolis, was
satisfied with the treasures he found there, and seems
not to have thought of wreaking his resentment upon

any part of the city itself. But one day having drunk to excess at a public banquet, and the conversation turning upon the cruelties committed by the Persians in Greece, and particularly at Athens, Thais, an Athenian courtesan, who was present, seized this opportunity of saying, that it was mean and pusillanimous, in the highest degree, not to take revenge for such repeated slaughters. "This day," cried she, "has fully repaid all my wander-ings and troubles in Asia, by putting it in my power, to humble the pride of the Persian monarchs. To insult over the palace of Persepolis will be a noble deed ; but how much more glorious would it be to fire the palace of that Xerxes, who laid the city of Athens in ruins ; and to have it told in future times, that a single woman, of Alexander's train, had taken more signal vengeance on the enemies of Greece, than all her former generals had been able to do !" All the guests applauded the discourse ; when immediately the king, in a fit of frenzy, rose from table (his head being crowned with flowers) and taking a torch in his hand, he advanced forward, to execute his mad exploit. The whole com-pany followed him, breaking out into shouts of joy, and in a riotous manner, with singing and dancing, sur-rounded the palace. All the rest of the Macedonians, at this noise, ran in crowds, with lighted torches, and set fire to every part of it. However, Alexander soon repented of what he had done, and thereupon gave orders for extinguishing the fire ; but it was now too late.

In the meantime Darius continued his flight, and at length arrived at Ecbatana, the capital of Media. But though he was able to escape the pursuit of his natural enemies, he could not secure himself from the secret designs of his treacherous subjects. Two of them in particular, Nabarzanes and Bessus, the one the general of the horse, the other the commander of the Bactrians, had entered into a plot to seize his person : and either deliver him alive into the hands of Alexander, if they were overtaken ; or, if they escaped, to put him to death, and afterwards usurp his crown, and begin a new war. They even found means to draw over to

their party all the forces of Darius, except the Greeks
in that monarch's pay; who, shocked at the baseness of
his natural-born subjects, generously offered to protect
his person at the hazard of their own lives. But Darius
was of too noble a spirit to accept of such a proposal,
and he therefore replied, that if his own subjects would
not grant him protection, he could not think of receiving it from the hands of strangers. The Greeks, seeing
they could be of no further service to him, immediately
threw themselves on the mercy of Alexander, who in
consideration of their gallant spirit, not only forgave
them, but enrolled them among his own forces.

Darius, being thus left destitute of all kind of re-
source, was seized by the traitors, who put him in
chains, and carried him along with them for some time;
but finding that the Macedonians were in close pursuit
of them, and that it was impossible for them either to
conciliate the friendship of Alexander, or to secure a
crown for themselves, they again set him at liberty, and
advised him to accompany them in their flight. This,
however, he refused to do; and calling upon heaven
to revenge the indignities they had already offered
him, he openly declared, that he would rather trust to
the mercy of Alexander, than continue any longer in
the hands of traitors. At these words they fell into
a furious passion, and thrusting him through with their
darts and spears, they left him, in that manner, to linger
out the remains of his wretched life. The traitors then
made their escape different ways; while the victorious
Macedonians, at length coming up, found Darius in a
lonely place, lying in his chariot, and drawing near his
end. However, he had strength enough, before he died,
to call for drink; which a Macedonian, named Polystratus, brought him. The generosity of the unfortunate monarch shone forth, on this melancholy occasion,
in the address he made to this stranger: "Now indeed," said he, "I suffer the extremity of misery, since
it is not in my power to reward thee for this act of
humanity." He had a Persian prisoner, whom he employed as his interpreter. Darius, after drinking the
liquor that had been given him turned to the Macedo-

nian, and said, that in the deplorable state to which he was reduced, he however should have the comfort to speak to one who could understand him, and that his last words would not be lost. He therefore charged him to tell Alexander, that he had died in his debt; that he gave him many thanks for the great humanity he had exercised towards his mother, his wife, and his children, whose lives he had not only spared, but restored them to their former splendour: that he besought the gods to give victory to his arms, and make him sovereign of the universe; and that he thought he need not entreat him to revenge the execrable murder committed on his person, as this was the common cause of kings.

After this, taking Polystratus by the hand, "Give him," said he, "thy hand, as I give thee mine; and carry him, in my name, the only pledge I am able to give of my gratitude and affection." Saying these words, he breathed his last.

Alexander, upon coming up, and viewing the dead body of Darius, was deeply affected; he generously paid it the tribute of a tear; he caused it to be embalmed and enclosed in a magnificent coffin; and he sent it to Sysigambis, in order to be interred with the honours usually paid to the Persian monarchs. At the same time he pursued the traitor Bessus, and having taken him prisoner, and cut off his nose and ears, he caused him to be conveyed to Ecbatana, there to suffer whatever punishment Darius's mother should think proper to inflict upon him. He was accordingly put to death in the following manner: Four trees were bent by main force, all towards the same point, and to each of these one of the limbs of this traitor's body was fastened; and then the trees being suffered to return to their natural position, they flew back with so much violence, that each tore away the limb that was fixed to it, and so quartered him.

It was about this time that Alexander is said to have received a visit from Thalestris, queen of the Amazons: but this circumstance, though related as a fact by some

Q

historians, is considered as a fable by the most judicious
writers.

Among the many good qualities of Alexander, his
gallantry and generosity to the female sex was not the
least remarkable. Of this he now gave a striking instance in his behaviour to a Persian female captive,
whom having discovered, by her modest and reserved
air while she was singing at one of his public banquets,
to be a princess of the blood-royal, he not only set her
at liberty, but returned her all her possessions, and
even caused her husband, Hystaspes, to be sought for,
in order that she might be restored to him.

The grandeur and elevation of Alexander's mind appears in nothing more conspicuous than this, that he
always accustomed his men to consider their present
possessions, however great, as nothing in comparison of
what he would one day bestow upon them. Perceiving
that they were now so encumbered with booty, as to
be incapable of marching with their usual celerity and
dispatch, he commanded them to carry all their baggage (excepting only such things as were indispensably
necessary) into a large plain, and there to commit it to
the flames.

We have hitherto beheld the fair side of Alexander's
character. We must now reverse the picture, and take
a view of his bad, as well as his good qualities; for no
man ever had a more mixed character, or united, in a
more eminent degree, the extremes both of virtue and of
vice. Hearing that Philotas, one of his chief favourites
(and who was likewise the son of Parmenio) had received intelligence of a plot formed against him, and
had neglected to inform him of it, he immediately concluded that that nobleman himself was concerned in the
conspiracy; and he accordingly had him first put to the
rack, and afterwards stoned to death. Philotas, in the
agony of pain, had acknowledged himself guilty, and
named several of his accomplices, and, among others,
his own father. The consequence was, that Parmenio,
though entirely innocent, was likewise put to death;
and in this act Alexander was at once guilty of injustice, cruelty, and ingratitude; for Parmenio had con-

tribnted more to the success of his arms than perhaps any of his other generals.

In order to prevent the ill humour that might have been excited in the army by these acts of severity, Alexander set out in quest of new nations whom he might subdue. He totally extirpated the Branchiæ, merely on account of their being descended from some traitorous Greeks, that had delivered up the treasures of a temple, with which they had been entrusted. The success of his arms against the Scythians is very problematical. According to Arrian and Quintus Curtius, he was able to make little or no impression on the bold and untractable spirit of these barbarians. Curtius even says, that the Scythians gave the Greeks so terrible a defeat, that Alexander made it death for any one, who had escaped from the battle, to make the least mention of it. He adds, that they sent ambassadors to Alexander, who had the courage to tell him to his face, that he, who pretended to have no other view in all his military enterprises than the extirpation of robbers, was himself the greatest robber that existed. It appears, however, that after taking and plundering the city of Cyropolis, and crossing the river Jaxerthes, he. defeated a body of thirty thousand Scythians, who were posted in a strong hold called Petra Oxiani, and having met with a more obstinate resistance than he expected, he reduced the common men to slavery, and caused their leaders to be fixed to crosses at the bottom of the rock that formed the pass.

Having thus opened to himself a way into the heart of the country, he advanced first into the province of Barsaria, and afterwards into that of Maracanda, of which last he appointed Clitus governor. But it was not long before this brave and deserving officer met with the same fate as Parmenio. For having taken upon him, at a public entertainment, where he had drunk too freely, to depreciate the king's achievements in comparison of those of his father Philip, Alexander, who was likewise very much intoxicated, was so transported with passion, that taking up a javelin, he laid Clitus dead at his feet. He had no sooner committed this barbarous action, than he was seized with the deepest and most bitter affliction. He threw himself upon the dead body; he forced out the javelin, and had he not been prevented by the by-standers, he would instantly have plunged it in his own breast. For some time he continued in a state of the deepest melancholy: but at last having recovered his usual serenity, he set out in quest of new adventures, and entering the country of the Sacæ, he was met by Axertes, one of its kings, whose daughter, Roxana, he married.

Having now subdued all the Persian provinces, he resolved to carry his arms as far as India, a country deemed at that time, as well as at present, one of the richest and most desirable in the world. This country, on both sides of the Ganges, was then inhabited by a people, not very unlike the present Gentoos, or native Indians. They were divided into seven casts or classes, which always kept separate and distinct from each other, no person of one class being permitted to intermarry with one of another; nor any one being allowed to belong to two or more classes, or to quit one class for another. The first class consisted of the guardians of religion; the second of husbandmen; the third of shepherds; the fourth of merchants and tradesmen, including pilots and seamen; the fifth of soldiers; the sixth of magistrates; and the seventh of persons employed in the public councils, and who assisted the sovereign in the government of the state.

Upon entering this country, Alexander received the voluntary submission of most of the petty princes that reigned in it. Having reduced Hagosa, he attacked the rock of Aornos, which was considered as impregnable, and was said to have foiled the prowess even of Hercules himself: but the garrison, struck with the vastness of his military preparations, delivered it up after a very faint resistance. This helped to inflame his natural pride and vanity, in having been able so easily to make himself master of a fortress, that had bid defiance to the might of the great founder of his race.

From thence he proceeded towards the river Indus, and continued his march to the banks of the Hydaspes, receiving everywhere, as he passed, the submission of the neighbouring princes, and, among others, that of Omphis, who made him a present of fifty-six elephants. There was one of them, however, (named Porus) who disdained to relinquish his independent situation without a struggle; and Alexander, therefore, resolved to compel him by force of arms. A bloody battle accordingly was fought between them; and though Porus behaved with extraordinary valour, and performed both the duty of an able commander and a gallant soldier, being as remarkable for his great strength and stature, as for his uncommon abilities, he was yet obliged, however unwillingly, to resign the victory to his antagonist. The loss of the Indians on this occasion was great, amounting to no less than twenty thousand foot and three thousand horse; whereas that of the Macedonians did not exceed two hundred and eighty foot, and between thirty and forty horsemen.

Alexander was so charmed with the extraordinary merit of Porus, that he was extremely desirous of saving him from the general carnage that followed the battle. He therefore sent a messenger after him, entreating him to return, which with some difficulty he was prevailed upon to do; and when he came into the king's presence, who, the nearer he viewed him, admired him the more, Alexander asked him how he wished to be treated? "Like a king," replied Porus. "But," continued Alexander, "do you ask nothing more?" "No," replied Porus, "all things are included in that single word." Alexander, struck with this greatness of soul, the magnanimity of which seemed heightened by distress, did not only restore him his kingdom, but annexed other provinces to it, and treated him ever after with the highest marks of esteem and regard. Porus continued faithful to him till his death. It is hard to say whether the victor or the vanquished deserved most praise on this occasion.

Alexander built a city on the spot where the battle was fought; and another in the place where he had crossed the Hydaspes. He called the one Nicæa, from his victory; and the other Bucephalus, in honour of his horse, who died there, not of wounds, but of old age.

Having now conquered Porus, he advanced into the interior part of India, and as the people of that country were never remarkable for their military spirit, he easily added it to his former dominions. Passing by a place, where there were several brachmans or Indian priests, he was seized with a desire of conversing with them, and of learning, if possible, something of the nature of their religion. But hearing that these priests never made visits, and thinking it below his dignity to visit them, he sent Onesicritus, the philosopher, to wait upon them. This man met, in the neighbourhood of the city, fifteen brachmans, who from morning till evening always stood naked, in the same posture in which they had at first placed themselves, and afterwards returned to the city at night. He addressed himself first to Calanus, an Indian, reputed the wisest man of his country, who, though he professed the practice of the most severe philosophy, had however been persuaded in his extreme old age to attend upon the court, and to him he told the occasion of his coming. The latter, gazing upon Onesicritus's clothes and shoes, could not forbear laughing: after which he told him, "That anciently the earth had been covered with barley and wheat, as it was at that time with dust; that, besides water, the rivers used to flow with milk, honey, oil and wine; that man's guilt had occasioned a change of this happy condition; and that Jupiter, to punish their ingratitude, had sentenced them to a long and painful labour; that their repentance afterwards moving him to compassion, he had restored them their former abundance; however that, by the course of things, they seemed to be returning to their ancient confusion." All nations, even in the very lowest stages of society, seem to have some notion of a happier state that preceded the present.

Onesicritus endeavoured to persuade two of them, named Mandanus and Calodanus, to accompany him to Alexander, telling them they would find him a generous benefactor. The former haughtily rejected the proposal: it was however accepted by the latter. Alexander's chief ambition was to imitate Bacchus and Hercules in their expedition into the east, and he therefore resolved to penetrate, like them, as far as he could meet with new nations to conquer. But now the Macedonians refused to follow him, satiated, as they were, with spoil, and worn out with repeated encounters; and though he used every argument he could think of to overcome their obstinacy, he yet could succeed no farther than to obtain their consent to attend him towards the south, in order to discover the nearest ocean, and to take the course of the river Indus for their guide.

In his voyage down this river, he gave a signal proof of his personal intrepidity, for which he was so remarkable; for having landed his troops, and attacked the capital of the Ox draci and the Mallis, he seized a scaling-ladder, and was the first that mounted the wall. His attendants, seeing his danger, endeavoured to follow him; but the ladder breaking, he was left alone; upon which, sword in hand, he boldly leaped from the wall into the city, which was crowded with enemies. He repulsed such as were nearest to him, and he even killed the governor of the place, who advanced in the throng. Thus with his back to a tree that happened to be near, he received all the darts of the enemy in his shield, and kept even the boldest at a distance. At last an Indian discharging an arrow of three feet in length, it pierced his coat of mail and his right breast; and so great a quantity of blood issued from the wound, that he dropped his arms and lay as dead. The Indian came to strip him, supposing him really what he appeared; but Alexander that instant recovered his spirits, and plunged a dagger in his side. By this time a part of the king's attendants had come to his succour, and forming themselves round his body, till the soldiers without found means to break the gates, they thus saved him, and put all the inhabitants without distinction to the sword.

Having recovered of his wound, in a few days, he continued his voyage down the river, subduing the country on each side as he passed along: and at last having reached the shore, he was struck with surprise at the high tides of the Indian ocean, especially as he had never beheld any thing of the kind but the gentle floods of the Mediterranean, where there can hardly be

said to be any tides at all.   Here he put an end to his
expedition; and casting his eyes wistfully on the broad
expanse of waters before him, he is said to have wept
at there being no more worlds left for him to conquer.
He now therefore resolved to direct his march home-
wards ; and having appointed Nearchus admiral of his
fleet, with orders to proceed along the Indian shore as
far as the Persian gulf, he set out with his army for
Babylon.

The first part of this journey was attended with the
greatest difficulties, on account of the poverty of the
country through which they passed, and the consequent
want of provisions; but upon their arrival in the province of Gedrosia, the richest district in that part of
the world, they found themselves surrounded with all
the necessaries, and conveniences, and even the luxuries of life, nor were they backward in enjoying them.
The fact is, like true soldiers, they gave themselves up
to every species of intemperance and excess.   Alexander, still wishing to imitate Bacchus, was drawn by
eight horses, on a scaffold in the form of a square stage,
where he passed the days and nights in feasting ; and
his men, at humble distance, did not fail to follow his
example.   Here he put Cleander to death, whom he
had left behind him as the governor of some provinces,
and who had grossly abused his authority during his
master's absence.   As this man had the chief hand in
cutting off the unhappy Parmenio, this act of rigorous
justice gave great satisfaction.   He likewise inflicted
the same punishment upon six hundred soldiers, whom
Cleander had employed as the instruments of his ex-
tortion.

In his way to Babylon, he stopped at Pasargada, in
order to visit the tomb of Cyrus, upon which was this
humble but significant inscription :—" O man, whoso-
ever thou art, or whencesoever thou comest, I am
Cyrus, the founder of the Persian empire; do not envy
me this little quantity of earth which covers my body."
Here Orsines, a Persian prince, being accused (though
falsely) of having robbed this tomb, was condemned to
suffer a capital punishment.   Here, too, Calanus the

Indian, having completed his eighty-third year, without disease or sickness, and now feeling the approaches of old age, resolved to put himself to a voluntary death, agreeable to the strange superstition of the enthusiasts of his country. A funeral pile accordingly was erected for him: this, after taking leave of his friends, he boldly ascended, and laying himself down upon it, and covering his face, he continued immoveably in that posture till he expired in the flames.

From Pasargada Alexander proceeded to Susa, where he married Statira, the eldest daughter of Darius; and at the same time gave her youngest sister in wedlock to his favourite Hephæstion, and fourscore Persian ladies of rank to as many of his principal officers.

But while he was thus amusing himself in Persia, a commotion had like to have been excited in Greece. Harpalus, governor of Babylon, having amassed immense riches, and wishing to acquire an independent authority, had gone over to Athens, and endeavoured to engage the leading men in his interest, and, among others, the illustrious Phocion, whom we have already mentioned. But this man lent a deaf ear to all his tempting offers, and showed himself to be as much proof against the seductions of Harpalus, as he had formerly been against those of Philip and Alexander. When Philip pressed him to accept of a large sum, if not for himself, at least for his family: "If my children," said Phocion, "resemble me, the little spot of ground, 'upon the produce of which I have hitherto lived, will be sufficient to maintain them; if they do not, I would not wish to leave them wealth, merely to inflame their luxury and ambition." And when Alexander sent him a hundred talents, Phocion asked those who brought it, Why their master had presented him with so great a sum, and did not remit any to the rest of the Athenians? "It is," replied they, "because he looks upon you as the only just and virtuous man in the state." "Then," rejoined Phocion, "let him suffer me still to enjoy that character, and be really what I am taken for." Harpalus, disappointed in his hopes of success from this quarter, was obliged to abandon the enterprise.

This commotion was scarcely suppressed when another ensued, and seemingly of a more dangerous nature. Alexander had published a declaration, by which all the Macedonians, who, from their age or infirmities, were incapable of bearing the fatigues of war, were ordered to return to Greece. This they considered not only as the highest affront, but even as the greatest injustice. They therefore, with seditious cries, unanimously demanded to be entirely discharged from his service, murmuring against him as a despiser of his bravest troops, and as a cruel king, who wanted their destruction and not their absence. Alexander, however, on this trying occasion, acted with that resolution which always marked his character. Being seated on his tribunal of justice, he rushed among the principal mutineers, seized thirteen, and ordered them to be immediately punished. The soldiers, amazed at his intrepidity, withheld their complaints, and with downcast eyes seemed to beg for mercy. "You desired a discharge," said he, "go then, and publish to the world that you have left your prince to the mercy of strangers; from henceforth the Persians shall be my guards." This menace was actually executed, and filled the soldiers with such grief and consternation, that they never ceased soliciting his forgiveness, till at last he was prevailed upon to restore them to his favour.

Being now secure from insurrection, he gave himself up to mirth and jollity; he spent whole days and nights in immoderate drinking; and in one of those Bacchanalian entertainments Hephæstion lost his life. As this was the greatest of all Alexander's favourites, his death made a deep impression on his mind. He seemed absolutely incapable of receiving consolation; he even put to death the physician who attended him; and, on his arrival in Babylon, he celebrated his funeral rites with the greatest pomp and magnificence.

As he drew near to that city, many sinister omens were observed; on which account the Chaldeans, who pretended to foresee future events, endeavoured to dissuade him from entering it. But the Greek philosophers displayed the futility of these predictions, and advised him to pursue the course which his glory pointed out. Babylon, they told him, was a proper theatre on which to display the greatest of his power, as ambassadors were there expecting his arrival from all the nations he had lately conquered. Accordingly, after making a most magnificent entry, he gave orders to the ambassadors with a grandeur and dignity suitable to his royal character, yet with all the affability and politeness of a private courtier.

As he intended to make Babylon the seat of his empire, he began to form schemes for beautifying and improving that 'city. But, amidst all his amusements of this kind, and though he had now attained to the height of his ambition, he was far from being happy. The recent loss of Hephæstion, and the sad remembrance he still had of the murder of Clitus; and of the barbarities exercised on Parmenio and his son Philotas; the recollection, I say, of these shocking events festered in his mind, and threw a gloom upon his spirits; to dissipate which it was necessary to have recourse to some powerful remedy. The remedy he employed was intemperance. In consequence of this he was often invited to entertainments, at which he drank immoderately. On a particular occasion, having spent the whole night in a debauch, he was pressed to engage in a second, which he unhappily did, and drank to such excess that he fell upon the floor, in appearance dead; and in this lifeless condition was carried, a sad spectacle of debauchery, to his palace. The fever continued, with some intervals, in which he gave the necessary orders for the sailing of the fleet, and the marching of his land forces, being persuaded he should recover. But at last finding himself past all hopes, and his voice beginning to fail, he gave his ring to Perdiccas, with orders to convey his body to the temple of Ammon. He struggled, however, with death for some time, and raising himself upon his elbow, he gave his hand to the soldiers who pressed in to kiss it. Being then asked to whom he would leave his empire, he answered, "To the most worthy." Perdiccas inquiring at what time he should pay him divine honours, he replied, "When you are happy." With these words he expired, being then upwards of thirty-two years old, of which he had reigned twelve, with a glory and renown that no prince, either before or since, has ever been able to equal.

As to his character, it may be summed up in a few words. Personal courage, military skill, unbounded generosity, unexampled continence, considering his youth, his rank, and the powerful temptations to which he was exposed; such were his chief and most distinguished virtues; but these were more than counterbalanced by his intemperance, his cruelty, his vanity, and, above all, by his wild and insatiable ambition. His victories, however, had one good effect; they served to show in how high a degree the arts of peace can promote those of war. In this picture we behold a combination of petty states, by the arts of refinement, growing more than a match for the rest of the world united; and leaving mankind an example of the superiority of intellect over brutal force. Alexander left one son behind him; he was named Hercules, and was born of Barsine, the daughter of Artabazus, and widow of Memnon. Both Roxana and Statira are said to have been pregnant at the time of his death.

CHAPTER XV.

TRANSACTIONS IN GREECE, FROM THE DESTRUCTION OF THEBES TO THE DEATH OF ANTIPATER.

WE now return to the affairs of Greece, with which Alexander's expedition is, in a great measure, unconnected; and hardly, indeed, bears any other relation to them, than that it was carried on by Grecian forces. When the general convention of the states of Greece declared Alexander their generalissimo against the Persians, the Lacedæmonians were the only people that refused to concur in this appointment. With a sagacity and penetration, which did them honour, they plainly foresaw, that if that prince should succeed in his ambitious scheme of subduing the East, it would not be long before he put a period to the small remains

of Grecian liberty. They therefore did every thing in
their power to counteract his views; they even entered
into an alliance for this purpose with the Persian monarch; and Agis, at that time their king, a brave,
active, and enterprising prince, son to Archidamus,
and grandson of the renowned Agesilaus, exerted himself so strenuously upon this occasion, that he actually
brought over a good number of the other states of
Greece to join in the confederacy against Macedon.
By this means he was enabled to raise an army of
twenty thousand foot and two thousand horse, with
which he attacked Megalopolis, the only city in Peloponnesus that had acknowledged Alexander for its
sovereign. Antipater, Alexander's viceroy in Macedon,
was not long in meeting him, and that too with an army
amounting to above double the number. Agis, however, did not endeavour to avoid the contest; a general action ensued; and though the Macedonians gained
the victory, yet it was with the loss of three thousand
five hundred of their best troops. The same number
fell on the other side, and, among the rest, Agis, the
Spartan king, one of the most illustrious characters to
be found in antiquity. His end was as glorious as his
life had been virtuous. Having received several wounds
in the course of the action, his soldiers endeavoured,
when the rout became general, to carry him off on
their shoulders; but Agis, seeing they were in danger
of being surrounded, commanded them to set him down,
and preserve themselves by flight for the future service
of their country. They did so: he was accordingly left
alone; and on his knees he fought and killed several
of the Macedonians, whom he continued to engage till
he was run through the body with a dart.

The subsequent reigns of the Spartan kings were
productive of few events that are worthy of notice.
Eudemidas, the son of Agis, succeeded him on the
throne; and happily, at least for the tranquillity of his
country, his mind was as much turned to the arts of
peace, as his father's had been to those of war. While
the whole nation was burning with resentment at the
loss of Agis, and calling out for a renewal of hostilities

against the Macedonians, in order to revenge it, Eudemidas alone restrained their military ardour. And
when a certain citizen asked him, Why he should
recommend the continuance of peace, when all his
subjects were for war? "Because," replied the king,
"I wish to convince them, that what they desire would
be injurious to them." When another of his subjects
was magnifying, in his presence, the victories which
their ancestors had won from the Persians, and was
from thence drawing arguments for recommencing
hostilities against Macedon, "You perhaps think," said
Eudemidas, " that it is the same thing to make war
against a thousand sheep, as against fifty wolves."
Going one day by chance into the school of Xeno-
crates the philosopher, and observing that he was very
old, he asked those who stood next to him, what was
the old man's profession. Upon being answered that
he was a wise man, who sought after virtue, "Alas!"
said he, "is he seeking it at these years? when then
will he make use of it?" And when, as we shall see
afterwards, Alexander caused the return of all the
Greek exiles, those of Thebes excepted, to be proclaimed at the Olympic games, "'Tis a hard case, O ye
Thebans," said Eudemidas, "but at the same time very
honourable; for it is evident that, of all the Greeks,
Alexander fears you only."

Antipater, having succeeded to his wish in crushing
the insurrection at Peloponnesus, and having cut off
Agis, who was the chief author of that insurrection,
resolved, if possible, to take out of the way every
other person that was likely to dispute his master's
authority; and the first he pitched upon with this
view was the celebrated Demosthenes, whom he contrived to bring under a suspicion of having proved
false to the interests of his country. For though Harpalus, as we have already observed, could not corrupt
Phocion, he is said to have been more successful with
Demosthenes, who was now accused of having accepted
a bribe of a golden cup and twenty talents. Certain it
is, that when he was to have given his opinion with
regard to the propriety of granting protection to a

Macedonian culprit, he appeared with his throat bound round with several rollers. This was probably owing to a real cold he had caught, though his enemies alleged it was only a pretended one ; and a wit observed on the occasion, " that the orator had got a golden quinsey." Be this as it will, he was tried for bribery in the court of Areopagus, and, being found guilty, was condemned in a fine of fifty talents : and as this was a sum he was unable to pay, he was therefore obliged to go into banishment. But from this charge of bribery and corruption Demosthenes is fully vindicated both by Plutarch and Pausanias, two of the most respectable authors of antiquity.

Antipater having now rid himself of almost the only man in Greece that dared to question his master's authority, Alexander resolved to try how far the minds of the people were prepared to submit to that yoke of slavery which he was determined to impose upon them. With this view he caused it to be proclaimed at the Olympic games, " That all the Grecian exiles (those only excepted who had been guilty of atrocious crimes) should be forthwith restored to their respective cities ; and that those cities which should refuse to admit them should be compelled to it by force of arms." This step however seems to have been rather premature. Cowed as the minds of the people were by the repeated acts of oppression they had suffered, they were not yet disposed to comply with an order which was a direct subversion not only of all free but of all regular government. They therefore began to make preparations for a bold and vigorous resistance ; and being headed by Leosthenes the Athenian, who had already collected a good body of his countrymen, they soon found themselves sufficiently strong to set Antipater at defiance.

Such was the situation of affairs in Greece, when the news of Alexander's death reached that country ; news which added greatly to the spirit and activity of the insurgents. It was at this time, too, that Demosthenes was recalled from banishment, as his eloquence and patriotism would be of the greatest service in uniting the different states of Greece in a general confederacy against the Macedonians. He was chiefly opposed, on this occasion, by Pytheas, a creature of Alexander's. "The Athenians," said Pytheas, "may be likened unto asses' milk, which is a certain indication of sickness being in any house into which it is brought; for when they appear in any city, we may with certainty pronounce that city to be distempered." "True," answered Demosthenes, "but as asses' milk is a restorative of health, so are Athenian counsels of distempered states."

Antipater, though greatly inferior to the confederates in number, had the courage to give them battle; but being defeated, he took refuge in Lamia, a city of Thessaly, where he resolved to hold out till a reinforcement should arrive. The Athenians were so elated with this success, that some of them proposed declaring war in form against the Macedonians; but from this they were dissuaded by Phocion, who well knew their inability to maintain such a contest. "When do you think," said one of the principal citizens to him, "will be the most proper time for going to war?"— "When the young men," replied he, "keep within the bounds of regularity; when the rich are liberal in their donations; and the orators cease to rob the state."

It was not long before Antipater received the supply of troops he expected; and now thinking himself more than a match for the enemy, he set out in quest of them, and coming up with them in the neighbourhood of Cranon, a city of Thessaly, he there gave them a complete overthrow. Enraged as he was at the Athenians more than at any of the other states of Greece, on account of their having been the original authors and chief conductors of this insurrection, he refused to grant them peace upon any other terms than their delivering up Demosthenes, and receiving into their city a Macedonian garrison.

Demosthenes, well knowing that he had incurred the resentment of Antipater beyond the possibility of forgiveness, fled immediately to Calauria, a small island in the neighbourhood, and there took refuge in the temple of Neptune. He was followed thither by

Archias, a player, whom Antipater sent after him, in order to bring him back. Archias used every argument he could think of to persuade him to return, telling him that Antipater would treat him humanely: but Demosthenes, who knew better than Archias what were the dispositions of Antipater, said, "O, Archias, I was never much moved with you as a player, and now I am as little moved with you as a negotiator!" When Archias began to press him hard, he begged leave to withdraw a little farther into the temple, in order to write a few lines to his family. When he had got to the place where he was to write, he put a poisoned quill into his mouth, and chewed it, as he usually did other quills, when he was very thoughtful. The poison beginning to operate, he turned towards the tragedian, and said, "Now, sir, you may act the part of Creon, in the tragedy, and cast out this body of mine unburied." He desired to be supported to the door of the temple, that he might not pollute it by his death; but as he passed by the altar he expired.

By the death of this great man, and that of Agis, Antipater established his authority in Athens, and in most of the other states, upon a firm foundation; and even so far gained upon the affections of the people, by the mild use he made of his power, that he received from them the honourable appellation of The father and protector of Greece. With the Ætolians, however, he was not equally successful. That people were so dissatisfied with the terms granted them at the late pacification, that they were determined either to obtain better, or to risk every thing in the field. With this view they raised a large army, with which they invaded the territories of Macedon; but though they gained at first some petty advantages (especially during Antipater's absence in Asia, whither he had been obliged to go in order to counteract the designs of Perdiccas, who was planning an insurrection in that part of the world), yet were they finally defeated, and compelled to submit to their former masters.

Even the Athenians, though less displeased than any of the other states of Greece, with the conduct of Anti pater, yet felt their pride hurt at their city's being defended by a Macedonian garrison; and they therefore wished to free themselves from this badge of slavery. They first entreated Phocion to use his good offices with Antipater for this purpose; but that patriot declined the commission, well knowing that his countrymen were now become too effeminate to be left entirely to their own protection. They therefore deputed the orator Demades to wait upon Antipater, and solicit the recall of the garrison. This is the same Demades we have already mentioned as the enemy of Demosthenes. He was a man of some abilities, but of more vanity, and of a most venal disposition. Antipater used to say that he had two friends at Athens; Phocion, who would never accept of any reward for his services; and Demades, who never thought he had received enough. Whether Antipater had discontinued his largesses to Demades, or whether Demades expected to be more liberally rewarded by Perdiccas, we cannot say; but he had entered into a correspondence with that commander, and had recommended him to come over and assume the government of Macedon and Greece. A letter of his to Perdiccas was found, in which were these words: "Come, and be the support of Macedon and Greece, which at present lean on an old rotten staff," meaning Antipater. This discovery was made at the very time that he and his son were endeavouring to obtain the recall of the garrison. Antipater immediately caused the son of Demades to be slain in his father's presence; and the moment he had expired, the father himself underwent the same fate.

Antipater did not long survive this incident. He had now attained to a great age; and the anxiety of his mind, cooperating with an enfeebled and declining habit of body, at last produced a violent disease, that soon left him but little room to hope for a recovery. His end was not unworthy of the high character he had maintained through life. Preferring, as he had always done, the interest of the nation at large to that of his own family, he contented himself with appointing his son Cassander to be merely a chiliarch, or commander of a thousand men, while he left the government of Macedon and Greece to Polyperchon, the eldest of Alexander's captains at that time in Europe. This noble and disinterested act raised him still higher, if possible, in the opinion of his countrymen, and made them consider his death, which happened soon after, not only as a national but almost as an irreparable loss.

CHAPTER XVI.

TRANSACTIONS IN ASIA FROM THE DEATH OF ALEXANDER TO THE DEATH OF ANTIGONUS.

THE expression which Alexander made use of on his deathbed, of leaving his empire "To the most worthy," would probably have produced a war among his principal officers, each of whom thought himself the most deserving, had it not been that, happily for the country, the ambition of every one of them was restrained by the no less ardent ambition of the rest. All of them, therefore, being thus obliged to relinquish for themselves every pretension to the crown, they placed it, and that too with general consent, on the head of Alexander's only brother, who was named Aridæus, or more commonly Philip Aridæus. This was a prince of very weak intellects; indeed he is said to have been absolutely insane: and to this circumstance, probably, more than to his being the son of Philip, did he owe his ready admission to the throne.

As to Hercules, the son of Alexander by Barsine, his right was easily set aside, as his mother was not of royal extraction. A share, however, of the supreme power was reserved for the child with which Roxana was then big, should it prove a boy; and as it actually did so, and was named by its mother Alexander, the empire henceforth may be said to have had two kings instead of one. Indeed, in a little time, it might probably have had a third, as Statira, Alexander's other queen, was then pregnant; but Roxana, a cruel and ambitious woman, took care to obviate this inconve-

nience, by secretly making away with Statira, as she
soon after did with her sister Parysatis, the widow of
Hephæstion.

Perdiccas, to whom on his deathbed Alexander had
bequeathed his royal signet, and who was supposed to
be his greatest favourite after the death of Hephæstion,
was the chief author of these, and of every other public
measure.   For though, in the outward distribution of
power, he contented himself with the humble station of
captain of the household troops, yet was he possessed
of more real influence than any other man at court, or
even than any of those who were appointed governors
of the different provinces.   As to these last, they were
disposed of in the following manner: To Antipater and
Craterus was assigned the government of Macedon and
of all Greece.   Lysimachus was set over the Chersonese
and Thrace.   Eumenes had Paphlagonia and Cappadocia.   Ptolemy had Egypt, and Antigonus Phrygia
the greater, Lycia, and Pamphylia.

Though none of Alexander's captains had been able
to raise themselves to sovereign sway, yet were they,
most of them, by far too powerful to continue long as
peaceable subjects.   In a little time, accordingly, a
civil war broke out, and it then appeared that there
were no less than three parties in the empire.   One of
these was headed by Perdiccas, and supported by Eumenes ; another was headed by Ptolemy, and supported
by Antipater and Craterus ; and the third, which ulti-
mately proved the most formidable of all, was raised
and maintained by Antigonus alone.   The events produced by the violent contentions of these different
parties, the narrow limits to which we are confined
will not allow us to relate at any length: nor, indeed,
were we to do so, would the detail, after all, be very
interesting.   Let it therefore suffice to lay before the
reader the most material circumstances.

Perdiccas marched into Egypt with a large army, in
order to crush the insurrection of Ptolemy, but was
there slain by his own soldiers.   Antipater likewise
assembled an army ; and having divided it into two
bodies, he put one of them under the command of Cra-

terus, who had orders to watch the motions of Eumenes, whilst himself, with the other, went over to Cilicia for the purpose of giving assistance to Ptolemy, in case there should be need. In his absence, Eumenes, seizing a favourable opportunity, attacked Craterus, who was not only defeated, but lost his life in the action. For this loss, however, Antipater found some consolation in being unanimously chosen protector of the kings, in the room of Perdiccas. This last appointment made it necessary for him to revisit Macedon, and he therefore left the prosecution of the war against Eumenes to Antigonus, and to his son Cassander, whom he privately instructed to keep a watchful eye on the proceedings of the former, as he well knew his bold and enterprising character.

Antigonus, though an excellent soldier, had to cope with a man who was but little, if at all, his inferior. A battle ensued between him and Eumenes; and though the latter was worsted, chiefly through the treachery of his officers, yet had he the address to retire with a handful of men to the castle of Nora, where, without any other provisions than corn, salt, and water, he defended himself for a whole year, and at last obliged the enemy to give over the siege.

Antipater died soon after his return to Macedon, and, as we have already observed, he appointed Polyperchon for his successor. This was a weak and vainglorious man; and he now gave a signal proof of his imprudence in recalling Olympias to Macedon, from which the policy of Antipater had always kept her at a distance. On the present occasion, however, she did not give way to those cruel and vindictive dispositions which had formerly marked her character, and which afterwards rendered her equally infamous and miserable; on the contrary, she discovered the greatest political sagacity and discernment. By her advice Eumenes was appointed to the chief command in the east, and was ordered to make head against Antigonus, who was every day rising into a dangerous degree of power. Eumenes executed this commission with great ability, and even with considerable success. Being much inferior to Antigonus in number of soldiers, he drew over to his own party some of the most powerful officers in that general's interest, and even the whole body of the Argyraspidæ, a set of hardy Macedonian veterans, who derived their name from the silver shields which they wore, and with which they had been presented by Alexander the Great, on account of their extraordinary valour. By these and various other means, he contrived to thwart all the designs of Antigonus for the space of three years, till at last the other, seizing a favourable opportunity, fell suddenly upon him in his winter quarters, and not only discomfited his forces, but took himself prisoner, and instantly put him to death.

Being now freed from such a formidable enemy, Antigonus began to execute those ambitious projects which he had long been meditating in private, but had never dared hitherto openly to avow. He first advanced to Babylon, of which he made himself master; Seleucus, the governor, having fled into Egypt, and thrown himself upon the protection of Ptolemy. He next invaded the provinces of Cœlosyria and Phœnicia, which he compelled to submit: and having built a fleet of five hundred sail in less than a twelvemonth, he attacked and reduced the city of Tyre.

In the mean time a league was formed between Ptolemy, Lysimachus, Seleucus, and Cassander, for checking the progress of Antigonus's arms. Ptolemy advanced with a large army to Gaza, where he attacked and defeated Demetrius, the son of Antigonus, who had been left to command in his father's absence. But Demetrius soon recovered the honour he had lost, by attacking, in his turn, one of Ptolemy's generals, and giving him a complete overthrow. Ptolemy, however, was enabled, by his victory at Gaza, to furnish Seleucus with a small body of forces, with which he returned to Babylon, and resumed the government of that city, which he continued to enjoy till his death.

Though not only Antigonus, but even Ptolemy, Lysimachus, and Cassander, had for some time acted as independent princes, still they affected to acknowledge a kind of submission to Alexander, the young king of Macedon. But this was a mere pretence to blind the eyes of the people; and that pretence being now no longer thought necessary, they all of them threw off the mask, and openly assumed a title to that sovereign power of which they were really possessed. Antigonus and his son were proclaimed kings of Syria; Ptolemy was declared king of Egypt; Cassander, king of Macedon; and Lysimachus and Seleucus took the same badge of royalty in the provinces they governed.

It is not to be supposed that such restless and ambitious spirits would long live in harmony and concord among themselves. The Syrian kings invaded Egypt, of which they hoped to make a conquest; but in this they were disappointed. They next turned their arms against Rhodes; but though Demetrius, who, on acount of his wonderful success in storming cities, was called Poliorcetes, employed against it the utmost efforts of his military skill, yet was he obliged to abandon the enterprise. For this, indeed, he was furnished with a plausible pretext, in consequence of an embassy from the Athenians, entreating him to come and free them from the oppression of Cassander, who was now besieging their city. Demetrius readily complied with their request, and not only compelled Cassander to give over the siege of Athens, but even to retreat with precipitation into Macedon.

By this time the power of the Syrian kings was become so formidable as to threaten the independence of all the neighbouring states, and a general combination was therefore formed against them. It consisted chiefly of the Macedonians, Thracians, and Egyptians, who assembled a large body of forces, amounting, in the whole, to about seventy-four thousand men. The kings of Syria were not long in meeting them with a still superior army, and a battle ensued in the neighbourhood of Ipsus, a small town in Phrygia. Both sides behaved with uncommon gallantry; but, after a fierce and obstinate struggle, the Syrians were completely defeated, and their king Antigonus left dead upon the spot. Demetrius escaped with about nine thousand men.

CHAPTER XVII.

REVOLUTIONS IN MACEDON AND GREECE, FROM THE DEATH
OF ANTIPATER TO THE FINAL OVERTHROW OF THE
FAMILY OF PHILIP.

CASSANDER, as we have already observed, had usurped
the throne of Macedon. The steps by which he attained
to that high dignity, it may not be improper here a
little more particularly to relate. Alarmed, as he justly
was, at the conduct of Polyperchon, in recalling Olympias to court, and intrusting her not only with the care
of the young king, but even with the direction of the
public councils, he began, in concert with his friends,
to adopt such measures as appeared to be the most
proper for securing themselves against the effects of
that woman's resentment; for he well knew that she
bore an implacable hatred to the memory of his father,
and to all that were either descended from or had been
connected with him.

One of the first steps, which Polyperchon took by
her advice, was to issue an edict, abolishing, throughout all the states of Greece, the aristocratic form of
government, which Antipater had revived, and restoring the democratic mode, which had existed a little
before it. His ostensible reason for embracing this
measure was the bestowing upon the people a greater
degree of liberty than they then enjoyed; but his real
motive was the displacing those governors whom Antipater had appointed, and thereby weakening the interest
of Cassander. The more intelligent part of the citizens
easily saw through the deceit; but the people in general were caught by it, and clamoured loudly against all
those who dared to oppose the execution of the edict,
and, among others, against the virtuous Phocion, who
fell a sacrifice to their prejudices on this occasion.
Being brought to a trial for this pretended crime, he
asked, whether he was to be proceeded against according to the regular forms of law? and being told that he
was, he replied, "How is that possible, if no hearing
is to be allowed me?" Perceiving, from the violence

of the popular résentment, that no opportunity of defence would be granted him, he exclaimed, "As for myself, I confess the crime of which I am accused, and submit cheerfully to the sentence of the law; but consider, O ye Athenians! what it is that these men have done, that they should thus be involved in the same calamity with me." The people called out vehemently, "They are your accomplices, and we need no farther proof of their guilt." A decree was then drawn up and read, by which Phocion and several others were condemned to death. As they were leading this great man to the place of execution, a friend asked him, if he had any commands to leave for his son: "Only this," replied he very coolly, "that he forget how ill the Athenians treated his father."

The revenge of his enemies was not satiated even with his death. They passed a decree, by which his body was banished the Athenian territories, and a penalty was denounced against any person who should furnish fire for his funeral pile. One Conopion conveyed the corpse a little beyond Eleusina, where he borrowed fire of a Megarian woman, and burned it. A Megarian matron, who attended on that occasion, raised an humble monument on the spot, in memory of the unfortunate orator; and having carried home his ashes, which she-had previously collected with great care, she buried them under her hearth; putting up, at the same time, this prayer to her household gods: "To you, O ye deities, who protect this place, do I commit the precious remains of the most excellent Phocion: protect them, I beseech you, from every insult, and deliver them one day to be deposited in the sepulchre of his ancestors, when the Athenians shall have become wiser."

A short time only had intervened, when the prayer of the pious matron was fulfilled. The Athenians, as in former instances of a similar kind, began to abate of their fury, and to have their eyes opened to the truth. They recollected the many services which the state had derived from the superior wisdom of Phocion's counsels: and on that recollection, they could not but wonder at the part they had acted. They decreed for the victim of their rage, a statue of brass; they ordered his ashes to be brought back to Athens at the public expense; and passed an act, by which all his accusers were to be put to death. Agnonides, who had a capital hand in carrying on the prosecution against Phocion, was seized and executed. Epicurus and Demophilus fled; but Phocion's son overtook them, and revenged the death of his father.

Polyperchon, having thus freed himself from so powerful an opponent as Phocion, proceeded to execute his decree with unrelenting severity; and whoever dared to thwart his will, in this particular, was instantly condemned to death. Olympias too, now thinking she might gratify her revenge without control, and without the fear of future retribution, began to wreak her resentment upon all those who were either the objects of her jealousy or hatred. King Aridæus, the son of Philip by a concubine, naturally fell under this predicament. She had already deprived him of his understanding by means of a potion she had given him; and she now had the cruelty to deprive him of his life, and even to inflict the same punishment on his queen Eurydice, who was likewise his niece, and grandaughter to Philip. She had, indeed, some shadow of reason for proceeding to such extremities against them. They had not only disapproved of her return to Macedon, but even raised an army to prevent it; but being deserted by their troops, they were both taken prisoners, and put in confinement. Aridæus was soon after murdered in prison by a party of Thracians, whom Olympias sent thither for the purpose; and in a little time she dispatched a messenger to the queen, with a poniard, a rope, and a cup of poison, desiring her to choose which she pleased. This message Eurydice received with the greatest composure; and after praying the gods, "that Olympias herself might be rewarded with the like presents," she took the rope, and strangled herself. Cynane, her mother, had some time before been cut off by the arts of the same vindictive woman.

Olympias's thirst of blood seems not to have been

quenched by the numerous murders she had committed. She now caused Nicanor, the brother of Cassander, to be put to death. The body of Iolas, another brother of Cassander's, which had long rested in the tomb, she ordered to be brought forth, and exposed on the highway; and a hundred Macedonians of noble birth were seized and executed, on suspicion of having been in the interest of Cassander. She had, indeed, great reason to hate, or at least to dread, that illustrious commander; but had she been as cunning as she was cruel, she would have endeavoured to soften, rather than inflame his resentment.

Cassander, sensible of his utter inability to make head against her and Polyperchon with any force he could raise in Europe, had applied for assistance to Antigonus in Asia, and having received a small supply of men from that quarter, he returned with them to Athens, where he was gladly received by Nicanor the governor, who had opposed the execution of Polyperchon's decree with great zeal and activity. Their forces being thus joined, gained several advantages over those of Polyperchon and Olympias: they defeated their fleet near Byzantium, and they rendered all their enterprises by land perfectly ineffectual.

Cassander, however, with all his good qualities, seems to have been as much transported with the lust of power, as any of the other great men of the age; and to this he was always ready to sacrifice every tie of justice, of honour, and of gratitude. Hearing that Nicanor was beginning to form a separate interest of his own, and aimed at no less than the sovereignty of Attica, he contrived to draw him, under pretence of an interview, into an empty house, where he had him murdered by some assassins he had prepared for the purpose.

For this barbarous act, indeed, he made the best amends in his power, by appointing, for his successor, a man of a most excellent character. This was no other than Demetrius Phalerus, the celebrated disciple of Theophrastus. Demetrius was at once a philosopher, an orator, and a man of virtue. Cicero makes mention of his oratory in a very favourable manner; but then he says, he was the first of all the Greeks, who changed the bold, nervous, and resistless eloquence of the earlier orators, into the mild and pathetic species of eloquence; which he thinks is as much inferior, in point of merit, to the former, " as the power of the gently gliding stream is inferior to that of the rough thundering torrent." Demetrius, however, executed, his important trust with so much justice and equity, and with such an invariable attention to the happiness of the people he governed, that the Athenians erected no less than three hundred statues to his honour, and many of these were equestrian.

Matters were now tending fast towards a crisis between Cassander on the one hand, and Polyperchon and Olympias on the other. Cassander, having divided his army into two bodies, gave the command of the one to Callas, with orders to march against Polyperchon, whose troops had been separated from those of Olympias. With the other he himself set out in pursuit of that woman, who, after trying various arts to stir up the Macedonians in her favour, was at last obliged to take refuge in the city of Pydna, which was strongly fortified. There she was immediately besieged by Cassander, who reduced her at length to such difficulties for want of provisions, that she was forced to surrender both herself and her army. In taking this mortifying step, however, she had the precaution to stipulate for her life; but the kindred of those whom she had murdered insisting on her death, Cassander pretended, that the stipulation related only to military execution, and he therefore gave her up to the civil laws of her country. The friends of those whom she had slain, assembled, and accused her before the people, by whom she was condemned without being heard. On this occasion Cassander offered her a ship to convey her to Athens, but she rejected the offer. She insisted upon being heard before the Macedonians; and said, she was not afraid to answer for all she had done. Cassander was unwilling to abide the issue of such a trial as she demanded: he therefore sent a band of two hundred soldiers to put her to death. When the soldiers entered the prison, they were struck with awe at her majestic appearance, and refused to execute their orders; but the relations of those who had fallen by her resentment rushed forward, and cut her throat. She is said to have behaved with much fortitude on that trying occasion. Cassander suffered her body to lie, for some time, unburied; to revenge, perhaps, the insult which she had offered to the remains of his brother Iolas. Roxana and her son (as we have already observed) were soon after murdered; and the same was the fate of Hercules, Alexander's other son whom he had by Barsine.

Not more than twenty-eight years had elapsed since the death of that conqueror, and not a single branch of his house remained to enjoy a portion of the empire, which he and his father had acquired at the price of the greatest policy, dangers, and bloodshed. Such, to the royal family of Macedon, were the effects of that ambition, which had lighted up the flames of war in Europe, Asia, and Africa.

CHAPTER XVIII.

REVOLUTIONS IN MACEDON AND GREECE, FROM THE OVER-
THROW OF THE FAMILY OF PHILIP TO THE CONFEDERACY
FORMED BY THE MACEDONIANS AND ACHÆANS AGAINST
THE ÆTOLIANS.

THOUGH Cassander had now established himself on the throne of Macedon, he did not enjoy all that tranquillity which he thought he had reason to expect. He found that Polyperchon and his son Alexander were forming a party against him in Greece; and therefore, in order to counteract their designs, he marched into Bœotia, where he not only defeated all their machinations, but likewise rebuilt the city of Thebes, about twenty years after it had been destroyed by Alexander the Great. This transaction he did not long survive. He died in a little time after, leaving behind him two sons, Antipater and Alexander, who, as usually happens in such

cases, soon began to quarrel about their respective
right to the throne; and the latter calling in the aid
of Demetrius Poliorcetes, this last contrived to make
away with the man he pretended to assist, and himself
got possession of the sovereign power. Of this, however, he was soon deprived by the joint efforts of Lysimachus, and Pyrrhus, king of Epire; the former of
whom, partly by open force, and partly by secret arti-
fices, found means to make himself sole king of Macedon.
But neither did he enjoy his newly acquired power for
any length of time, his army being routed, and himself
slain, in a great battle, which he fought with Seleucus,
king of Babylon. Seleucus, upon this victory, resigned
his Asiatic dominions to his son Antiochus, and came
over to Macedon, in the fond hope of passing the re-
mainder of his days in the quiet enjoyment of his native
country. But he was treacherously murdered, about
seven months after by Ptolemy Ceraunus, the brother
of Cassander; who, to add to his guilt, prevailed upon
the widow of Lysimachus to marry him; but he had
no sooner got her and her children into his power, than
he put the young princes to death, and banished the
mother into Simothrace.

Crimes so atrocious did not long go unpunished.
His kingdom (for he had now seized on the throne of
Macedon) was soon overrun by a body Gauls, who
suddenly attacked and defeated his forces, and having
cut off the head of the king himself, they fixed it to
the end of a long pole, and thus carried it in triumph
through their ranks.

The progress, however, of these barbarians was at
last put a stop to by the united states of Greece. They
several times attempted to force the straits of Thermopylæ, but were always repulsed with considerable loss.
At length they found a passage into the interior parts
of Greece, by the way of Mount Œta, and directed their
march towards the temple of Delphi, which they intended to plunder. But the inhabitants of that sacred
city, inspired by religious enthusiasm, made a desperate
sally upon the barbarians, who, struck with a panic,
fled with precipitation. The pursuit was continued

for a whole day and night; and a violent storm and piercing cold cooperating with the fury of the victorious Greeks, most of the enemy perished either by the sword or the severity of the weather. Brennus, their leader, unable to bear the smart of the wounds he had received, and distracted at the same time with religious horror, put an end to his own life. The few that survived, having assembled together, endeavoured to effect a retreat from so fatal a country. But the different nations rose upon them as they passed, and of all those multitudes, which had poured out of Macedon into Greece, not one returned to his native land. Justin says they were all cut off; though other historians allege, that a remnant of them made their escape into Thrace and Asia.

The Delphians did not depend entirely on their courage in repelling the barbarians; they employed two very ingenious and successful stratagems against them. They procured an order from the oracle, commanding the inhabitants of the adjacent villages to abandon their dwellings, and to leave them well stored with wines and all kinds of provisions. The consequence was, that the Gauls, who, like all other barbarians, were naturally voracious, and had their appetites sharpened by a long want of sustenance, fell ravenously upon these dainties, and thus through intemperance lost much of that vigour, which had hitherto been the principal cause of the success of their arms. The other stratagem was this: Mount Parnassus, which stood close by the city of Delphos, was furnished with many caves and hollow windings. In these numbers of people were stationed, with instructions, on proper occasions, to set up loud shouts, and to make the most frightful yellings and screams. These issuing forth without any visible cause, filled the barbarians with terror, as if they proceeded from something more than human; and therefore believing they were warring with superior beings, not with men, they betook themselves to a precipitate retreat, even almost before they were attacked. This body of Gauls formed only a part of that immense shoal, which to the number, it is said, of no less than three hundred thousand, poured out of their own country in quest of new settlements; and though they were defeated and cut off in Greece, yet they had the courage to take and to plunder Rome.

The Macedonian throne, after the death of Ptolemy Ceraunus, was filled by Antigonus, the son of Demetrius Poliorcetes; he was deposed and succeeded by Pyrrhus, king of Epire: but, upon the death of this last prince, Antigonus once more assumed the sovereign sway. Nothing remarkable happened during the reign of either of these kings, except that Pyrrhus, the most warlike prince of his time, and, in the opinion of Hannibal, the greatest general that ever lived, made an attempt upon the liberty of Sparta; and advancing to the gates of the city with a powerful army, the inhabitants were struck with so much terror, that they proposed sending off their women to a place of safet But Archidamia, who was delegated by the Sparta ladies, entered the senate-house with a sword in her hand, and delivered their sentiments and her own in these words: "Think not, O men of Sparta! so meanly of your countrywomen, as to imagine that we will survive the ruin of the state. Deliberate not then whither we are to fly, but what we are to do." In consequence of this, the whole body of citizens exerted themselves with such undaunted courage, that they repulsed Pyrrhus in all his attempts to destroy the city. They even pursued him in his retreat, and slew Ptolemy his son, who was bringing up the rear of his army. Pyrrhus himself soon after perished in a like attempt upon Argos.

Antigonus, upon his reascending the throne, defeated a body of Gauls, who had made a fresh irruption into Macedon; and encouraged by this success, he began to entertain thoughts of making himself absolute master of Greece. He even proceeded so far as to compel the Athenians to receive a Macedonian garrison; and he would probably have imposed the same badge of slavery on the other states of Greece, had not death put an end to all his ambitious projects. He was succeeded by his son Demetrius, and this last by his kinsman Antigonus, neither of whose reigns were distinguished by any remarkable events.

About this time the republic of Achaia began to make

GREECE. **257**

a capital figure, and bade fair for restoring that spirit
of liberty in Greece, which had in a great measure been
extinguished, partly by the dissensions of the different
states among themselves, but chiefly by the encroachments of the Macedonian monarchs. This republic consisted originally of twelve towns, that were associated
together for their mutual defence. They had the same
friendships and the same enmities; the same coins,
weights, and measures; the same laws, and the same
magistrates. These magistrates were elected annually,
by a majority of voices throughout the whole community. Twice in the year, or oftener, if necessary,
a general assembly, consisting of deputies from the
different cities, was held for the great purposes of
~islation and government. The magistrates, who
ᴤ invested with the supreme executive power,
. ᴜre styled generals of the states of Achaia. They
commanded the military force of the republic, and possessed the right of presiding in the national assembly.
Their number was originally two; but from the incon-
veniences attendant on a divided government, was at
last reduced to one. A council of ten, called Demiurgi,
assisted the general with their advice, and examined
all matters intended to be brought before the national
assembly, and proposed or rejected them at pleasure.
The power of the Demiurgi, in this last respect, was
exactly the same as that of the lords of articles in the
ancient government of Scotland. Besides these superior magistrates, every town had also its municipal
magistracy, consisting also, as is generally supposed,
like the national constitution, of a popular assembly, a
council, and a presiding magistrate. With respect to
the laws of the Achæans, the most material object in
the history of any people, our knowledge is extremely
imperfect. Such of them, however, as have come down
to us, are proofs of their political wisdom.

It was enacted, that whatever individual or town,
belonging to the Achæan confederacy, should accept
of any gratification whatsoever, in its public or private
capacity, from prince or people, should be cut off from

s

the commonwealth of Achaia: that no member of the Achæan league should send any embassy, or contract any alliance or friendship with any prince or people, without the privity and approbation of the whole Achæan confederacy. The unanimous consent of the whole confederacy was necessary for the admission into it of any prince, state, or city. A convention of the national assembly was not to be granted at the request of any foreign prince, unless the matters to be offered to their consideration were first delivered in writing to the general of Achaia, and the council of ten, and pronounced by them to be of sufficient importance. The deliberations of every assembly were to be wholy confined to the matters on account of which they had been convened. In all debates, those who spoke were to deliver a short sketch of the arguments they employed, in order to their being considered the ensuing day; and within three days at farthest, was the business before them to be finally determined.

The general tendency of the Achæan league was so favourable to the liberties of mankind, that most of the neighbouring states associated themselves with it; but when the power of Macedon became paramount to that of all Greece, many of the members deserted the confederacy, and fell under the dominion of various tyrants. From this state of slavery, however, they were, in a little time, freed by the spirit and activity of Aratus, a native of Sicyon, who having first delivered his own country from the tyranny of Nicocles, its sovereign, and being in consequence of this chosen general of Achaia, proceeded to attack one petty tyrant after another, till at last he reestablished all the states of Greece in the possession of their ancient freedom. But this happy situation of affairs was not of long continuance: it was soon overturned by the jealousy and ambition of those very parties, from whose love of liberty it had originally sprung.

CHAPTER XIX.

FROM THE CONFEDERACY BETWEEN THE ÆTOLIANS AND
SPARTANS AGAINST THE ACHÆANS, TO THE INVASION OF
GRÆECE BY ANTIOCHUS KING OF SYRIA.

THE Ætolians were the first that began to look with a
jealous eye on the superiority of the Achæans over the
other states of Greece; and they laboured, and that
with but too much success, to infuse the like prejudices
into the Spartans. The manners of this last people
were now totally altered. They had exchanged poverty
and hardy discipline for opulence and a luxurious style
of living. The lands, which were formerly divided, in
equal portions, among the whole body of the people,
were now engrossed by a few families, who lived in
the greatest splendour and magnificence, while the rest
of the citizens were plunged in the utmost poverty and
distress. Agis, one of their most virtuous kings, was
put·to death, for attempting to restore the Agrarian
and sumptuary laws of Lycurgus. Cleomenes, however,
his successor, was more fortunate. He actually did
restore these laws, though not till he had acquired
sufficient popularity to set all opposition at defiance.
This popularity he owed chiefly to the success of his
arms against the Achæans and their allies, several of
whose towns he attacked and subdued; and he even
defeated their army in two pitched battles, the one at
Leuctra, and the other at Hecatombæum.

Aratus, provoked at the conduct of Cleomenes in thus
making war upon the Achæans without any visible
cause, threw himself on the protection of Antigonus,
king of Macedon; and, in order to induce him to grant
the aid he requested, he entered into a compact with
that monarch, the conditions of which were, That the
citadel of Corinth should be delivered into the hands of
the king; that he should be at the head of the Achæan
confederacy, superintend their councils, and direct
their operations; that his army should be supported at
their expense; that neither embassy nor letter should
be sent to any power without his approbation; and
that no city, state, or people, should be, from that time,

admitted into the Achæan league without his consent.
From these articles it is evident, that the liberties of
Achaia were now no more, and that the real sovereign
of that country was Antigonus.

The conduct of Aratus in making this treaty, was
more unpopular than that of Cleomenes in attacking
the Achæans: the consequence was, that most of the
states of Greece abandoned the cause of the former, and
espoused that of the latter, whom they now considered
as the only protector of their liberties. But Antigonus,
besides being an excellent general, was possessed of
greater resources than any Cleomenes could command; '
and thus having contrived, after various manœuvres,
to bring him to an engagement, he not only gave him
a complete overthrow, but compelled him to fly into
Egypt, where, being suspected of forming designs
against the government, he was cruelly put to death.

Antigonus himself died soon after, and was succeeded
by Philip, the son of Demetrius, the last of the Macedonian kings of that name. This prince, treading in the
steps of his predecessor, resolved to give effectual aid
to the Achæans; which he accordingly did, by carrying
the war into Ætolia itself, and reducing a great number
of its strong holds. Though naturally possessed of
great moderation, he now began to entertain the hope
of making himself master of all Greece, by forming a
junction with Hannibal, who was then carrying on war
against the Romans. He sent ambassadors to the Car-
thaginian general, and a treaty was concluded between
them, importing, that Philip should furnish a fleet and
army, to assist Hannibal in making a conquest of Italy;
after which, Hannibal should pass into Epire, and having
completed the reduction of the whole country, should
yield up to Philip such· places as lay convenient for
Macedon. Philip performed his part of the agreement.
He entered the Ionian gulf with a large fleet, and took
Oricum, a seaport on the coast of Epire; but being
surprised and defeated by the Romans, he was obliged
to return disgracefully into his own country.

The Romans had their hands too full of the war with
Hannibal to think of carrying their arms into Macedon;
but they took care to find employment for Philip, by

encouraging his enemies in Greece to attack him. For this purpose they entered into a treaty with the Ætolians, of which the following were the principal conditions: That the Ætolians should immediately commence hostilities against Philip by land, which the Romans were to support by a fleet of twenty galleys; that whatever conquests might be made, from the confines of Ætolia to Corcyra, the cities, buildings, and territory, should belong to the Ætolians, but every other kind of plunder to the Romans. The Spartans and Eleans, with other states, were included in this alliance; and the war commenced with the reduction of the island of Zacinthus, which, as an earnest of Roman generosity and good faith, was immediately annexed to the dominions of Ætolia. These things happened about two hundred and eight years before the birth of Christ.

The Romans having thus obtained a footing in Greece, soon extended and established their power throughout the whole of that renowned country. Agreeably to their usual policy, they availed themselves of the credulity, the dissensions, the ambition, and the avarice of the different chiefs; ever vigilant to support the weaker against the stronger party, that the diminished strength of each individual state might lead the way to the conquest of the whole.

Meanwhile the war continued to be carried on between Philip and the Ætolians with equal vigour, and almost with equal success on both sides, till at last the former was obliged to return into his own kingdom, to suppress a rebellion which had there broke out. The Achæans, however, though deprived of the aid of so powerful a monarch, were still able to make head against their enemies. They were now commanded by Philopœmen in the room of Aratus, whom Philip had poisoned, on account of his opposing the ambitious design which the latter had formed of subduing all Greece. They even defeated the armies of Ætolia and Elis in a great battle; but after the war had continued for the space of six years, it was at length terminated by a peace between the Romans on the one hand, and Philip on the other.

This peace, however, was but of short duration. For

Philip having invaded the dominions of the king of
Egypt, as also the territories of several of the states of
Greece, complaints were brought against him on that
account, before the Roman senate, who immediately
dispatched an ambassador to him, strictly charging him,
in the name of the republic, to desist from all hostilities
against those powers, and to refer the matters in dispute
between him and them to a fair arbitration.   Marcus
Æmilius, who carried this order, delivered it with all
that dignity and firmness which distinguished the Roman
character.   "The boastful inexperience of youth," said
the king to him, "thy gracefulness of person, and still
more, the name of Roman, inspire thee with this haughtiness.   It is my wish that Rome may observe the faith
of treaties; but should she be inclined again to hazard
an appeal to arms, I trust, that with the protection of the
gods, I shall render the Macedonian name as formidable
as that of the Roman."   These events happened about
one hundred and ninety-nine years before the birth of
Christ.

Philip soon found, that the style of the Roman ambassadors was not more imperious, than their power
was irresistible; for Titus Quintus Flaminius, being
appointed to command against him, reduced him, in a
little time, to the hard necessity of accepting a peace on
the following conditions: "That all the Greek cities,
both in Asia and Europe, should be free, and restored
to the enjoyment of their own laws; that Philip, before
the next Isthmian games, should deliver up to the
Romans all the Greeks he had in any part of his dominions, and evacuate all the places he possessed either in
Greece or in Asia: that he should give up all prisoners
and deserters: that he should surrender all his decked
ships of every kind, five small vessels, and his own galley of sixteen banks of oars, excepted; that he should
pay the Romans a thousand talents, one half down, and
the rest at ten equal annual payments; and that as a
security for the performance of these articles, he should
give hostages, his son Demetrius being one. This event
happened a hundred and ninety-three years before
Christ.

CHAPTER XX.

FROM THE INVASION OF GREECE BY ANTIÓCHUS TO THE TIME OF ITS BECOMING A ROMAN PROVINCE.

THOUGH the Romans, by their treaty with Philip, pretended to reestablish the Greeks in the possession of their ancient freedom, yet nothing was farther from their intention. On the contrary, they meant to reduce them under their own dominion. The question was not whether the Greeks should be enslaved, but who should be their masters; and the Romans thought, and it must be owned with some shadow of justice, that there was no people in the world better entitled to such a distinction than themselves. They therefore sought for a plausible pretext of carrying their arms a second time into Greece; and it was not long before this was afforded them, by Antiochus king of Syria. For that prince having invaded Greece under pretence of supporting his own rights, was opposed by the Romans on the specious plea of defending the public liberty; and who not only defeated his forces, but compelled him to retire into his Asiatic dominions. The Ætolians too, though they formerly cooperated with the Romans as allies, could not think of enduring them as masters; and they therefore endeavoured to thwart their design of usurping the sovereignty of the Grecian republics; but the consul Acilius Glabrio soon reduced their power to so low an ebb, that they were glad to accept of a peace upon any terms, and even virtually to give up their independence, by promising to pay observance to the empire and majesty of the Roman people.

The efforts of the Achæans, to prevent the establishment of the Roman empire in Greece, were not more successful. Above a thousand of their leading men were transported to Rome, in order to answer for the pretended crime of having secretly abetted the king of Macedon, who had had the courage or temerity to oppose the Romans in the field. But that prince, whose name was Perseus, and who was son and successor to Philip, was not only defeated in a great battle; but being taken prisoner, was carried to Rome, and thrown into a dungeon, where he starved himself to death. His only surviving son, Alexander, became a clerk to one of the Roman magistrates. Macedon was immediately formed into a Roman province, as were likewise, in a little time after, all the different states of Greece. These things fell out about a hundred and sixty-three years before the birth of Christ.

From this time forward few events of any great consequence happened in Greece, and those that occurred belong more properly to Roman than to Grecian history. We shall therefore pursue them no farther at present, but conclude with observing, that depressed as the Greeks now unhappily were under a foreign yoke, and consequently deprived of their national character as a free and independent people, they yet retained, amidst all their calamities, that strength of genius and delicacy of taste, that quickness of invention and acuteness of discernment, for which they had ever been remarkable : that they helped to polish their haughty, and as yet but half-civilized conquerors; that, upon the destruction of the western empire, they successfully cultivated the arts and sciences, while all the rest of the world was sunk in the grossest ignorance and barbarism ; and that, upon the taking of Constantinople by the Turks, they carried those arts and sciences with them into Italy, and there paved the way for the revival of that learning, which has ever since enlightened, and still continues to enlighten mankind.

THE END.

C. & C. WHITTINGHAM, Chiswick.

Lightning Source UK Ltd.
Milton Keynes UK
UKHW02f0943310718
326554UK00011B/496/P